DREAMERS

DREAMERS

How Young Indians Are Changing the World

Snigdha Poonam

HARVARD UNIVERSITY PRESS
Cambridge, Massachusetts
2018

First published as *Dreamers: How Young Indians are Changing
Their World* in India in 2018 by Viking, an imprint of
Penguin Random House India Pvt. Ltd
7th Floor, Infinity Tower C
DLF Cyber City
Gurgaon - 122 002 Haryana

Typeset in Aldine401 BT by Manipal Digital Systems, Manipal

First Harvard University Press edition, 2018
First printing

Cataloging-in-Publication data is available from the Library of
Congress

ISBN 978-0-674-98817-0 (pbk.)

For my parents

Contents

PART I: 'There Is No Plan B'

1

The Click-Baiter

It might be any other editorial meeting, in any of a million new clickbait start-ups: a set of editors huddled around a table to discuss what news and gossip to feed their audience next. The process is quick and brutal. Ideas are thrown around like bids on a trading floor:

> *Why your best friend is your true love, just like Mila Kunis and Ashton Kutcher.*
> *This is what you need to know about Amanda—Justin Bieber's new girlfriend.*
> *How your face would look if you survived a car crash.*
> *Fifteen times Donald Trump was trolled hilariously.*

Fifteen minutes is all it takes the team to go over the whole range of American obsessions, from Kardashians to belly fat, from sex confessions to life hacks; and fifteen seconds is the average time they spend making a decision. Poor Amanda is peremptorily ditched for Victoria Beckham, who has just kicked up a parenting scandal by posting a photo on Instagram in which she is kissing one of her children. The editors opt

tand, and argue the former Spice Girl did nothing
, as the published article will later put it, 'This is
g your kids on the lips is not a bad idea.' They have
a reason for choosing the story: 'Child kissing is trending in
the US,' a young woman wearing black eyeshadow informs
the room. The car crash idea is tweaked to imagine the impact
of *two* car crashes on someone's face at once. Everyone agrees
it should only be a visual story. Americans, apparently, simply
adore accident horror. Kim Kardashian loses out to Kylie
Jenner. Another enterprising young woman volunteers a
DIY experiment as research for the story 'How to get lips like
Kylie Jenner without going under the knife'. ('Kylie Jenner
lip challenge' is also, apparently, trending.) No changes to the
last item—Donald Trump is, of course, always hot. Ideas are
approved not because of their news value but on account of
how they appeal to base emotions. And in this quarter of an
hour, these ten youngsters have tapped into the whole range
of American emotional triggers: what excites Americans, what
terrifies them, what makes them sad, and what makes them
curious.

This isn't an editorial meeting somewhere in the US.
Everyone here is less than twenty-three years old, and they're
perched in an all-glass office in a shopping mall in Indore,
a medium-sized city in central India. They're deciding, a
few hours before America wakes up, what it will read when
it does.

They are hardly ever wrong—or so say the numbers.
Millions of people visit their website, WittyFeed, every day.
Of them, 80 per cent are foreigners and half these people are
from the US. WittyFeed is one of the world's fastest-growing
content farms; over a billion people follow it on Facebook
alone. The only website of its kind visited by more people
is BuzzFeed, the world leader in viral content. Currently

valued at only 30 million dollars, WittyFeed is giving itself a couple of years to beat BuzzFeed. That's not its ultimate goal, though. What the plucky youngsters who run it want to do is to build the world's largest media company ('bigger than BBC, CNN'). How do they hope to do it? By following their maxim: 'It's emotion that goes viral.'

Few people have heard of WittyFeed, even in India. The only reason I'm here is because I noticed its crazy numbers: 82 million monthly visits, 1.5 billion page views, 170 million users, 4.2 million likes on Facebook. WittyFeed is news by the same parameter that it uses to define news: the WTF factor. How can a bunch of kids in a small Indian town who have never seen the world dream of ruling it by simply *getting* the internet better than anyone else?

In May 2016, I went to Indore to decide for myself if WittyFeed could indeed become the biggest media company in the world. Whether or not I found an answer to that question, I would at least get to hang out with a bunch of Indians who live *in* the internet. Flying in from Delhi, Indore looks small along every dimension: the width of its roads, the height of its buildings, the price of one night's stay at a mid-scale hotel. The signs of aspiration are all there, however. Cool coffee shops are coming up on cow-populated lanes; rock concerts are advertised on billboards; and youngsters wander its streets in Instagram-ready outfits.

But Indore's new spirit of enterprise peaks in WittyFeed's 10,000-square-foot office on the ninth floor of the town's tallest commercial tower. It is decorated in a wide-eyed image of Silicon Valley. The walls are a canvas for everything central to the company's self-image, from an elaborate graphic illustration of WittyFeed's journey to icons of their favourite social media companies—Facebook, Twitter, Instagram, Google and Snapchat—to the collage of a 'start-up alphabet' (creativity, crazy, courage . . .). Between these colourful walls, the open-plan office is a window into the company's hopeful, global soul: exposed brick and espresso machine, beanbags and a ping-pong table, a corner where the employees can wind down and an enclosure where they can work out. The office is designed such that, if you're not staring into your slim laptop, you're forced to look at something inspirational. Something that's meant to make an employee think as big, and American, as possible. It could be the blown-up face of a celebrity—Marilyn Monroe, perhaps, or Madonna. It could be nuggets of espresso-shot motivation—'99.9 per cent is not 100 per cent' or 'Set Goal. Reach. Repeat'. Or it could be a triptych of the most inspiring Americans according to WittyFeed—Abraham Lincoln, Steve Jobs and Elon Musk. Should they be hit by self-doubt amid this architecture of inspiration, all they have to do is stand outside the office of the company's CEO and look at the image of an enormous Aladdin voicing the words that power millions of dreams across India every day: 'The universe is a genie . . . it always says, "your wish is my command".' The CEO's office has a name: Winterfell. So do the bathrooms: the men's is called 'Khal' and the women's 'Khaleesi'. Like the violent medieval world of *Game of Thrones*, WittyFeed runs on the hunger for power, and for other people's territory.

The twenty-something workforce live together in a couple of large bungalows, are told to regard each other as brothers and sisters, and reach out to the Chief Content Officer, or CCO, if they are out of shampoo or toothpaste. To enter the world of WittyFeed, they must leave their past at the door. It feels almost like a cult designed by millennials, for millennials: The chance of getting in goes up the less of a past they have to begin with. The conditions are stated clearly to anyone who wants to work at WittyFeed. This must be their first job, and they must want it *bad*. The company actually prefers people with poor work experience and education. What it wants from a candidate in an interview—which can stretch over a whole day—is the answer to a question it considers central to their eligibility: Who are you? The answer can be a monologue or a manic dance around the room; the second may win more points.

Most young Indians who take that interview will have been asked that question for the first time. It isn't something that young people in India have ever been encouraged to ask: Who *are* you? In a society where who you are—caste, class, region, religion—is decided for you long before you are born, 'wokeness' is a luxury. This is the defining difference between this generation of Indians, and most of those that have come before.

Applicants put themselves through this existential interrogation because they are desperate for a job and this is their only chance. Of the first three WittyFeed employees I met in Indore, two had recently lost their fathers and found themselves supporting their entire family. Fitting into WittyFeed's world is an experience most of them described to me as strange but life-changing. A week at the company is all it takes them to go from not knowing anything about the world to deciding what the world should know. It is not easy. You don't just wake up and write a definitive cure for American break-up blues if you are an eighteen-year-old girl in Indore who has never been on a date. You start by learning how to think like the audience you want to reach: an American kid who wants an 'AI butler like Iron Man's Jarvis', or a hipster looking for an app that will allow him to 'teabag' American politicians, or a Tinder user who wants to master the art of 'bread-crumbing'—flirty yet non-committal texts. And you then get into the spirit—or the spirit gets into you. Every thought in your head is a potential idea for a viral post; it flashes before your eyes complete with the number of people who are likely to click on it. If you're good, some of them come attached with a thumbnail image. Sometimes you think you are going crazy; then you look around and no one appears any saner.

'One day Parveen bhaiyya—the CCO—was on a flight back to Indore from somewhere. He was using the loo when an idea came to him: Where does your poop go in an aeroplane? The moment he was back, he came over and shared the idea with us. We published a story around it the same day. It went super viral. 315,000 views. The idea was copied across the content industry.' Lavanya Srivastav is showing me around the office. We have just come out of the editorial meeting and everyone's *on it*. Someone in 'content' is tracking Selena Gomez on Instagram, someone in 'tech' is building a hack to beat Facebook's audience limit, and someone in 'engagement' is updating a list of topics likely to trend over the next two hours. In every corner of the office, a screen is flashing the number of people on the website at any second. 'Nine thousand people now,' says Srivastav, with a flick of her shoulder in the direction of a screen.

Srivastav looks even younger than she is: chubby, curly-haired, twinkly-eyed. She joined WittyFeed two years ago, when she was twenty. 'They didn't ask me what I had done before. They asked me to sing. It was hard to sing in front of strangers, but I went along with the moment.' She needed the job. 'When my father died, it was hard for my mother to return to work because of her age. I have a little sister. I was in college in our home town in Gujarat, but I started looking for a job. One day I came to know there is a start-up in Indore that was hiring.' Srivastav's now the chief of content at WittyFeed. She began her writing career with a post on relationship advice. 'At first I didn't know what to say. You can't just write something like that. You have to be genuine. I started digging deep within myself, reading up. It was very important to put sentiment in such a piece. With time, we found our tone. Now we know how to write stories of great transformation. Say, someone who has a scar but is living her life. Ladies out there who we are trying to reach get inspired by these stories.'

She has helped contribute several other categories to WittyFeed's content mix over the two years: cats, beards, OMG. Her OMG instinct is seldom off: It's where she slotted the poop story. Written by WittyFeed's resident 'poop expert', 'What Happens to Your Poop in an Airplane Toilet Will Leave You Surprised' swiftly got to half a million views. The thumbnail shows a pair of legs in front of a toilet seat, red panties pulled down to its knees. Her first viral story—a photo puzzle titled 'A Husband Divorced His Wife after Looking Closer at this Picture'—was about a guy who comes home to find a man hiding under his wife's bed. Over 3 million people have viewed it so far. Her second viral story featured a lip-sync battle between Dwayne Johnson and Taylor Swift. 'It was shared by George Takei, of *Star Trek*. Suddenly, there were 50,000 people on the website. I was so thrilled. People were liking it, sharing it, commenting on it. That's when I knew, you know, that there is something right about what I do.' Her faith in the power of sharing validated, Srivastav threw herself into the WittyFeed life. Her mother and sister moved to Indore to live with her in a rented house. They have given up wondering about her unusual lifestyle. 'You are feeding American curiosity. There is always a story to do at three in the morning. You can't come into office at ten and do it; virality doesn't work like that.'

With every day at her job, she says she gets better at relating to her audience, no matter how different their world is from hers. 'I wrote a DIY story on how to make a swimming pool in your garden. Title—we kept it very relatable—"This Man Couldn't Afford a Swimming Pool but What He Did Next Is Truly Fantastic". It went viral. We have other ways. The moment you tell someone you are doing something wrong, automatically they will want to know. My story "The Way You Brush Your Teeth Is Wrong and You Don't Even Know about It!" got 2 million views. After the success of the airline poop story, we started to do a lot of "ever wondered" stories. "Ever Wondered What Female Astronauts Do When They Get Periods in Space?" One of our writers explained.'

Not every story hits a million views, but they are supposed to reach a minimum of 100,000. This is why so few survive the editorial wringer. 'You know the moment when you are scrolling through your Facebook feed, going through links without paying much attention, and then suddenly you scroll past something, and it makes you so curious you scroll back to click on the link—that's the kind of pull we put in our content. It should force you to click on it.' No law of clickbait science is overlooked. 'We have a system where we track every keyword that is important for virality—terrifying, shocking, inspirational.'

With every passing minute of our conversation, Srivastav's tone becomes more authoritative. She still looks like a teenager, but one who talks like a Silicon Valley boss. 'Together we control 1 million reach on Facebook alone through 50,000 pages as affiliates—popular pages on nail art, relationships, health and lifestyle. They should have at least 40,000 followers. They share our posts, we share revenue with them based on how many clicks they enabled. Ninety per cent of our traffic comes from Facebook. Usually, Indian and other clicks are non-premium. US, UK, Canada, Australia are premium. If I give $1 for 1000 clicks for India, I will give $7 for an American click.' She uses a similar formula to calculate the payment for the company's writers. 'Over 150 writers across the world—Philippines, China, Spain.' We are sitting at her desk, a long table she shares with eight other members of the content team. Some of them are currently reaching out to freelance writers in South America who can power exclusive Spanish-language content on their website. 'The demand has been insane.'

Srivastav clearly no longer works just to support her family. She doesn't even see herself as an employee. 'Everyone here is an entrepreneur. Everyone wants to be something.' The last thought to hit her before she falls asleep in the early morning is not about the next day's tasks but the next global city for the company's expansion. 'We want to open an office in LA. We are already setting up one in Singapore. Our main audience is America, so why should we think small?' Before I can applaud her ambition, she is off to interview a nineteen-year-old who has showed up at the reception. A couple of hours later, Srivastav tells me she wasn't impressed by the college student's attitude. The girl didn't have enough hunger.

The standard is set by the CEO, who constantly surveys the level of hunger around the newsroom from his seat in Winterfell. Like Ned Stark, the upright lord from *Game of Thrones*, he sits flanked by his trusted commanders—the CCO, who happens to be his younger brother, and the CTO, his best friend from college. Singhal's right hand is encased in plaster of Paris. 'Got upset about something and hit a wall,' he says.

Singhal seems to be aware that he is not entirely a normal person. He is thankful for his madness, though; it has brought him this far. Singhal grew up in a small village in Haryana where his father worked as a middleman, connecting farmers to the grain market. The first madness to grip him, at the age of sixteen, was to make money—lots and lots and lots of it. 'I wanted to be the richest person in the world. Starting with my village, then my block, then my district, then my state, then my country, and finally the world.' He had no idea how anyone became so rich, however. Most people in the village worked in and around farms; not one had made it past the tenth grade. Singhal decided to become a software engineer; it's what young people across India seemed to be doing to get rich. He moved to Delhi and started preparing for entrance tests to engineering colleges.

And then the second biggest madness of his life struck him. 'In Delhi I started reading newspapers, watching news channels and I realized that assholes were running our country. I was always patriotic—I love India and can literally do anything for it—but now I took a vow to claim the country back.' In 2009, the Congress party was about to enter its second term in power, and disillusioned youth across the country were gunning for change. In 2010, Singhal went to an engineering college in Tamil Nadu to get a degree in computer engineering. 'I really wanted to do something with the computer, some kind of business around it, but I realized I didn't have it in me to become a programmer.' Then, he discovered the internet, and shortly after, the world. 'The internet is the most powerful tool the world has ever invented. I became obsessed.'

Singhal realized he could employ the internet to achieve both his ends: become rich and fix the country. He already had a team that included his younger brother, who had followed him to the same college, and several classmates who wanted the same things as him. 'We started two things: a small business where we charged companies for developing their websites, and a website, Badlega India ("India will change"), where we posted things we thought young people should know about the country, from noteworthy news to personalities to monuments.' Badlega India was Singhal's idea of what India should be, powered by completely imaginary facts (India has lost ₹7,30,00,00,00,00,00,000 to corruption since Independence—enough money, among other things, to build 1.4 million low-cost houses) and extreme prescriptions (Should there be a 'citizen's charter' in public service offices, and severe punishments for not completing the jobs according to this charter?). 'My patriotism had hit its peak. I was blind with anger. A great country spoilt by some idiotic people chosen by us because of lack of awareness, who make wrong laws.' When he was not publishing articles calling for 'a youth revolution', he organized meetings and candlelit marches to the same end.

Nothing came of this, however, neither his business nor his activism. But his team did hit a gold mine where they were least expecting it. In late 2011, Singhal's younger brother, Parveen, then seventeen, set up a Facebook page to post 'amazing Indian things'. 'I had just discovered the internet. I was blown away by the things you could do,' says Parveen Singhal, now twenty-two and a proud digital native. 'I spent months watching every available movie on YouTube. It was so much fun. Then I discovered Facebook. I signed up, created a profile, started making friends, talking to them. I found it so interesting. Then I realized that you could create a page to post things you wanted to share with the whole world.' The page was called 'Amazing Things in the World', but all he posted on it were photos of Indian monuments like Akshardham and the Lotus Temple in Delhi. Within a month, thousands of people liked it. 'The interest was building. We thought why only buildings, why only India. There are so many things we see interesting in life. People, places, adventure, technology. Soon enough, half the likes on that page were from the US, the UK, Australia, Canada. Within a year the page had

1 million likes. It changed our whole story. The page has 4.2 million likes today. Whatever we are today, it's because of that single page.'

Once the Singhals figured out the market for content, it quickly led them to the idea of a website where they would only publish stuff that people couldn't resist—'junk food for the brain', as some now call viral content. The brothers applied to the publishing business the same formula that they had seen their father use in the grain market: arrive early and sell hard. They cared neither about the language—neither had encountered English before leaving their village—nor the substance of the stories they put up on WittyFeed. They cared only about their ability to hit the spot emotionally, from horny confessions to parenting disasters. It's not one's grip on facts that works in the business of clickbait, Vinay Singhal tells me about his post-truth world, but one's grip on people. 'Viral is in my head.' He had cracked the route to at least one of his dreams: becoming rich.

In 2014, the Singhals moved to Indore, where the third partner in their viral news business had grown up. The city was big enough to be full of young job aspirants and small enough to present them with few options. The young men pooled family resources, rented a small office in a shopping mall, hired a group of youngsters low on education and experience, and started churning out listicles: Seven Secret Tips to Please Your Boyfriend, Fourteen Secret Confessions by Horny Girls, Ten Weirdest Faces of Katy Perry. A couple of months after Srivastav joined the company, WittyFeed hit the million mark. The Singhals bought their first bungalow in Indore and brought their parents down from their village in Haryana.

Their father now spends his days running the city's trendiest clothing store in a swanky shopping mall. 'We started this shop for him where we sell only one fashion item of one kind. If you buy a dress from this shop you can be sure no one else in town has it.' The business model is another win for the brothers, but their father is still dealing with the shock of going from selling grains to selling cropped tops. 'He feels a little low, a little depressed. It's only college girls who come to the shop, they all speak to him in English. He gets disturbed by the short, cut-up clothes that are in demand. He used to work hard in the village. At forty-five, he has nothing left to do.' Later that evening, I stopped by the shop. Surrounded by stacks of the latest arrivals in halter dresses and torn jeans, Singhal senior appeared bored. I asked him if there was anything he likes about his new life. He nodded vaguely. I bought a long skirt to make him feel less hopeless about the world.

The father continues to judge everything by the standards of the village. But so do his sons. Parveen Singhal repeatedly calls himself a simple boy from a small village in Haryana—a simple boy from a small village who hashtags 'beard' and grooms his man bun. His brother too brings up the village to make every other point. 'I am the most successful person to come out of my village. One of my proudest moments was last year when my eighty-year-old grandfather came to Indore, saw the new office and said, 'Wow, this is as big as the village *mandi* (market).' Shortly after, Vinay Singhal married his village sweetheart, in what he calls the biggest adventure of his life. While he put together a company meant to prove India can lead the world, Singhal was also plotting his future wife's escape from confinement by her family, her punishment for loving a man outside her caste.

After he married her on the run and brought her to Indore, Singhal made his wife a senior editor at WittyFeed. She's currently in charge of the website's expansion into Spanish-language content. The twenty-three-year-old is *bhabhi*—

sister-in-law—to everyone in the office other than her
husband; she isn't only in charge of WittyFeed's content but
the well-being of the eighty youngsters whom her husband
considers his 'children'. Dressed as a newly-wed in a bright
red salwar-kurta and matching bangles, she walks through the
office passing around her blessings.

Bhabhi is the latest enforcer of what everyone at WittyFeed
calls the 'WittyFeed culture'. It's a jumble of Silicon Valley
ideas and village values. A day at WittyFeed begins with
a chanting of 'Om' and ends with a dance party. Every
celebration is broadcast live on Facebook and every conflict
sorted out in a panchayat, or village council. Relationships
are encouraged and emotions provoked. The Singhals believe
they have an edge over an American start-up because they
have turned theirs into a big, joint family. The millennial
workforces of their rivals may put their interests above that of
their companies, but there is nothing these eighty youngsters
who see Singhal as big brother wouldn't do at his command. 'If
you let Indian values guide you, you can beat any competition
in the West. Indians are not inferior to other people. We
are better than them because we have the institution of the
family,' says Singhal. 'Family is at the core of everything. The
company as family. The families of these kids—when their
parents come, we touch their feet.'

As the patriarch of this for-profit family, Vinay Singhal
takes great pride in being a template for the life of his young
employees. He wants them to be the kind of young Indians he
was earlier trying to create through his activism: with global
ambition and Indian values, youngsters who want to take
over the world without losing their pride in being Indian. Of
course, it's Singhal again who gets to decide what passes as an
Indian value. Partying is fine but with the family. 'Once every
month we hire the rooftop bar and throw a huge party for

them. Everything is arranged—whatever they want to have.'
I am assuming drinks and drugs come under 'everything'.
He is not as cool about smoking, though. 'I don't allow
them to smoke inside the office or anywhere outside.' The
youngsters are too captivated to mind. They talk about him
like brainwashed citizens talk about dictators.

'Vinay bhaiyya wants to change the country.'
'Bhaiyya becomes very angry if anyone criticizes India.'
'He is a guy who motivates me every single day. The way he talks,
the way he lives his life.'

He addresses them every Sunday morning in a monologue that
sounds like a motivational speech. Hours go by as he paces the
corner stage—'King's Landing'—setting goals for himself, his
team, his company and his country. 'For the next five years,
I will build the company, then for the next ten years I will
work on the country.' Behind him, they can see through the
towering floor-to-ceiling glass the flattened outline of Indore.
'I wanted them to feel on top of the world.' The architectural
strategy works. The view makes you giddy—especially if you
have been listening to the greatest man you know talk about
the greatest men he knows. Steve Jobs keeps coming up. Jobs'
spiel speaks directly to a bunch of kids who want to believe
they have as much of a claim to world domination as anyone
anywhere.

'Live your life as if you were to die tomorrow.'
'Sometimes life hits you in the head with a brick. Don't lose faith.'
'Stay hungry, stay foolish.'

Lately, Elon Musk shows up more and more. 'I am not proud
of it but I haven't read many books. I have read only one book

from cover to cover. The biography of Elon Musk. It changed my life,' Singhal told me. His world view is increasingly shaped by the tech demigod's sci-fi inspired existential philosophy.

> *'The future of humanity is going to bifurcate in two directions: either multi-planetary existence or extinction event.'*
> *'If humanity doesn't land on Mars in my lifetime, I would be very disappointed.'*
> *'The only thing that makes sense is to strive for greater collective enlightenment.'*

The other half of his motivational mother lode is also borrowed from America. Like his younger brother, Singhal has spent much of his time since his discovery of the internet meticulously exploring American pop culture. Most of his lessons for life and business come from American movies and television shows. '*Game of Thrones*: strategy, passion, principles. *Prison Break* for the idea that "There is no Plan B, there is Plan A1 A2 A3." Captain Jack of the Pirates of the Caribbean movies for undying attitude. At the end of the second movie, his ship's in the middle of a tornado and surrounded by enemy ships, when he brings out a sword and says, "Let's do this." *Breaking Bad*: Negative message but the guy does everything for his family. *Rocky*: Life is about how hard a hit you can take and move forward. I have faced eight bankruptcies. I thought back to the film at the point when I was ₹3 crore in debt and had ₹22 in my pocket.'

His motivational oeuvre expands every day. He may already have repeated to his team every noteworthy line from start-up billionaires and Hollywood heroes. The latest person to have motivated the literature-averse CEO is a nineteenth-century English poet who was once no stranger to India. 'Have you heard of Rudyard Kipling? Someone sent me a poem by him this morning. It's called "If". I have sent it to the whole team.'

I reread 'If' later that night, and realized which bit of it appealed to him and his team:

'If you can make one heap of all your winnings
And risk it on one turn of pitch-and-toss,
And lose, and start again at your beginnings
And never breathe a word about your loss.'

Entrepreneurial success is the biggest achievement in Singhal's Trump-era view of the world, and like the billionaire-turned-President of the United States, he thinks running a successful company makes him the most suitable candidate for running a country.

'My company, I look at it as a version of the country. When I lead it, it performs on every indicator. Everyone knows they have a job to do; there is a reason they are here and only if they are doing that properly will they be staying here. Why can't politics be the job of making this country better?'

His ideas of leadership too seem right out of the Trump playbook. 'A good leader is half democratic, half dictatorial.' I ask him if there is an Indian political leader who inspires him. I am not surprised by the answer. Like millions of young men rooting for India to take over the world, Singhal sees hope in Prime Minister Narendra Modi. The tech-savvy strongman has everything a man like Singhal wants in a leader. His stress on government accountability online has made those like Singhal believe he can run the country like an efficient company. 'Today one can tweet to a minister in his cabinet and get a response. It's one of his biggest achievements. Before 2014, I never thought your leaders could be so accessible to you. He addresses the public on the radio every week. People feel he is there.'

Loyal to his ilk, he rates politicians on how well they are using technology to make an impression. Rahul Gandhi is dismissed for not personally running his Twitter account. Arvind Kejriwal is admired for the 'multi-camera set-up' of his Facebook Live speeches. 'So mature, so professional. Really makes you believe he is connected to the youth.'

Singhal thinks he can do a better job than all of them. 'There is something that needs to be done and for that the right kind of people need to go into politics. If you want to change something, politics is the only way.' He feels that if he can build a $30 million company telling American audiences things they don't need to know, there is nothing he can't do. Lately, though, he has started feeling that Indian politics is a very small game for him to get into. 'I no longer want to just be the prime minister of this country.'

I didn't go to Indore to listen to Vinay Singhal's plans to change India and the world. I merely wanted to know how he built one of the world's largest content farms without leaving that city. But Singhal just isn't that interested in talking about business. He has made his point with the website's stats. All he wants to discuss is his 'vision'. The deeper he sinks into it, the more distant he appears from our physical surroundings. I am sitting right across the table from him in the peppy WittyFeed Café—'the best in town'—but he is clearly not with me. His eyes are fixed somewhere behind me and I turn back to trace their focus in the motion-blur workings of the after-hours newsroom—America will wake up any time now—but he's not looking at anything I can see. His next words come to me after a pause. 'I want to lead humanity. Humanity is bigger than a country. I want to go outside the earth. I want humanity to be a multi-planetary existence. I want to lead Mars.'

* * *

I noted that down calmly. This was by no me

thing someone told me that year. Between 2014

talking to youngsters in the far corners of In

when I seemed to be able to finish their senten

my notebooks overflowed with statements of their extreme

emotions: their hopes, plans, fears, dreams. More than half

of India's population is under the age of twenty-five. It is

the largest number of young people of any country on earth.

'Never before have there been so many young people,' a 2014

UN report noted in a clearly overwhelmed tone. And then it

distilled the meaning of India's unprecedented demographic

edge into the plainest possible words: 'Never again is there

likely to be such potential for economic and social progress.

How we meet the needs and aspirations of young people will

define our common future.'

The world's future depends on young Indians meeting

their aspirations, but it's a pipe dream at this point. As

developmental economists have been warning for years, India

needs urgently to take care of its '3E' problem. What that

means is a majority of India's youth bulge falls into one of these

three categories: uneducated, unemployed or unemployable.

A country that depends solely on its youth bulge to become a

superpower hasn't yet figured out how to turn the numbers

into an asset.

The logistics of the challenge befuddle even the most

hopeful of India cheerleaders. To call the shots in the global

economy, India will need to educate about 100 million young

people over the next ten years, a task never before undertaken

in history. At least 1000 universities will need to be built

over this period and nearly 50,000 colleges. (To put things in

context, the United States has a total of 4200 colleges.) Even

if the country magically achieves this feat, questions about the

quality of education in these schools and colleges will persist.

At the moment, fewer than 17 per cent of India's graduates are immediately employable. Only 2.3 per cent of the Indian workforce has undergone formal skill training (compared to 80 per cent in Japan and 96 per cent in South Korea). They want jobs nevertheless; to choose to be unemployed in India is a privilege few can afford. The country is struggling to create jobs for its young, though. Around 117 million people need to be absorbed into new and more productive jobs. The growing gap between jobs and jobseekers may lead to what the International Labour Organization calls a 'scarred generation'. It predicts the 'collective frustration' will spark off protest movements and social instability.

The slide has begun. Over the last three years, large sections of young Indians in many Indian states have hit the streets rioting over job quotas. In Andhra Pradesh, they shut down road and rail networks. In Haryana, they cut off the flow of water to the country's capital. In Gujarat, they locked down factories and were fired at by the police. In Maharashtra, they threatened annihilation of those covered under affirmative action. Things are going to get worse.

The majority of India's youth bulge still lives in its backwaters. The provincial masses make up the heart of modern India, but one rarely hears about them. They only show up in my newsfeed before a major Indian election, when my colleagues, on sweeping tours of the hinterland, gauge the mood of 'the young voter'. They come back with the same conclusion: A wave of aspiration is sweeping through the Indian hinterland.

It almost seemed as if the farther you lived from a big city, the bigger your dreams. We could tell what they wanted— more choices, in opportunity and income, personal values and political views, love and lifestyle—but not what drove them to want those things. Figuring that out wasn't as easy.

A crucial period of time separated us. Seen one wa
about their lives is any different from that of th
or grandparents at their age—from where they li
they live. Shift perspective slightly, and nothing is familiar. A
twenty-year-old in Indore has the same access to information
as someone his age in Iowa—and could very well have the
same desires. They see no connection between where they
live and what they want from their lives.

What happens when 100 million people suddenly start
dreaming big, in a place where no one is prepared for it—
families, teachers, employers, governments? They realize they
are on their own. They reconcile themselves to the idea that
they must build a world in which they can be what they want
to be, where how well you do depends on how badly you want
to do well. Once they have created this bubble of aspiration,
they chase their dreams like their life depends on it—do or
die.

Young Indians are using their imagination to create
options—economic, political, cultural—in the unlikeliest of
spaces. Could WittyFeed become the biggest media company
in the world? I had no more reason to believe so now than
before I stepped into the small-town fairy tale. By the time I
discovered Singhal and his empire, the magic of clickbait was
beginning to fade. Among other reasons, Facebook was less
interested in letting other players profit from its popularity. If
WittyFeed wanted to keep up the numbers, it would have to
reinvent its game. It wasn't what went viral that interested me,
but the fact that an obscure company in Indore played a role in
the global rise of clickbait news.

I would see Singhal a couple more times at big-city events
pondering the rise of small-town spirit; the moment he was
put on a stage, the CEO went on and on about being a 'simple
guy from a small village'. Holding forth in his imperfect

English, he told his audience of nervous youngsters to take pride in their imperfect English. Projecting his page views on life-size screens, he told them to believe the future of the world depended on their ideas. Staring straight into the soul of his desperate generation, he told them they needed to make India great again.

Eyes red from sleepless nights of plotting his and his country's rise to glory, Singhal seems like the face of the new India. This new India is not always easy to like. To begin with, it's more male than female. Men are frequently under more pressure than women to take charge—of family, society, nation. Between 2004–05 and 2009–10, more than 24 million men joined the workforce, while 21.7 million women dropped out of it. Avid investigators of the trend such as World Bank blame it on 'social norms: marriage, motherhood, vexed gender relations and biases, and patriarchy'.

This is a generation of Indians hanging between extremes. They are hitting adulthood with the cultural values of their grandparents—socially conservative, sexually timid, God-fearing—but the life goals of American teenagers: money and fame. They have the bleakest chance at a real opportunity—a million Indians enter the job market every month; perhaps 0.01 per cent of them find steady jobs—but the fanciest possible ideas about success. They are the most global young Indians ever, but with the narrowest ideas of what it means to be Indian, based on language, region, religion, and an exaggerated notion of the country's precolonial glories. A majority of them are frustrated with India's old politics—synonymous in their minds with the Congress party's stodgy, heavy-handed liberalism—but their idea of a new politics is that of the ruling Bharatiya Janata Party's, one of exclusionary nationalism and sectarian division. This is the most desperate generation of Indians since Independence—86 per cent of

them have been found to feel 'anxious' about their future—
but also the one most bent on world domination. No matter
how poorly placed they find themselves now, they make up
the world's largest ever cohort of like-minded young people,
and they see absolutely no reason why the world shouldn't
run by their rules. The consequences for the rest of us, inside
and outside India, of young India's determination, won't just
be economic. The idea that only they can help themselves
will lead this generation of Indians to redefine everything
according to their perspective: work, success, morality. It will
change our world in ways we can't yet imagine.

At first I thought I knew what it meant to be young in an
India changing around me every day. I knew the frustration
of not being able to find your place and the urge to turn
everything upside down to forge it. As a girl growing up in
a middle-class family in small towns in a newly liberal India,
I constantly recalibrated who I was, what I thought of the
world, and what I wanted from it. Fortunately for me, the
most difficult part of this process was to convince myself that
I ought to think bigger. I didn't have to fight for survival or
success but only for individual freedoms—to leave home, to
work for joy, to marry for love, and to set my own rules for
life. My fight wasn't against state or system, but tradition.
Protected from the harsh realities of other people in a high-
caste, upper-class cocoon, the only entity I had to fight was
my family, and it didn't put up much of a fight.

Unlike young Indians today, I couldn't be angry with
the world, because I didn't have enough of a reason. I was
too busy being fascinated by it. The country had just let the
world in through a hole in its iron door, and I was enchanted
by its colourful brilliance. I could access thrills available thus
far only to teenagers in luckier parts of the world: cable TV,
pop music, high-school comics. I was equally thankful for the

variety it brought to my everyday life, starting with being able to choose from more than one brand of soap. Growing up in an India better in so many ways than the country in which my parents were young, I wondered how anyone could find anything wrong with it. As far as I could see from where I stood, India was rising.

This was what everyone else was saying, too, including hardened cynics. Touring India during the early '90s, V.S. Naipaul saw the country embracing 'the idea of freedom' and achieving 'liberation of spirit' in spite of its usual challenges— 'group excess, sectarian excess, religious excess, regional excess.' One of every five headlines featuring India in the *New York Times* in that decade announced the signing of an exciting business deal with a foreign corporation. The things that were being built could send India soaring into the future, from space technology to personal computers.

But unlike the young people I now encounter, a twenty-year-old me didn't want India to rule the world. I was happy just to see my country become one with it. My politics were the politics of my parents, who then identified as voters of the Congress party. It had been the party their parents had voted for; it was the only party to vote for. Not only did it win freedom for India, but the party of Jawaharlal Nehru and his descendants established what India would be at home—secular, socialist, democratic—and in the world—an advocate of equality and justice. No one thought the Congress was perfect—it enabled nepotism, corruption and authoritarianism—but it shaped India into a modern, technological and scientifically advanced nation, at least during its early period in power. More than that, though, people saw it as a party that *got* India and kept it going in the face of its extremes. The Congress, I heard growing up, was a party for everyone: Hindus and Muslims, rich and poor, old and young. I question the faith now, but I believed it then.

I similarly inherited my parents' prejudices, rarely voiced, of class, caste, region and religion. Unlike the twenty-year-olds of 2017, though, I was fortunate enough to become a thinking adult before post-truth—so I didn't read books and articles to validate my ideas but to question them. And mostly ended up embarrassed.

I began researching and reporting this book prepared to see young Indians as younger versions of myself—barely a decade had passed since I too had been an anxious eighteen-year-old —but it took me only a few full days with the eighteen-year-olds of the 2010s to realize they couldn't be more different.

Unlike a younger me, they have no trouble believing they were born to be big—it is, in fact, the first thing they often know about themselves. Their problem is that no one else cares what they think of themselves. Such lack of interest should make them wary of their ideas and sceptical of their expectations, but oddly that's not happening. Left to their illusions, they keep stretching and strengthening them until they can stand as a wall between them and the indifference of the world.

I knew little of this when, in a Delhi distant from the Indian heartland, I started thinking about my country's great baby boom generation. All I knew at that point was that decoding them—perhaps 600 million people—was crucial to decoding contemporary India. Everyone agreed the country was going through the trickiest phase of its transformation— political, economic, cultural—and no one had more at stake than people starting out their adult lives. I specialized in stories of young Indians making sense of a world spinning off its axis. I wrote earnest reports about their attempts to adapt to its whims. I sat in 'personality development' classes in Delhi where young men from villages in Haryana and Rajasthan learnt how to *present* themselves. I spent nights chatting with men in distant corners of the country—from Saharanpur in Uttar Pradesh to Salem in Tamil Nadu—on the first internet dating website to try the Indian market. I spent days reading self-published novels in which young Indians who had made the journey of self-discovery through jobs, places and relationships addressed other young Indians about to undertake it.

Most of my subjects were men: awkward, anxious, aggressive. I always kept a distance, probing into their deepest emotions from behind a screen—books, internet, classroom. I was afraid of what I would find if I went too close.

But the more I talked to them, the more I felt the need to go closer. They were happy to tell me everything about themselves, but some of them shared the intimate details of their lives with the caveat that I wouldn't understand it all sitting in Delhi. I once asked a young man in a distant suburb of Mumbai who cheated foreigners for a living how he got into the business. He said, 'I can tell you everything on the phone, but once—just once—come down and let me take you to my neighbourhood, my home, my workplace.'

In mid-2014 I began travelling to small towns and villages to find out what young Indians want, how they intend to get there, and how their dreams will change their world and ours. The year marked a test for the possibility of a new India. The dreamers had elected as their prime minister a man who spoke to their anxieties and hopes: of jobs, progress, glory. The country was finally going to be cast in the imagination of its most demanding voters. Young Indians had brought Narendra Modi to power; now they expected him to keep his end of the deal. He knows what they want, but can he help them make their dreams come true? What will the country's future look like if he does? And what happens if he can't?

I went, first, to my home town. Ranchi used to be the
kind of town where if you grew up middle-class, everyone
your family knew worked in a government office or in the
family business. Few people outside of India's east had heard
of its name until a decade or so ago, when it produced, out of
nowhere a captain for the Indian cricket team. For years, every
youngster in Ranchi who could leave, left. It was the only way
to make something of yourself, as a doctor, engineer, lawyer,
journalist, company man.

It's not only my friends and I who left. Anyone who
was barely of working age did the same, joining the global
economy of big cities as factory workers or delivery men. On
an average day in Delhi or Mumbai, I could conceivably meet
more people from my grandfather's village in Bihar than those
native to these megapolises. Over the years, I asked many
why they left. Irrespective of what they did—teaching yoga
in south Delhi or shopping for expats in Bandra—the answer
was the same: to move up.

Before 2014, I had only flown back to Ranchi for the
occasional family reunion on Holi or Diwali. My parents still
lived there, as did my sister. Like every Indian city of its size
and scale—the growing towns of a few million called 'Tier-2
cities'—Ranchi had changed over the decade from a dot on
India's map to an aspiring 'global' city. It looked enormously
different to me every time. The markers of Tier-2 modernity
added up over the years: airport, apartment complexes, token
chain-brand hotel, token shopping mall. So did the markers of
Tier-2 mess: traffic, pollution, crime, sewage. I saw the process
of its makeover as an insider who'd rather be an outsider. It
was easier to change its appearance than its thinking; I wasn't
too hopeful about the latter.

The smallest thing about an Indian small town isn't, after
all, its physical area or population—Ranchi is bigger and more

populous than many sovereign republics—but its imagination.
I was back to challenge my notions. I also travelled to other
towns and villages, places so small they made Ranchi seem like
a vast, shining paradise. I was looking for places where someone
young would go in pursuit of success in a new India, zones of
opportunity you could enter without being armed with the
qualifications of the past, neither academic cut-offs nor important
contacts. You could become, for example, an 'event manager'.
After three years of roaming second-tier India, I came back
with more visiting cards from event managers than from people
engaged in any other profession. Every occasion was an 'event'
and nothing was above being managed, from company galas to
government functions. Everyone was managing weddings; so,
when the competition got tough, private pastimes had to be
turned into public spectacles, beginning with the morning puja.

Or you could enter the 'media'. Not the media as I
understood it as a journalist, a job that needed you to be good
with language or general knowledge or the ability to find the
truth of things. The only instinct that attracted my young
friends to a media job was the desire to influence what people
think. Vinay Singhal wasn't the only young man I met who
was drawn to the thrill. The first youngster I befriended in
Ranchi was the twenty-six-year-old host of the city's most
popular radio show, Josh Factory—'40 per cent information
and 60 per cent entertainment.' R.J. Shanky was more
interested in the information part. Not plain information,
but his take on information. 'Take. Take is most important,'
he once explained his media motto to me. 'You have to take
90-degree news and spin it 360 degrees.'

Like Singhal and his team, Shanky doesn't offer his
audience—nearly a million listeners—news, but the emotions
with which to react to it: pride, relief, shame, outrage. Just out
of college, Shanky had followed many of his friends to Delhi

and ended up at a call centre of a big IT company.
back before completing a year. 'If I hadn't, I would
just another call centre guy in Delhi.' Now, eight years after the
epiphany, R.J. Shanky is a legitimate celebrity who spends most
of his time building his brand. In his free moments, he—like
everyone else—offers his take on how to fix the country.

'The problem with our country is that no one knows their
job: politicians, bureaucrats, police. Indian politicians are not
efficient for their profession. They know politics, but they
can't execute what they are elected to do.'

If he could, he would run his country like a company.

'There should be a meeting every three months for
elected representatives where they prove themselves fit for the
job, show what they have achieved. There should be a rating
system for them, the public should score them on the basis of
term-based performance.'

If a country was run like a company, he imagines everyone
would do according to his or her merit—no special ground
for discrimination and none for privilege.

'Why are we still creating policies on the basis of caste,
religion or place of birth?'

His favourite Bollywood film is one in which young
idealists like him take over the Parliament in Delhi.

'It's about time.'

You can always enter politics to court money and power in
India—old or new—except now a young man who wants to
be an MP or state legislator doesn't feel the need to fit the type.
He doesn't need a vote bank or electoral funding or even the
ability to herd 5000 people into a political rally, but simply the
confidence that he knows better than everyone else in charge.
I have lost count of the number of young men who told me a
country should be run like a company. Most of them dreamt
of running their own companies, of course.

Was that the new Indian dream? It certainly seemed a break from the past. For generations, ordinary young Indians didn't have an option but to work for wages; now every second one of them has an idea for a start-up. Perhaps they need an idea like that—after all, they know they have a poor chance of landing a salaried job. But, more crucially, they have consulted their smartphones and learnt that one no longer has to be rich to dream of running one's own company. All over the world, they are aware, people like themselves are building the companies of their dreams from hope and thin air.

The current government is happy to pump the dream with promises that make India sound like the ultimate destination for a young entrepreneur. In May 2017, cornered about a 'job apocalypse', the BJP's president and Modi's lieutenant, Amit Shah said, 'It is impossible to provide employment through jobs in a country with more than a billion people.' Three years into a regime won by promising jobs, the BJP said it was going to give Indians 'opportunities for self-employment'. Lurking behind the buzzwords pushing a smart and self-made India is a message the target audience is too busy to notice: 'We can't deal with your dreams—but we are very happy to leave you in charge of them.'

I never had to look around for dreamers; they were crawling out of corners like zombies in a horror movie. But I was drawn only to a few. Some things were obviously common to the people I chose to follow: For one, they had the biggest dreams. Each of them wanted to end up at least one of the following: rich, important, famous. Their ambition went beyond what seemed reasonable: Reading my notes at the end of a day spent with any of them, I would be surprised by the number of times I had used words like 'crazy' or 'insane'. Mostly, that was a record of what they had called themselves or of what other people had called them—but on some occasions, I had just failed to find another word that fit.

Except for a couple of them, who wanted only to be important, most people I followed wanted money and influence. And in each of their cases, I didn't know or understand how they could dream of these things starting off from where they were. I couldn't get over the gap between their reality and dreams; they, on the other hand, couldn't care less. Even the fact that they had no one else to help them but themselves made no difference. They were obsessed with their dreams and I was obsessed with their attempts to make them real.

No two of them went about it in the same way. They could be naive or shrewd, honest or crooked, cynical or idealistic— often at the same time. But there was something about them, beyond the single-mindedness, that I couldn't define. I kept returning to their lives to discover the answer. And to find out if they would—could—become as rich or important or famous as they wanted to be. Like every journalist covering the everyday drama of frustrated hopes, I was curious about what the future looked like.

But also, while I had no way to divine it, I had a feeling that in these people's ability or inability to meet their dreams lay some clue to the future of India. I wondered what kind of people have a chance at their dreams and what kind of dream has a chance of coming true; I was equally interested in what happens to those who have no chance at all.

I followed some for years, some for months, and some for days—in no particular order. I first met some of them on reporting assignments and wrote parts of their stories for newspapers and magazines. I had to ask each of them if I could enter their lives for some time and they were happy to let me in. I have changed some of their names, either

on request or to spare them trouble. I also followed their
lives the way they preferred, on social media. There, they
construct elaborate personas that came ever closer to making
their dreams real; there, they share regular, and elaborate,
updates about life, work and everything in between. Their
timelines sometimes read as neat accounts of their lives; but,
also, it is only on social media that Indians of a particular age
were willing to present a complete picture of themselves:
personal, political, professional. If they had something to
say to me—an important update to pass on—they left me a
message on Facebook or WhatsApp, their two main channels
of communication with the world. Often, they only spoke to
me through photos and videos.

I observed some of these journeys from the outside and
occasionally entered the others. I offered my advice if they
asked for it. I didn't always approve of their decisions and they
didn't always care what I thought. It was hard not to be affected
by the developments in their lives, nevertheless. I celebrated
their successes and mourned their failures. They saw me as
half-outsider, half-insider. It wasn't a great place to occupy.
It meant, for example, that they refused to understand why I
couldn't help them beyond telling them what was wrong and
right—especially since they asked so rarely. *But can't you see
that I need your help right now?* I disappointed one by refusing
to buy him a train ticket to escape a dead end, and another by
saying that I couldn't pay the interest on his car loan.

Our relationships couldn't help but be shaped by the fact
that they were mostly men and I, a woman. Often I happened to
be the only woman in their lives outside of family—and unlike
any they knew. I lived alone in a big city, travelled to the ends
of the world to talk to random men, and couldn't stop asking
questions. Our interactions rarely started smoothly. It could
go either way: They could be respectful or patronizing, smitten

or suspicious, vulnerable or protective. We got around the tension at some point. They had their obsessions to return to and so did I. Everyone I followed knew exactly what I was doing; not one of them was surprised at the fact of being chosen. Long before I showed up with a notebook and pen, they had known that someday someone would.

2

The English Man

I HAD BEEN hanging out in Ranchi for a year before I stepped into The American. I saw the signboard every time I drove along Lalpur Road; and I drove along Lalpur Road every time I left the house. The long, narrow strip is a crucial link between major localities in the city. It serves as a crucial link of another kind, too: between the career ambitions of most kids in and around Ranchi, and their chances of succeeding. The gulf between jobs and jobseekers is what drives business along Lalpur Road. This is how it has been as long as I can remember. The wider the gap is, the more alluring the promise of closing it. When I lived in Ranchi, Lalpur Road was largely a middle-class refuge; it's where your parents sent you to train for entrance exams to professional institutes and jobs worthy of respect in society: medicine, engineering, management, banking, administrative services. You couldn't imagine a career to which a coaching centre on Lalpur Road didn't promise an entry.

But there were only so many careers you could imagine in 2001. Things have changed now. The number of jobs in the market may not be growing at an ideal rate, but there is a new kind of job in the market every day. If a job promises a decent amount of money and status, it is sure to come with an entrance exam tailored to take in as few people as possible and a coaching centre on Lalpur Road selling success in said exam. And unlike the blissful days of middle-class monopoly over 'decent' jobs, everyone who is eligible is in the race.

Today the area is a jungle of coaching centres. Every inch of real estate has been claimed by one-room establishments selling success in one or the other entrance examination: MBA/APMT/SSC/PMT/NTSE/NEET/SLEET/MCS/JAC/ BPSC. The road even has a three-storey shopping mall just for coaching centres, each flashing a different acronym on its glass front. The skyline is a battle of billboards, flashing blown-up mugshots of star teachers, the currency of the coaching economy—Sunil Kumar (PHY) IIT, IIM/Rakesh Sharma (CHEM) BHU/Nitin Mehra (Calculus) Roorkee, IIM. The tougher an entrance exam a teacher claims to have cracked himself, the greater his value in the market.

English makes a side entry into this universe; all this coaching will come to naught if you can't answer questions in English. If you are lucky, you can choose to write your answers in a regional language, but you can't crack an interview in India without explaining to a suited man in English why you deserve the job. So for every five coaching institutes offering proficiency in maths or reasoning, there is one simply selling 'Spoken English'. Or these days, just 'Spoken'. And the people who 'speak' are 'The Speaking People'.

That, at least, is what they are termed by the American Academy of Spoken English, a fast-growing chain of coaching centres seizing the market for upward mobility. It's a branding brainwave the organization is visibly proud of. And going by the rate at which The American is spreading through the interiors of north India—from slums in Delhi to hilltops in Dehradun—the message seems to have worked. The American has four branches in Ranchi alone, the largest of which is suitably perched on Lalpur Road. A big red arrow indicates a turn off the main road. One day in March 2015, I took that left turn. Five youngsters were waiting in a queue at the reception, where a man not much older than them was taking a father and son through the rates for various 'packages'. I could see his face on a newspaper clipping stuck to the wall behind him. Three youngsters were poring over a pamphlet on a sagging sofa in a corner, the only other piece of furniture. The anxiety level in the room was rising by the second. 'What can I do for you?' the man asked me when we came face to face. I asked him about the courses on offer. 'Basic Communication, Personality Development, Group Discussion, Interview,' he rattled off, each capital letter loaded with the weight of practice. 'Why should I join The American?' I asked him. 'Because we believe that *anyone* can speak English.' From this brief exchange we had in English, Moin Khan knew I wasn't really there to learn spoken English. Crossing his arms on the table, he asked me what it was I actually wanted from him. I said I was there to understand spoken English as a tool for life improvement. I told him I wanted to attend a course in Basic Communication. We made a deal: He would let me attend his classes for spoken English if I paid the fee (₹1800). 'Come with me then,' Khan motioned me out of the room and up a flight of stairs, 'I have been teaching a new batch. It's a good place for you to watch the process. People who join this course don't know their ABC.' What I had to do at my end of the deal was to keep my mouth shut in class.

* * *

Moin Khan didn't know his ABC himself until ten years ago. He was seventeen years old when he heard about the free English class. He remembers where he was at that point: in the village market, selling balloons. He hadn't spent much time in a classroom. His family's income came from their two cows; from the time he could handle a pail, Khan spent most of the day delivering milk from one doorstep to another. In the evenings, he spread a sheet on a pavement and sold things—'firewood, toys, anything.' Not in a position to waste precious daylight in a classroom, Khan enrolled in a local college where he had to show up once a year—to sit for the annual exam. He knew a few things for sure: that he would have an undergraduate degree in arts at the end of the three years; and that he had no idea what he was going to do with it. He knew that people could become rich and powerful through education; and also that he didn't have that option. Moin Khan could neither become a software engineer and join the new elite, nor enter the administrative service and join the old. His father didn't have the money to hand that Vinay Singhal's had, which allowed access to a coaching centre in Delhi—or even to one on Lalpur Road.

But there was one respectable job he could land without taking an entrance examination—at a call centre. It was the ultimate cheat's guide to the white-collar world. All he needed to do to get in was speak English. Not the English of English literature or that of official project reports, but a cut-price version called, simply, Spoken English. It required of its user barely the ability to speak a set of sentences to get through basic communication in a globalizing India. Spoken English was going to be the operative language of the new India, the currency of communication at 'multi-cuisine resto-bars', shopping malls, airport check-ins.

Most notably, spoken English enabled the phenomenon that was the Indian call centre. In 1998, an entrepreneur in Delhi hung two intersecting rows of saris from the ceiling of his office, installed a landline and headphone set in each of the 'booths', hired a team of eighteen to answer the phones, and set in motion his brainwave: routing the customer calls coming into American businesses to India and charging the companies a fraction of what they'd been paying for the same service back home. As he pointed out to his interviewers in the following years, someone had to monetize the combined English-speaking skill of 100 million Indians.

From 2000 to 2011, India cornered more than half of the world's call centre market. In 2005, the Indian call centre industry peaked, its revenue growing 38 per cent. By 2006, when Moin Khan heard his first-ever burst of spoken English by making a customer service call on a borrowed cell phone, it had sparked the curiosity of the whole nation. In 2006, over 2 million Indians were employed in the call centre industry. The first lot of call centre employees was crammed with urban English-speaking college-goers for whom the night shift was a short cut to financial independence. All their 'multinational' companies in Gurugram or Bangalore had to do was allot them American names—Harry for Harish, John for Janardhan—and train their accents until their 'r's became softer and their 'v's differentiated from their 'w's. Towards the latter half of the 2000s, the industry was growing faster than college students were joining it. To keep up its pace, the call centre industry needed to tap into the next level of human resources—non-English speakers who could be trained to speak English as if they knew the language. So did an India gunning to be a global powerhouse. The business of spoken English soon took over the landscape of aspirational India. If you wanted to know the state of development of a place, you ran your eyes around the local market and counted the advertisements for spoken English centres. They followed the same formula as coaching centres preparing you for entry into engineering colleges or the administrative service, but with some crucial differences: No previous qualification was demanded, the training lasted only as long as you could spare, and regardless of how much English you managed to learn, you came out a winner.

In the summer of 2004, Natural Creative English Vision opened a coaching centre in Khunda. The village may only be an hour's drive from Ranchi, but it's 100 years in the past. You simply don't drive down there unless you have to. And someone finally had a reason. To get things started, the man in charge sent out word to the whole village inviting youngsters to attend a free class. Moin Khan was one of the seven teenagers who showed up the next day. It was the first time Khan saw someone speak English. He was enchanted. Everything the man said over the next hour seemed to Khan to be full of knowledge he'd no idea existed in the world. As he shuffled out of class that day, feeling like a thief who'd found the treasure while looking for coins, there was only one thing running through his mind: 'I want to be just like this man.'

After a week of free classes, the teacher invited the youngsters to join a six-month course by paying ₹550. Khan didn't have the money. But he knew he had to come up with it. Over the next two months, he offered his services to everyone in the village who had a cow. After two months of milking cows, Khan counted his funds: ₹350. He put the cash in his pocket, walked to the coaching centre and told the teacher there was nothing in the world that he wanted more than to join the classes, but he was still short of ₹150. The man asked him to start the next day.

The new students were supposed to begin with an introduction before the whole class. It took Moin Khan eleven days. It wasn't the part about having to speak English that he feared. What got his tongue every time he tried to get up from his seat was his 'level'. He recognized everyone else in the class; he knew they came from 'respectable' families, and had actually sat in a classroom before. He feared they could smell the cow dung on him. He wasn't going to be able to address them as an equal until his English was equal to theirs. And so, Khan hardly slept for the next six months. Every night when he came back from the market, he sat in a corner of his house with his notebook and repeated aloud every single word the English teacher had uttered in the day's class. Not only did he try to copy his teacher's pronunciation of words, but also the manner in which they were delivered—whether it was with a pause or a drawl or a chuckle. The teacher used to make his English sound effortless by dropping in words from the local dialect. That's the effect Khan strived for in his private practice sessions.

And so it was that by scripting and performing this lively mimicry night after night as his village slept that Moin Khan learnt spoken English. One day at the end of it, he stood before his class and made his first public address in English: 'Good morning to all. It's a gala day for me.' He wasn't satisfied, though. No matter how much he tried to learn by copying, he could tell that when a sentence in English came out of his mouth, it sounded false. He knew there was only one way to solve the problem: to speak more English. That was his 'new mission'. And one day walking back home, he invented a way to execute it. When he woke up the next day, Khan borrowed his father's mobile phone and dialled 121, the toll-free customer service number for the cell phone service provider. It was the only contact he could summon with an English-speaking person outside of the class. So he spoke and spoke to the call centre executive in whatever English he had picked up so far. It became a daily routine. Often the person at the other end hung up after the first few seconds of his ramble. But every once in a while, they listened as Khan told them 'everything that came to my mind—my friends, my family, my dreams'.

The more Khan tried, the more he felt it wasn't enough. He was about to reach the end of the coaching programme. If he couldn't transfer to daily life the English he had learnt in the class, not only would he have lost dozens of business hours, but also any chance of moving up in life. So a few weeks before his course was to wrap up, Khan gathered his closest friends and took them to the bank of a river that flowed near the village. There, standing in a circle with the only six people he could trust, he made them take an oath to which the river was witness: 'We shall speak only English for a month.' They followed it for thirteen days. It included days when Khan's family thought he had gone mad because he wouldn't speak to any of them.

The last day of the course in spoken English began with a speech by the teacher. Concluding his role as mentor, the man asked the graduating batch to go out and chase their dreams. Before the class ended, he asked Moin Khan to come and see him in his office. Five minutes later, he asked the jittery seventeen-year-old standing across from him to take over as the new teacher. Khan was supposed to feel on top of the world, but all he felt in that moment was cold horror: 'I was only thinking about the reactions of the people I was supposed to teach. I was the same person who dispatched milk to their houses in the morning—"this *gwala* (milkman) will teach us English!" they would say the moment I stand before the class!'

English encodes class in India. It does so by sliding into the DNA of social division: income, caste, gender, religion or place of belonging. The threat it poses to social cohesion is persistent enough that it has worried public commentators across the political spectrum. Even Mahatma Gandhi, who once famously claimed that 'to give millions a knowledge of English is to enslave them'.

In another address, delivered as independent India's Parliament dilly-dallied over the suggestion to replace English with regional languages as the medium of instruction for higher education, Gandhi said, 'This blighting imposition of a foreign medium upon the youth of the country will be counted by history as one of the greatest tragedies. Our boys think, and rightly in the present circumstances, that without English they cannot get Government service. Girls are taught English as a passport to marriage.'

A hundred years after Gandhi's first address, during which English became a part of the country's global game, the language continues to be seen as a tool of exclusion. The problem now is not about the imposition of a colonial language on clueless natives, but an inequality of access. 'To be denied English is harmful to the individual as well as our society,' writes Chetan Bhagat, self-appointed leader of a class war set off by unequal access to English. Bhagat, an engineer-turned-investment banker, wrote his first college romance in English in 2004, the same year Moin Khan's village got its first coaching centre for spoken English. Then only a certain kind of person—someone who grew up reading, writing and speaking the language—wrote books in English. And that, too, in a certain kind of English—big words, long sentences, literary pretension, heavy with Orientalism. In the ten years since Bhagat put the popular in 'popular' English fiction, he has written six other novels and sold millions of copies all told. With every new book, all written in a deliberately simple English, Bhagat has recruited thousands of new soldiers in his crusade against what he calls the 'caste system around the language'. Bhagat even has a term for Indians who 'have' English: E1. 'These people had parents who spoke English, had access to good English-medium schools—typically in big cities, and gained early proficiency, which enabled them to consume English products such as newspapers, books and films. English is so instinctive to them that even some of their thought patterns are in English. These people are much in demand.' The people E1 presumably control, through a nexus of privilege built on ownership of English, are E2: 'probably ten times the E1s. They are technically familiar with the language. [But] if they sit in an interview conducted by E1s, they will come across as incompetent, even though they may be equally intelligent, creative or hard-working.'

The situation may not be so comically stark. The haves and have-nots may not exactly fit into Bhagat's stereotypes of urban, sophisticated rich people and provincial, uncultured poor. His argument does not factor in many other walls around English in India. You are more likely to learn English if you are born a man rather than a woman, high caste rather than low caste, south Indian rather than north Indian. There is more than one kind of E1 and more than one kind of E2. And there is more than one way E2s can overthrow E1s. One is to speak it like they know it. Central to this coup is the spoken English institute.

* * *

The Moin Khan who stands before a class of fifty in Ranchi's number one coaching centre for spoken English looks anything but nervous. It has been ten years since he first entered such a classroom and stood next to the blackboard. The twenty-seven-year-old currently pacing the podium is a study in nonchalance. He's neither handsome nor tall, but he has the attribute that truly counts in the imagination of the people he's about to address: cool. Dark locks of hair fall on his forehead on either side with a flair that makes his small face, covered in careless stubble, interesting. His clothes, a mix of casual and formal—collared T-shirt, linen trousers, pointed black shoes—make his small, slight build look fashionable. When he finally faces the class, his expression is focused, his round eyes glowing with intensity.

It's a small room with two rows of wooden benches divided by a narrow aisle. Girls sit on one side and boys on the other. It's poorly furnished—a beige curtain covering the entrance, a split air conditioner unit, a small whiteboard, a rickety podium. The set-up is redolent of urgency. It's visible on the faces of the students, who are checking out each other for weaknesses like boxers dropped into a ring. English is the kick each of them needs at this point in their life—whether they are facing a job interview, getting a promotion at work, preparing to move to a big city, or raising their profile in the marriage market—but some need it more than others.

On 10 April 2015, the day I joined the 3 p.m. batch at The American, it had been running for a month. Khan began by telling his students a mantra he would repeat in every class: Grammar doesn't matter. 'The fat grammar books, my friends, with their rules and restrictions, they are only to keep people like us from ever dreaming of speaking fluently in English.' It was time to reverse the process. We weren't going to do words-sentences-story. We were going to begin with stories. We were going to learn how to use a verb in active and passive voice: the difference between 'doing' and 'is being done'. So he conjured a character, 'Sharmaji, an ordinary man—middle-aged and middle class'.

In the story, Khan, who is always the protagonist of his stories, is going somewhere on his motorbike when he runs into Sharmaji and his wife on a road. The sweating Sharmaji is dragging his punctured scooter to a repair shop with his overweight wife perched on the back seat. 'I join him as he *looks* for a puncture-repair shop and give him company as his scooter *is being looked at*. His wife, she has been waiting outside and she is getting very impatient. Huffing and puffing, she orders him to get back on the road immediately. Sharmaji is a very mild man who never upsets his wife. He tells her in response: Sweetheart, the scooter *is being repaired*. See how he describes the action? Not by translating from Hindi, which would have been "the scooter is repairing". That's not how you should ever put it. You must use "repair" in a passive sense by adding "is being".' In showing them the active and passive ways to use a verb, Khan was teaching them some of the oldest rules of English grammar. It wasn't grammar itself being subverted in Moin Khan's class, but the idea that you have to go to school or read a book to learn it. Except for the operative bits, Khan narrated most of this story in Hindi. It was more or less the format for his class. The students only noted the operative bits in their notebooks; they were never going to forget the stories. But what he did in the class was more than tell stories and jokes, as I would soon figure out. What one learnt at the end of a class wasn't just how to convey an idea in English but how to have ideas that were worth conveying.

'Truth has nothing to fear,' Khan was telling students as I entered the class one day, his words captured in notebooks as soon as they left his lips. It was a class on English proverbs and Khan was trying his best to convince his students to live by them. 'Beauty is in the heart not in the face,' Khan read from his diary next (a personal syllabus put together from his extensive reading routine: 'Motivational, self-help, philosophy, life, health, wealth, money, attitude, human psychology, child psychology, religion'). 'How many boys here will fall in love with a girl based on her looks?' he asked, his stern gaze raking the male section of the class. 'Aren't looks important?' asked one brave young man, raising his hand. 'No, my friend,' Khan seized the moment. 'Beauty is short; it will go away with age. Someone who is beautiful today will not be beautiful tomorrow. But if she has a good heart, then she will always have a good heart.' To hammer in his point, he even quoted a line from a book by former President Abdul Kalam, famous for speaking entirely in motivational nuggets: 'I am not handsome, but I can give my hand to someone who needs it.'

I wondered how seriously students took his lessons, or if they felt they weren't learning enough spoken English for the fee they had paid the academy—₹2000 for three classes a week for three months—but the rapt attention with which they listened to him was reassuring. One day shortly after I'd joined the classes, Moin Khan asked the students to come up on the stage one by one and use the English they'd learnt so far to introduce themselves to the class. Everyone followed the same script on the stage: their names, their family details (what their parents did, where they lived, where their siblings attended school) and their final ambition (government service, entrepreneurship, MBA).

Some of the students provided details perhaps too private to share with strangers—except that the circumstances in question were precisely the reasons why they were in the class. In one young woman's case, it was her single mother forced to take care of the family after the father got up and left one day. In a young man's case, it was a farming loan his family needed to pay back. After patiently listening to all of them, Khan took the podium and told the class he wasn't interested in their problems, but only their plans to fix them.

As we excavated the deepest meaning of every ancient proverb Moin Khan could throw at us, I thought back to that day of introductions. Perhaps what the students needed even more than ready-made answers for job interviews was the push to go out there and kill it. That's what Khan gave them as he ended the class. 'Every difficulty in life comes with an equal opportunity. What does it mean? Problems and difficulties are like a washing machine, my friends, they will turn you, beat you, wash you, but finally you will come out brighter, cleaner, smarter, lighter.'

* * *

What does speaking English have to do with the building of character? What does it even have to do with the development of personality? A lot. A spoken English classroom might be the only place where most young Indians would ever be asked to express themselves. For a society whose model of education depends on students silently receiving knowledge, this sudden freedom can throw up strange complications.

One such is the opening up of personality. It turns out that speaking English doesn't just connect you through a shared language to over 500 million people elsewhere in the world, but as an extension opens up your mind, your whole view of the world. So, what Moin Khan expected of everyone who walked into his class was not to learn English but to use the language to think—think for themselves, think outside the box, think big.

One day as we were leaving the class, Khan asked everyone to prepare themselves for a debate the next time. Topic: love marriage vs arranged marriage. It was an altogether strange situation. It was safe to assume that the whole class would engage in this debate. But as far as I knew, no one on the girls' side had ever ventured a word across the aisle. Despite the touted links between the English language and modernity, many coaching centres maintain the standard Indian classroom practice of segregating the sexes. On my first day as a student, I was asked to join a group of girls in a ladies' waiting room. The boys waited in the classroom if they arrived early; the girls filed in after the teacher. There was palpable strain in the classroom on the day of the debate. On the girls' benches, there were loud prayers to not be called to speak first. On the boys' side, there was laughing and backslapping. Things began cordially enough, with students rising from their seats, facing the person they were going to respond to, and following Khan's instructions to remember to say 'my dear friend', 'as far as I am concerned' and 'allow me to' before launching into arguments and counterarguments.

The first one to speak was a boy from the front bench: 'Friends, we have assembled here to give our opinion on topic of which marriage is best—love or arranged. Every marriage has advantage and disadvantage, but I would like to favour love marriage versus arranged marriage. I need my family's support because I have to spend my remaining life with my family, but I have to spend more time with my life partner.'

The thought got a sharp response from a girl across the aisle from him: 'According to my point of view, I favour arranged marriage. Love marriages are candles that burn brightly but for a short period of time. Parents have more experience of life than us, and they'll choose the best partner for us. In Chetan Bhagat's novel, *2 States: The Story of My Marriage*, he has written few lines about love: "A boy loves a girl and a girl loves a boy, but in India a girl should love the boy's family and a boy should love the girl's family, and the girl's family should love the boy's family and the boy's family should love the girl's family, because in India marriages are not between two persons they are between two families."'

It's a debate that can heat up any room in India. The class soon slipped into chaos. Students forgot they are not meant to lapse into Hindi at any point, or to cut others off mid-sentence, or raise their voice, or launch into personal attacks. As Khan struggled to bring things under control, the two rows stood up and faced each other in an all-out war: girls shouting at girls, girls shouting at boys, boys shouting at girls, boys shouting at boys.

'Girls promise before marriage that I don't want any kinds of things; after marriage they demand a lot of things.'

'So what are you saying? Have a relationship, date her, take her around, do everything, and in the end you don't marry the same person. What the hell is he saying?'

'In arranged marriages also, you can get time to understand each other, you can tell your parents that you want to understand each other.'

'Yes, but only after engagement, no? So what's the point?'

'After one or two years, after you have a child, your family always gives up, so one should go ahead with love marriage.'

'How can you cheat your parents? They have made the foundation of your youth.'

'In love marriage we have the freedom to decide our partner: how they look, how they behave, how much they love, how much they care.'

'But I love my family!'

'Yes, dear, you love your family. I also love my family, but I have the power to say that "Mamma, I want to marry this boy."'

'People are forgetting about dowry system. In my village, there are girls who are educated, smart, who are married to boys who are divorced, handicapped or less educated because of lack of money for dowry.'

'As far as dowry is concerned, it's not just girls who are victims. Giving a personal example, I have a younger brother, who's employed in the government, but I don't have a job.

Rishtas come only for him not me. My family has not published a tender demanding dowry from girls' families.'

'Because, my dear friend, this is how society works, it's not the fault of girls' parents. Even if they didn't want to, so many people would have gone to them and talked about what great catch your brother is.'

'In this age and time, we have to understand first what is love. Beauty fades away, character stays forever. Don't fall in love looking at a face.'

'Love *also* happens in arranged marriage.'

'The thought of Indians is if you live with a dog, you will fall in love with that also.'

'If you want to go for love marriage, go for it!'

'I will!'

* * *

The first branch of the American Academy of Spoken English opened in Uttar Pradesh's Meerut district in 1991—the same year India opened its doors to the world. A few years before that, a twenty-year-old man from Meerut, Vikram P. Lamba, was rejected at an interview for an entry-level position in the Indian army because of his poor English, although he had passed the written test and proved himself physically fit. 'It was there, at the interview, that Mr Lamba realized how badly students from villages and towns in north India fared in comparison to those from cities, from convent-run schools. In those times, children in government schools in UP and Haryana didn't come across English until they were in the sixth class. Mr Lamba saw that nobody was doing anything for people like them,' said Amod Kumar Bhardwaj, CEO of the American Academy of Spoken English and an old friend of its director, the selfsame Vikram P. Lamba.

Bhardwaj's spacious office at The American's headquarters was midway along a street crammed with coaching centres. Three of them were run by The American. The institute has a total of seven branches in Meerut, a city of 1 million. In the twenty-five years since the first centre was established there, the institute has trained, Bhardwaj told me, hundreds of thousands of local residents. 'In 2003, when we had a commemoration in Meerut where we invited all our ex-students to come, three hundred thousand showed up,' said Bhardwaj.

The American launched its operations with a single room in 1991. Lamba came up with a 'training module' by roping in his younger brother, a software programmer who'd migrated to America and claimed to have backward-engineered American English. 'It was the fad during that time so they branded the institute accordingly,' said Bhardwaj. The logo was designed by a student from their first batch: stars and stripes running across the letters AMERICAN. It was time for business.

Bhardwaj has been working with the company since 1995. When he arrived in Meerut to teach at The American, the institute had expanded to five classes of twelve students each. The American charged ₹300 for a three-month course in basic English communication. 'No one used to believe in those days that you can teach someone to speak English in three months. And we also knew that it was not going to be easy. How to teach someone who doesn't know the alphabets of a language to speak the language? We started by telling parents who were coming with their children that we were not going to teach them grammar, but only how to use it. We started to teach spoken English by telling stories. We also made sure to connect with our students using local dialect.' Everything had to be kept attuned to local terms and conditions, including separate waiting areas for boys and girls. 'Before they sent their daughters to study with us, parents used to come and make sure there was nothing in our set-up that would cause trouble. There was no ban on girls talking to boys—but best if that happened inside the classroom under the supervision of the teacher.'

The modernity-meets-tradition formula seems to have worked for the company. At last count, there were 325 franchise outlets of The American all over north India, most of them run by ex-students. 'They have to pay us ₹2 lakh annually for operating under our name.' Bhardwaj took great pains to stress that The American was less a business empire and more a social-service initiative, outraged every time I brought up profit or revenue. The ₹65 crore the company makes out of the franchise system is small change, he said, when placed in the context of the entire industry around English in India—'coaching centres, books, call centre training, GRE/TOEFL classes'—that he speculated was worth 'hundreds of crores' of rupees. What drives The American, Bhardwaj said, is knowing that the company has made the first moves in what's a game without any end point. 'Surveys reveal that only 1.3 per cent of Indians are proficient in English. There is a long way to go.'

* * *

Two months into the classes, Moin Khan announced to his students that they already know enough spoken English to get by. They knew by now the various ways one can use 'would'— 'as past tense of will (he said he would go), to express desire (I would like to have a word with you), polite request (would you be able to do this for me?), hope (I thought you would come)'; that you can 'get' something as well as 'get' someone to do something; a list of common verbs whose past tense did not end in '–ed' ('leave', 'shoot'); that you must (used here 'not to show certainty but as in the same way as 'have to') show 'great pleasure' at meeting someone and thank them 'from the core of your heart'.

I marvelled at his ability to package spoken English as a band of arrows to be loosed when needed. Even after attending his class for weeks, I couldn't perceive the logic behind Khan's method—one moment he'd be differentiating between the usages of transitive and intransitive verbs and the next moment he'd list five things to say before a handshake. But he pressed on, confident that when these fifty students left The American, they could get through most scenarios.

This wasn't a confidence unique to Moin Khan; it is indeed the axis of faith on which the wheel of spoken English rotates. How else could anyone make sense of the categories under which sentences of daily use appear in books on spoken English? According to 'Simple and Perfect Hindi to English Speaking Course', there are four kinds of sentences: Exclamation (Hello!; All right!; Oh, dear!), Order (Look here; Go away; Stop the car; Don't be late; Mind your own business), What (What movie is on today?; What is your occupation?; What's the menu for dinner?), How (How do you do?; How kind of you!; How old are you?); and Negative (Do not smoke; I do not know; We are not late today). At the end of the section on English for daily use, a general list of sentences takes care of situations readers may find themselves in: I have taken my breakfast; The school will remain closed tomorrow; She is a woman of good nature; When will you pay a visit to us?; Is it a holiday today?; What kind of food do you serve?; My kids are not as mischievous as yours are.

Whether or not it adds up, it's a formula that works. If it didn't, these books wouldn't be stocked in corner shops or hawked on highway buses. Nor could a company like

n go from one centre in Meerut in 1991 to 550
n 2015. Thousands must have graduated from
n in these twenty-five years. Most will be the
... ...milies to speak English. Even a rough estimate
of the expansion of the spoken-English business over the
same period would suggest that such first-generation English
speakers number in the tens of millions.

Here is what this vast expansion in numbers means:
that when these fifty from my class at The American go out
into the world, it is likely that they will deal with people
who have also learnt their spoken English from books and
coaching centres. The version of English they speak—with
colleagues, waiters, customer care executives—will define
the future of the language in this country, and, in fact, the
future of English worldwide. With India expected to have
the largest number of English speakers in the world in the
next ten years—overtaking the US—the English they speak
will be the English of the future.

When a nineteen-year-old is creating content at WittyFeed
she isn't worried about the correctness of her grammar, but
only its punchiness, its ability to get the point across. An event
can drive home a fact or 'drive us home to the fact'. Who cares
as long as the WittyFeed reader clicks on the link?

There's only one rule to speaking English in Moin Khan's
book: Speak like you own it. It's the maxim with which he
ended every class, and an implicit rebuke to Gandhi's claim of
'slavery' if ever there was one. It's not about how many things
you could say in English, he told the students, but how you
said it.

Three years into teaching spoken English in his village,
Khan came to Ranchi to face an interview at a call centre run
by a big IT company. They weren't impressed by his English.
'The mother tongue influence was too strong.' But Khan is

glad today that things didn't work out according to his plan. A few months after his rejection, a friend recommended him to The American's first branch in Ranchi for a coach's position. He was called in for an interview. 'They asked me to list topics I could speak on in English. I listed a hundred—my mother, my family, my childhood, my life, my dreams . . .'

Job in hand, Khan moved to Ranchi with a suit, a tie and a pair of dress shoes, all borrowed from a friend who ran a tailoring shop in the village. 'I started to groom myself to look like someone who was going to teach at The American,' said Khan, amused as he thought back to the makeover, which included a French beard. 'There is an image people have in mind for someone who speaks English. People find it difficult to believe I teach people to speak in English if I don't look like someone who would. My neighbour didn't believe me about my job until he saw me dressed up for work one morning.'

Khan has now been at The American for seven years: In this time, he has moved on from being a trainer to 'head of faculty'. His first class of the day begins at 7 a.m. and the last ends at 11 p.m. It's a really long day to be spending at the workplace, I remarked. 'I know,' Khan said, 'but it gives me happiness. Today, my students, they are in America, they are in London, they are in Saudi Arabia, they are in IIT [Indian Institute of Technology], they are in IIM [Indian Institute of Management], twenty of them are POs [probationary officers at banks]. This is what keeps me going.'

Khan told me he knew the effect his speaking English has on people and used it to 'show my importance. Wherever I might be in India, knowing in my heart that I can speak in English gives me confidence to face anything. In a bus, at the airport, in the bank, anywhere I can get people to pay attention to me. When I'm in Delhi I feel confident, I feel like I am in a better position than most of the people since 90 per cent of

India aspires to speak in English.' It also means he can never go back to living an ordinary life. The ability to speak English is his own superpower. 'There is a craze for me everywhere I go. When I go home to my village, people come home to hear me say something in English, "*Kuch bol ke sunao na* (Say a few lines in English)". It's awkward to be treated as if I am a singer or dancer, but I say a few lines on any subject to make them satisfied.'

We had most of these conversations sitting in a prefab enclosure behind the reception that he used as his office. He rarely had much time between classes, but he didn't mind me barging in during the breaks. Khan didn't have time for friends, and I think he liked speaking to me, someone with whom he could chat in English about things that interested him. And nothing interested him as much as English, of course. After all, we had something in common: We had both built our careers on using the language. So we spoke in English about how much English mattered to our lives. Khan wasn't particularly curious about my life otherwise. I had sent him links to my articles, but the only one he had read was a review of a Chetan Bhagat novel. I had critical things to say about it. I had argued that Bhagat is losing his grip on his recurring subject: aspirational young Indians. Khan never told me if he agreed with me or not.

While he spoke, he often ran his eyes around the room, a space he has filled with books that have helped him become the person he is today—the Quran, Rapidex English phrases, motivational speaking, body language, self-improvement. What Khan represents to his students is not just knowledge, but wisdom, sophistication and the complete belief in oneself that comes from conquering one's worst fears. Ten years ago, it was Khan trying to become a copy of the man who taught him to speak English; today every move he makes is watched by hundreds of students every day as the key that unlocks their dreams.

* * *

'If you realize what is your power, you can do anything. I have realized what is my power,' said Anoop Kumar, known to the class as the earnest young man who arrives first, sits in the same spot on the front bench every day, and is the first to raise his hand in response to a question. From the moment he entered Moin Khan's class five months ago, the young man has been on a mission: 'I can scan any person with any talent, transferring the talent to myself, and these days I am scanning Moin sir. I want to be like him.' For days I'd been plotting to find him alone. Given the regulations on interaction between the genders, Khan had advised me against approaching him after the class; it could encourage 'ideas'. Coming early and waiting in the classroom wasn't an option, either, since I was supposed to be huddled with the girls until the class began. Finally, after my repeated appeals to Khan, he proposed to take my message to Kumar himself. The next day, I entered the girls' waiting room to find Kumar alone and seated on the front bench. He had been baffled by Khan's message, he said, but it excited him to be singled out nevertheless. 'He told me you wanted to talk to me about myself. I was very excited. Last night, I called up many of my friends and told them that this was happening. I could hardly sleep,' Kumar said, almost whispering.

This wasn't the first time I was having a private conversation with a classmate. I had previously hung out with a couple of girls from the class—two fellow backbenchers who'd hijacked me on their scooter and got us drunk in a darkened bar. Before we got to that stage, I'd asked them what they wanted out of these three months at The American. One of them needed to pass the entrance interview for a bank job so she could delay her arranged marriage for a few years; the other wanted a promotion in her IT company so she could continue living in Bangalore on her own. For both of them, spoken English offered escape.

For Kumar, it was do-or-die. This was his second round of 'basic communication' with Moin Khan. Each course cost ₹1800 and lasted three months. 'I will do another one, even if I have to pay ₹1800 again because I am not finished with scanning Moin sir,' said Kumar with the unblinking expression in which his face was set most of the time. Anoop Kumar came to The American because he'd heard of Moin Khan. 'Other people had told me about how he talks in our language, how he teaches you how to live in society. It would be very difficult for me to learn from someone who did not understand where I came from.' Kumar came to Ranchi three years ago from a village in Jharkhand, along with his two brothers, to make something of himself. 'We all came to study. Two of us are enrolled in a college, one in a school. Education is important to us. My father is a farmer, my mother works in the field of someone else.' His family is of the Koeri caste, classified by the Indian government as 'most backward'; his parents had sent the three brothers to Ranchi so they didn't end up ploughing fields like them.

Anoop Kumar's time in Ranchi is limited, and he has planned out every second of it. 'I have time limits for everything. Right now my goal is to finish speaking fluent English by 10 August, a day before my birthday,' Kumar said, pausing after every sentence to make sure I understood him. 'So I am ready to do another round of the same course, because I am still not comfortable speaking to people like you, like Moin sir.' Once he's accomplished that, he'll move to other goals. 'I will have to find a job, since I will be done with college by then. For my family's sake, I will join any company that pays me ₹20,000, and keep working on my long-term goal, to find a good public-sector job.' This was 20 April 2015, which meant Kumar had less than four months to be fluent in English. He told me there was nothing he wouldn't do to make it. He began his day listening to English news on his radio. 'When other people listen to news, they listen to it for news. Not me. You will notice that the news anchor begins by saying, "Good evening, I am Ankit Mukopadhyay, giving you the news." This is what I did in the class that day in my introduction—"Good evening, I am Anoop Kumar, giving you information about me."'

As per Kumar, the world around us is full of lessons in spoken English. All one has to do is pay attention: 'There is a girl in the class who finishes all her answers with "thank you for listening to me very carefully". That's what I say these days when I finish a sentence.' Kumar carries around a fresh sheet of white paper every day, on which he writes down everything new that he learns or feels curious about. This day's sheet is already full. On the top right is the word 'should': 'In the class sir was teaching about how to use "should". I have been trying to make sentences with it.'

Like a seventeen-year-old Moin Khan, the only friends Kumar considers true are those with whom he can practise his English. His best friend is someone willing to spend an entire night talking to him—eight unbroken hours of spoken English. 'In this morning, my friend who works at the post office asked me this question—"What is the antonym for ignore?" I don't know the answer. I know the answer in two or three words but not in one word. I search in the dictionary. "Notice" is the correct answer. English is not easy.'

I first noticed Anoop Kumar when he was introducing himself to the class. Kumar had said once he is done learning spoken English and landing a suitable job, he would like to 'motivate people'. By the time we were having this conversation, I had begun to understand the appeal of spoken English to India's massive market for 'motivation'. If you speak English, you can get people to listen to you. If people listen to you, you can ask them to follow your advice, from how to speak English or how to make friends or how to lose weight.

English is like magic. That's how the 'scientifically developed' English-training devices are branded in the market: English magic, English mantra, English magic mantra. And the person peddling the contraptions in home-shopping programmes on late-night television is always some version of Anoop Kumar.

> 'I am a salesperson. My customers never listened to me earlier. My boss used to shout at me.'
> 'No girl used to speak to me because I couldn't speak a word of English.'
> 'My husband didn't take me to his office parties because I was an embarrassment.'

The solution to all their problems is a shot of spoken English. The salesperson can now sell his company's broadband service; the college lover is asked out by his dream girl to a coffee shop; and the new wife is now the pride of her husband. In short: Once you have taught yourself to speak English, you can either use it to improve your life or make a living telling others how they can improve theirs.

People might even pay to listen to you.

* * *

Motivational speaking is what twenty-three-year-old Santosh Dev Thakur does for a living. I learn about him from a friend who works at an English newspaper in Ranchi. His brief is to discover everything happening in the city that satisfies some cosmopolitan notion of cool—online dating, tattoo parlours, women riding motorbikes—and write vastly exaggerated reports about them. He is always at cool places covering cool things, be it the launch of a hookah bar or the auditions for the next big fashion show. He is also friends with anyone who's doing anything noteworthy. So when he suggests that I check out the Facebook page of Santosh Dev Thakur, I do so immediately.

The page is scattered with nuggets of motivational advice from the big names in the motivation business:

Teachers open the door, but you must enter by yourself: Chinese proverb
The only way to do great work is to love what you do: Steve Jobs
Those who want to live, let them fight, and those who do not want to fight in this world of eternal struggle, do not deserve to live: Adolf Hitler

And then there is Santosh Dev Thakur himself; standing tall against lapping waves or on the top of a mountain with his own words—or words his followers believe are his own—running across posters that testify to the awesome and uncanny power of Photoshop.

Never let other people stand in your way. Turn adversity into advantage.
It's your decisions not conditions which shape your life.
Climbing the mountain may be difficult, but the best view is from the top.

His thoughts—expressed in posters, videos and occasional Facebook updates—are not restricted to tricks for success; they make up a larger meditation on life. They range in content from the difference between money and wealth ('A wealthy person is having peace of mind') to the pursuit of happiness ('Where do we seek happiness—in job, promotion, something big that we don't have yet'). The first time I spoke to Thakur, he had just turned twenty-four. After he told me his story, I felt I could have made it up. It consisted of the same series of trials and triumphs that made Moin Khan's journey the stuff of a motivational seminar.

Poverty: Thakur's father drove a steamroller for Ranchi's public engineering department and the family of six lived in an office room by erecting an asbestos partition across the space.

Determination: At the age of fourteen, Thakur sold his grandmother's gold pendant, opened a tuition centre for physics and math, and started saving money.

Escape: For Moin Khan, it was the spoken English classroom. For Thakur, it was a new place where no one knew him. By the time he passed high school, he'd saved enough money to get himself into a private engineering college in Bhubaneshwar in the neighbouring state of Odisha. So off he went, determined to never look back.

Learning: Over the next four years, Santosh Dev Thakur taught himself everything he needed to succeed in the world coming up around him: spoken English, sales and marketing skills, the formula for entrepreneurship. He began by reading motivational books, hundreds of them: 'Jim Rohn, Tony Robbins, Nicholas James.'

The first book he read was Shiv Khera's *You Can Win*, the book which, in 1998, introduced the self-help genre to Indian English. He'd just joined a network marketing company to keep himself going in the new city. 'It's the book they give to everyone who joins a network marketing company in

India.' Why this book, I asked him. 'It's because Shiv Khera understands what we need. Not something other motivational writers from abroad will get. They take spoken English and confidence as granted. But Khera starts with these things. In his book, there are three chapters on confidence.'

Perhaps that is why the book has been translated in every Indian language and sold 2.5 million copies. It's through *You Can Win* that Thakur picked up the basics of English. 'I wasn't concentrating on grammar then.' He wanted merely to express himself in English. When young male students in his college hostel gathered to drink cheap rum and discuss the state of Indian politics—or, more precisely, how the Congress party had ruined the country and left people like them without any future—the conversation was dominated by those who made their points in English. 'I too started to read up on our history—books on Partition, on Gandhi, on Pakistan. After a point, I was able to stand up and share facts in English, like the country's GDP before and after Independence.' These 'facts' weren't very different from those cited on the website Vinay Singhal created as an engineering college student furious at the state of the nation. Like the proud patriot aiming for Mars, Thakur knew by this time that he was meant for bigger things. In another year, he'd have had a mid-level degree in software engineering and the chance of joining an IT company and making his way up. But the overload of motivation had started messing with his head. 'You don't want to do something common.'

His father too had been a rebel, Thakur told me. At fourteen, the senior Thakur had run away from home after being pulled out of school. Thakur's grandfather owned a lychee plantation in rural Bihar and saw no reason why his son had to take orders from ordinary teachers in school. So, the fourteen-year-old plopped himself in the back of a lychee truck and travelled to Ranchi to find a school and get himself enrolled. What he'd left behind was a secure future as a landowner; what he chose was a bold new way of life—an education, a government job, a pension.

For his son nothing could be more depressingly banal. If he rolled out his mediocre engineering degree and got a mediocre job at a mediocre company, he'd be a drop in an ocean of mediocrity that surrounds Indian middle-class ambition. So, following the advice of his motivational gurus, he sat down and made two lists running parallel to each other: things he was good at and things he liked to do. 'When I used to interact with children at my tuition centre back then, they used to come and tell me that they felt good when I was talking to them. I had a positive effect on them. It was something I was good at and I liked to do.' Thakur had found his calling.

Cashing in on the name he'd built in Bhubaneshwar's student circuit for his speaking abilities, he started offering his services to engineering colleges. He offered them a deal: For ₹5000, he'd come and advise their students on life and career. There are fifty private engineering colleges in Bhubaneshwar alone. There must be tens of thousands across India. Most of them charge hundreds of thousands of rupees for admission; a degree in computer engineering is the only way, after all, to have a chance at the IT-enabled Indian Dream for the millions of students who fail to 'crack' the entrance examination to the elite and exclusive Indian Institutes of Technology. Their business model depends on keeping this hope alive.

Thakur offered to make it easier. 'I told students they don't have to join a company. I told them about the potential of internet commerce, of start-ups, entrepreneurships. Of doing uncommon things.' Sometimes he shared with them the motto he'd picked up from a ten-year-old boy who had never gone to school. 'I went to a paan shop and asked a boy who seemed to be in charge of it for a cigarette. He was sweeping the ground outside and kept on doing that in spite of my request. After standing there for five minutes, I got tired of waiting and decided to leave. But before I did that, I asked him, "Do you not care about losing the ₹5 you could have made from selling me the cigarette?" He said he wasn't into small change. The boy gestured at the sky and said, "See, money is flying in the air. You need to know how to catch it." It's the best advice anyone had given me.'

When I first spoke to him, Thakur was a year out of college. He was travelling to engineering colleges across small towns to teach uninspired students how to catch the money flying in the air. It's what earned him his fan following on Facebook; the high-voltage posters were a way to keep them in thrall.

It's never too early to start, equally it's never too late to restart.
It's your decisions, not your conditions, which shape your life.
If you wait for perfect conditions, you will never get anything done.

For two years between 2014 and 2016, he sent me a stream of updates over WhatsApp. These were mainly photos of him addressing students in one or the other obscure engineering or management college, from Bihar to Haryana. I finally met him in Delhi in late 2016. Thakur was in the city to receive an award—'emerging motivational speaker of the year'—presented by an education magazine.

Thakur seemed unaffected by this distinction when I met him at a Café Coffee Day outlet the next day. He had gained considerable girth over the past two years, a sign of success. He was now the owner of a registered firm in Bhubaneshwar. Seventy people worked for him. Some worked on content; some called up schools, colleges and small companies offering

his services; and some spoke on his behalf. He charged
colleges ₹25,000 for a motivational talk and companies,
₹65,000. He told me he'd been spending a lot of time
thinking about life and developing his own content. 'So far I
used to take things I liked from other people's books, videos,
but now I have my thoughts to share. When I go on stage, I
take blank paper with me. After I have spoken for two, three
hours, I hold it up and show everyone that it was blank.' I
asked him if he continues to work on his spoken English. He
spoke the language fluently but not always correctly. He said
if he polished his speech any further, he'd lose his connection
with his target audience. 'The first thing they tell me after I
have finished a talk is that they loved how I spoke in their
language, in their accent.' Clearly, a generation of Chetan
Bhagat's readers had reached the point where he had begun,
and they were using his bestselling formula to capture the
same market.

Thakur had recently become the state coordinator for the
ruling Bharatiya Janata Party's youth wing. It seemed like a
natural next step. He was drawn to Narendra Modi for the
same reasons that Vinay Singhal was. The prime minister, he
said, was a self-made entrepreneur like him. 'Have you read
his biography? He was the only politician who was using a
laptop in the early 1990s. He knows the importance of youth
in politics.'

Thakur told me he was crucial to the party's attempts
to win the youth over. As one of the party's 'campus
ambassadors' during the campaign for 2014's national
elections, he'd motivated thousands of students to enrol as
party members. It didn't take him much work. The same
principles drove electoral politics and network marketing in
his view. What sells a product in both fields, he explained, isn't
the excitement of the manufacturer or the consumer, but the

salesperson. As someone selling the idea of Narendra Modi to the youth, Santosh Dev Thakur was excited about the product. Like other self-starters I met in small towns, Thakur doesn't plan to move to a bigger city. There are too many people to compete with. And too much traffic. 'I hate waiting,' he said, pointing at the line of customers at the coffee shop's payment counter. He may be important enough in Bhubaneshwar now to never have to queue for anything.

He also owns a house and a car in the city. Yet none of this has impressed his family back home in Ranchi. 'They can't understand what I do. I sometimes tell them how much I earn, but it makes no difference. They have never come to Bhubaneshwar in eight years I have lived there.' Thakur is like any Indian man when it comes to family. He wanted to be rich so he could give them a good life; he wanted to be successful so they could be proud of him. Unlike Vinay Singhal, though, Thakur hasn't yet been able to convince them to leave their life and enter his. To be important in the eyes of his family, Thakur will have to be important in their neighbourhood. It's his standards for success that have changed, not theirs. They have never left Ranchi since they moved there, not even to be with him on his big award night in Delhi. 'There was no one there in the audience who knew me before I was big.' Thakur has decided to fix that now. Next year he is going to organize the biggest event his neighbourhood has ever seen ('5000 people') and have someone big in Ranchi present him with a trophy.

* * *

Moin Khan had just ordered a book on the internet when I met him the next time: *The Alchemist,* by the turtleneck-wearing Brazilian New Ager Paulo Coelho. The meandering

book about a Latin American pilgrim to the Pyramids
who talks to spirits and discovers a 'universal language' is
a permanent bestseller in India, sold on every pavement
in every small town; it continues to inspire thousands to
chase their dreams every day, in what is one of the world's
biggest markets for motivational books. Even Vinay Singhal,
not a reader of books, has read it, or so I assumed from the
genie on his wall. And now Moin Khan planned to force
the universe to make his dreams come true. Five months
after I attended my last class at The American, Moin Khan
left the empire and launched his centre for spoken English
and motivational guidance. He named it Lingo. He hadn't a
fraction of the company's resources, but he had the skill that
most mattered in the business: 'I can make anyone speak.'
Khan himself now mostly spoke, like President Kalam, in
motivational quotes.

Profits are better than wages.
If god can feed a dog in the street, how can he leave me starving.

Khan was constantly in a motivated state of being. When
I asked him how he was doing—we were meeting after
over a year—he said he was doing 'fantastic'. Not fine,
or good, or even great. His new office—bigger, better-
furnished, better-lit—was certainly an improvement. Even
the classrooms looked less gloomy. He still worked from
seven in the morning to almost nine at night, teaching nearly
300 students in a total of six batches. He showed me his
curriculum for Lingo. It reflected his invigorated frame of
mind. The students no longer just took notes on how to use
words but were made to participate in mysteriously named
activities: Hot Seat, Media Session, Speedo, Drilling and
Facing and Speaking. At the time of admission, they could

choose along with spoken English a set of additional lessons: standing posture, sitting posture, self-belief, self-image and developing inner power. He had been reading a lot, he said. Parts of the curriculum were derived from nineteenth-century Hindu thinker Swami Vivekananda's teachings on 'character building and man-making'.

The common promise of spoken English centres is to turn losers into winners. At Lingo, Moin Khan was trying to turn his students into 'good people'. A month before launching Lingo, he made a new Facebook page titled 'Moin—Life Coach' to test his appeal as a professional motivational speaker. Five hundred people—most of them his previous students—liked it right away. For a year now, Khan has posted a motivational thought a day on its home page.

> *Fear is enemy no. 1, kill your fear before fear kills you.*
> *How far you will go in life it depends upon how far you can see.*
> *Taking no risk in life is the biggest risk of life.*

The page also has videos of his speeches at Ranchi's edition of Toastmasters International, the franchise-based network of clubs for enthusiasts of public speaking. He had paid £15 for a six-month membership. The twelve members of the club meet every Sunday in a classroom of a medical college and speak for seven and a half minutes on any topic of their choosing. One of the first speeches he delivered to his fellow speakers was titled 'Yes, we can'. The one most popular with his followers is titled 'Don't tell your dream that how big your problem is, tell your problems that how big your dream is.'

In comments, people write about being inspired by these videos to follow their dreams. Like the target audience of Santosh Thakur, the followers of Moin—Life Coach—relate to the way he speaks English: his simple vocabulary, his strong accent. He has never had any trouble understanding them, either, Khan pointed out to me:

Wearer knows where the shoes are pinching.

In another year, Khan aims to start a new career as a paid motivational speaker. In five years, he wants to be travelling the world spreading his wisdom. In none of his elaborate plans for the future is he ever living anywhere but in Ranchi. 'Why should I be anywhere else when my market is opening here?'

I don't want to compete—I want to complete.

Khan said another reason he won't leave the town is because he doesn't like the rushed atmosphere of big cities. Besides, 'if everyone goes to New York and London, who will work for the country?' Like the 'village boy' Vinay Singhal, Thakur and Khan can never detach their success from the distance they have travelled to reach it. Every time Thakur comes home to Ranchi, he goes to the rundown house where he spent his poor childhood. 'I sit outside for hours, alone. It gives me a sense of how far I have come.' He also forced his father to preserve the old bicycle he rode to deliver newspapers, before he got the driver's job.

One of things we'd been taught in Moin Khan's classes at The American was that there was no worse transgression than forgetting where one comes from. It was evident in the story he told us to conclude the class on the phrase 'used to'. The story is about a friend from his village who has made it in Mumbai and now looks down on the banality of life back home. "'*Aao kabhi aao, dekho duniya, zindagi kya hai, kuen se baahar aao* (Come out of your well sometime, and let me show you what the world outside is like)," he said to me every time he came back home. Finally, one time when I went to Mumbai on work, I decided to take him up on his offer. I had his address noted down in my wallet, so I went looking for him in the city,' Khan said, nodding at his mesmerized audience. Khan told us how he traced the address to a slum, packing his description with telling and useful detail—of lanes so narrow the man walking in the opposite direction had to lift you up and place you behind him; of the ground beneath him going from 'bumpy' to 'muddy' to 'sludgy', drawing out the differences between the three words; of a house so small the children were wrapped in bedsheets and hung from pegs in the corners. Eventually Khan found his friend: 'I asked him, looking at the compromises he has made to survive in a city like Mumbai, "How do you live like this?" He said to me in response, "What to do! I have become used to this life."' Khan finished, pleased with the horror on the faces of the students. 'Is it a true story?' asked a girl sitting on the front bench. 'Every story has truth,' Khan said with a twinkly smile.

* * *

Is it possible for an Indian to love both English, a foreign language, and the motherland? This is perhaps the trickiest dilemma the global Indian faces. You need to learn spoken English to be successful; but once you go through the grind, you no longer want to just be successful, but also motivated— and what indeed was the point of motivation if you couldn't, as Moin Khan argued, work towards something bigger than your own future? The ultimate end to which you can motivate someone, he believed, was to do something for the country. But how could you be loyal to the nation if you were still enslaved by the language of your past rulers?

At a motivational seminar in Delhi on 'How to Become Rich', I heard the most rabid critique yet of the slow poison that the British had injected in India's veins. His eyes bloodshot, thirty-two-year-old Shahnawaz Chaudhary ventriloquized the anger of eighteenth-century Indians: 'Who are you to assign yourself our master? How dare you come into my country?' Most people in the audience of about fifty in a rented conference room in central Delhi were young; only two of them were women. Like me, they had seen the event advertised in that morning's newspapers. Chaudhary has a dynamic presence: tall, well built, well groomed. His dark face wears permanent outrage, and his voice sounds like a thunderstorm. His audience remained frozen in awe as he moved on to remind them of their glorious history, of brave kings—Maharana Pratap, Shivaji, Chandragupta Maurya— and bountiful kingdoms. He reminded them their country once had the most advanced universities in the world, called *gurukul*s. Centres of such enlightened learning and research in the fields of medicine, management and technology, they made India the envy of the world. If we didn't believe him, he said, all we had to do was look up India's history on the internet. 'Just Google it.'

How did the British destroy it? 'They dismantled gurukuls and set up schools and colleges. They gave us textbooks. They gave us English.' And why did they do that? 'They invented a system of endless exams and cut-off marks such that if they were made to leave, Indians would still be ruled, except by other Indians.' A man of dramatic imagination, Chaudhary painted in vivid colour a scene inside the British Parliament in which Lord Macaulay, architect of the colonial education system, rubs his hands together in villainous glee as he informs his devious colleagues of his plot.

So this is how, he continued, seventy years after the British left the country, Indians remain enslaved by each other, first as students who are graded for marks and then employees who are appraised for salaries and incentives. Chaudhary ran his eyes over the room and pronounced each one of his listeners a slave. Was there any hope for them? 'You have to take control of your future. Don't expect a thing from the world.' He told them they didn't need a single thing to self-start. No education, no experience and no money. 'Let no one tell you that you need money to make more money.' All they needed to begin was a dream. 'Not the kind of dream that comes to you sleeping, but one that doesn't let you sleep. Our biggest problem today is that our dreams are turning into desires. What's a desire? A dream without fire. You need fire in your dreams.'

There is no dream as worth pursuing as the one to become rich, he said. And there is only one way to make it happen: business. 'To do well at salaried work is a petty objective. I was watching the news the other day and they said 87 per cent of IIT students want to work at a company. This is our tragedy.' Of course, the first mistake they made was to go to an engineering college, he said. 'Most of them want to work at Microsoft. It's run by Bill Gates. Did he go to college? Did Henry Ford?' Nobody got rich without thinking big, he told the room. '*Agar woh paana chahte ho jo aaj tak nahin paaya toh woh karna padega jo aaj tak nahin kiya* (If you want to achieve something you have never achieved, be prepared to do something you have never done)', Chaudhary said, now practically fuming. Only then could India become a nation of 'first-generation rich', he added.

And if you can't reach your destination alone, you could always recruit the universe in the pursuit, Chaudhary said, repeating the promise of Paulo Coelho. 'How did I come so far? By believing in myself. Every time someone doubted my ability, I said to myself, "you carry on, my friend, you are about to make history.'"

Nobody got rich being stingy either, Chaudhary reminded us at the end. His nine-day workshop, which covered topics such as 'how rich people became rich' and 'what's stopping you from becoming rich', cost ₹55,000. I didn't know if his advice could change the lives of all the fifty people in the room. But even if it worked for five of them, Chaudhary himself would be a successful man. In ten years, he aims to have enough influence to become President, and thereby serve the motherland. When he is not making people rich, Chaudhary runs a different set of classes in a different part of Delhi training people in 'how to contest elections'; students pay anywhere between ₹15,000 and ₹1,00,000 for classes that could run for a few weeks to a whole year. Since 2006, when Chaudhary first advertised in the newspapers, the institute has produced eight batches of aspiring politicians.

When he was fourteen years old and the son of a mid-level government employee from Amroha in Uttar Pradesh, Chaudhary had decided to grow up to be President of India. Everything he had done since, he told me, was a part of this plan. 'If I train enough people in politics, I will have enough people who are with me when I enter politics myself. If I make enough people rich, I will never lack for campaign funding whenever I contest.' There has never been a better time in this country for dreaming big, he said. Since he was a boy, Chaudhary told his audience, he has travelled to the President's house every night ('first on a bicycle, then motorbike, and now a luxury car') to stand outside the regal building and stare at it. Until he makes his way in, Chaudhary will continue to harangue college students and middle-aged professionals about the importance of thinking Indian.

While his life-size cut-out fluttered on University Road calling on the youth of Ranchi to change their lives through English, the real Moin Khan sat inside his office telling me about the damage done to India by Lord Macaulay. 'In India we are still obsessed with English-medium school, English-medium college. If you don't know English, there are no opportunities for you.' The problem, he said, was not only the superiority of the English language in our eyes, but also the superiority of the English-speaking world. 'We are embarrassed about everything Indian—our culture, our traditions. We think anything produced by America is good. We buy Amway products, because it is the American Way.' I didn't point out the fact that he makes his money selling the American way of speaking English. I knew what he would have said: He wouldn't be doing what he does if he didn't have to. He knows he is as much a winner as he's a loser; the same goes for India by that logic. English is the language of our subjugation, Khan would have said, first by Britain, then America, and now each other.

Unlike Shahnawaz Chaudhary, Khan is content ranting about the situation. He may be more self-made than Vinay Singhal and Santosh Dev Thakur, but Moin Khan hasn't the slightest inclination to enter politics. The furthest he would go is to home-tutor local politicians who might secretly wish to learn English in order to move to the national level (it's included in the special packages at Lingo). His aim is only to keep growing his audience.

I don't want to be successful, I want to be significant.

According to a mantra of motivational classes, the first step towards becoming significant is *feeling* significant. Khan is there already, as is more than evident in how he talked about his journey at this point. We were once again talking about the first class he taught in his neighbourhood back in the village where he grew up. It had been entirely about imperative sentences. 'Order, request, command. Go there. Sit here.' He remembered, as he had before, how some of the parents had pulled their kids out of the institute after they realized who the new teacher was. In his new telling of the story, he reserved no pity for himself.

Even Prophet Muhammad was not respected in his own neighbourhood.

No matter where he ends up, Moin Khan will always be teaching spoken English. Five minutes after his rant about Macaulay, he entered his afternoon class at Lingo and asked his students how they were feeling that afternoon. 'Fantastic,' they said in a chorus. One of the first times I spoke to him at The American, Moin Khan had told me he would never get used to the thrill of the moment when he enters a room and begins a sentence in English. 'When I speak in English, my heart sings, like it's doing right now as I speak to you.'

3

The Fixer

The first time I saw Pankaj Prasad, he was standing outside my sister's official residence holding a plastic bag in one hand and making a phone call with the other. As a stringer for a regional newspaper, part of his job was to follow my sister around, a government official in charge of a 'block' of sixty-nine villages in southern Jharkhand. As the Block Development Officer, she oversaw the affairs of what is the last link in the long chain of the Indian administrative system, and the hardest to manage. We knew this from having spent the earliest years of our lives following our father, a bureaucrat, from one remote posting to another. She had officers' quarters of her own now, one among a set of stodgy buildings spread across a large expanse of land enclosed within high walls. What I didn't know staring at this colonial design was that my sister wasn't the only one cultivating power in the block.

The 'sarkar', or the government, is an intimidating thing for the average villager—an entity as inscrutable as it is inaccessible. I grew up amidst dusty stacks of files and folders containing literature so convoluted I would wonder how anything ever got done. Framed by high-level bureaucrats in Delhi, the average government programme in India is notorious for its complexity, cumbersomeness and distance from the people it's meant to empower. And so Indian villages are full of people either unaware of or deeply confused by state schemes. The gap between the regular Indian and *sarkar* is widest at the very bottom, where the government deals with the people least aware of what they are owed.

That policies for rural governance are crafted in an urban bubble might have something to do with the prejudices of colonial administrative culture. Those at the highest level of governance are still seen as efficient and honest and those at the bottom as incompetent and untrustworthy; and besides, the higher-ups have passed more difficult examinations. The execution of welfare policies is equally tedious; it requires a mastery of paperwork and the energy to run between government departments. Most ordinary people leave it to a fixer.

The fixer is usually a man, and in large parts of provincial India, he's called *'pyraveekar'*. The existence of an old Urdu word—*pyravi*—for the act of furthering one's case before a government authority tells you a great deal about the nature of governance in South Asia. Pyravi is an art form and it needs the practitioner to be skilled in a variety of persuasive powers: persistence, pursuit, lobbying, liaison and, most importantly, the building and peddling of influence.

Rural fixers have been around in India for as long as anyone has tried to govern the lives of villagers. It is, in fact, one of the most lucrative career options available in an Indian village. Not only is a fixer indispensable to his village community, he's also a decisive part of the state's developmental machinery. The core of what they do and how they do it has remained the same over the decades, whether it's the mode of getting information, cultivating links with officers and politicians, or inspiring awe among their clients.

What's new about the rural fixer is the knowledge that he's playing a bigger game. He knows he needs the government to make a living, but he knows the government needs him more. He continues to be deeply embedded in the life of a village, but he's increasingly interested in the affairs of the world. He knows not only how to exploit the utility of a person to his advantage, but also to do the same with technology—mobile phone, computer, internet. His job may currently be limited to dealing with block officials, but he foresees himself as a go-to man for anyone—entrepreneurs, banks, consumer companies—eyeing the disposable income of Indian villages. When he measures his success, it's not by the standards set by his predecessor, but those of the men the world considers successful.

Of course, I couldn't tell this just by looking at Pankaj Prasad. A slight man with a long oval face and large, curious eyes, he looked much younger than his twenty-four years. He did his best, though, to look like a man who could get things done—well-combed moustache, side-parted hair, buttoned-up striped shirt, ballpoint pen in breast pocket, ironed pants, black belt, dress watch. Within the first ten minutes of our introduction, he'd asked me a torrent of questions about the profit-and-loss account of a journalism job in Delhi: how much I earned, how much I had in the bank and how many important people I knew. He frowned in disapproval at my answers.

I had travelled to the block to chase a story on a potentially historic day for the district. The Nehru-Gandhi heir and the Congress party's leader going into 2014's national elections, Rahul Gandhi, was coming to address people at a fairground a couple of miles from the block. The election campaign was in its final—and most heated—stage and appealing to the region's vast tribal vote bank could be the key to victory. Five thousand people were expected to assemble at the rally.

My sister was on law-and-order duty. An hour before Gandhi's helicopter was to land in a closed-off corner of the maidan, the three of us set off from the block. Two hours after the scheduled time for Gandhi's arrival, we were still waiting, along with thousands of men, women and children settled on their haunches, all eyes to the sky, for any sign of the helicopter. Flitting between various groups of people—officers, local leaders, stringers—Prasad told me Gandhi would be wasting his time even if he came. Long abandoned as a backwater wasting its mineral wealth, the tribal belt was dying for development. And we stood in the middle of what was euphemistically called an 'affected' district; as a local police officer once whispered to me, 'In these parts, every day, five or six young men get together and form a Maoist group.' The region's insurgent youth wanted opportunities, not the earnest good wishes of a distant dynast. Prasad told me they had made their choice: They were going to vote for Gandhi's rival, the Bharatiya Janata Party's Narendra Modi. By early evening, local Congress workers had exhausted their paeans to the Gandhi family and moved on to extemporize personal poems. As another hour passed and restlessness turned into commotion, party volunteers announced what they had known for some time: Gandhi wasn't coming. His helicopter, they said, had developed a snag. Turning back to tell Prasad he was right, I realized he had already left. He had no personal objection to the Congress or Rahul Gandhi, but he believed simply that it was time for change. Six weeks later, the BJP won twelve of the fourteen parliamentary seats in Jharkhand. The Congress got none.

* * *

By June 2014, Narendra Modi was perched in Delhi and I was back in the block, this time to follow Pankaj Prasad around. He represented the new ingenuity of the provincial young man. He believed, first of all, that he was born to be important. He had known from an early age that he would need a plan to make that happen. And by the age of fourteen, he'd already put it into action.

The country had shifted on its axis in the one month I'd been away, but back in the block everything was functioning as it had since 1930. At 10 a.m. every day, my sister's car would roll up outside the main office building with the Indian flag on its crown and, as if acting out their role in a play, the villagers sitting under a gulmohar tree would break into a bustle. Of course, they never bothered with the names of the officials they strove so desperately to see; everyone in the block office is known by an acronym—CO (Circle Officer); BPO (Block Programme Officer); DSO (District Supply Officer); JE (Junior Engineer); MO (Marketing Officer). Block officials are mainly the sum of their powers, sign-and-stamp authorities that keep changing faces. Irrespective of the dramatic pace of block-level postings and transfers, villagers streamed into the headquarters every day for the same two things: to enrol in welfare programmes, or to complain about being left out. When they noticed the red of my sister's car through the film of thick brown dust, they wondered if this would be their day.

While she settled into a tall black chair and looked across a large table at a colour-coded map of her jurisdiction, they ran about the place looking for peons to carry their files inside. Once inside her cabin, my sister immediately switched on her work face: authorizing in-house purchases, approving—or rejecting—leave applications, receiving invitations to grace this or that social occasion. There is no power, our father always told us, like the one the state gives you to act on its behalf. After years of living the big-city life—bars, late nights, shopping malls—she upped and left one day, as if to test his words. Now, five years into her job, I had the opportunity to watch her as she executed decisions that had the power to affect thousands of lives. Most of her work involves dealing with men. They usually don't know how to deal with her. Ageing clerks address her as 'sir'; feudal lords put on a gentle persona; and middlemen answer looking into a vague distance.

Since the day he could think for himself, Pankaj Prasad had eyed a job placing him between the government and the people. He had had a very basic education, acquired no professional skills and possessed little money. His situation was closer to Moin Khan's, for whom even going to school was a luxury, than that of Vinay Singhal and Santosh Thakur, who had breached the gates guarding professional opportunity only to realize they could do better on their own. Prasad wanted to be as rich and powerful as any of them, but without leaving his village.

There is only one way to get rich and powerful in a place where the flow of money and power is controlled by the state. But, unlike my sister, he wasn't authorized by the state to execute its decisions. Nor had he sat for an entrance exam that tested his general knowledge, or faced an interview that judged his elocution and confidence. He certainly didn't have the money or connections to edge his way in. So he undertook the political equivalent of the method by which millions of enterprising Indians leech power from the official supply—hooking their own lines on to the main cable. At the age of sixteen, Prasad became known in his village as the passport photo guy.

Eight years ago, when his father, a small-time construction supervisor, had been unable to find any work for months, Prasad urged him to buy two things with his savings: a computer and a digital camera. Prasad proceeded to hang a blue sheet from a wall of his old house, the size of a prison cell, and announced the making of passport-sized photos—₹60 for a set of eight photos, ₹120 for sixteen. His family thought he had gone mad, but Prasad didn't care. They hadn't shown any particular faith when he, then a sixth-grade student in the village school, had pestered his father for a mobile phone, the first in the village. They learnt what he was up to after he went home to home in the village offering it to people to make calls—₹10 for every minute.

Few favours can be demanded of the Indian government without the submission of a passport-sized photograph, the 3.4x4.5 cm reproduction of one's blank face that goes on the top right of an application form—and makes it count. The idea had to work; there was no reason why people would travel 12 km to the district headquarters to get a service that was available within a mile. It was 2006; the two-year-old Congress-led government was announcing one welfare scheme after another; its rural wage guarantee programme of the previous year (Mahatma Gandhi National Rural Employment Guarantee Act, or MGNREGA) had stirred even the sleepiest of villages, and everyone needed passport photos. At first, the villagers were hesitant to enter Prasad's studio, but within weeks he had a stream of people posing against the blue sheet—hair oiled, faces powdered—throughout the day. The photographs came out awful, he told me, holding up one from four years ago. All he had for lighting equipment was a white tube-light, after all, but nobody complained. It was the beginning of Prasad's life as the block's go-to man.

Between 2004 and 2009, the Congress-led government set up a series of welfare schemes touching almost every aspect of village life: health, housing, drinking water, schools, roads, child nutrition. The party had decided to put the rural poor above all other categories of the voting public. Over the last year of its term, the government announced a massive welfare policy promising ration subsidies and waived farmer loans totalling crores. In 2009, the Congress came back to power with the help of a coalition of smaller parties. It saw this as a reward for its welfare efforts, and launched its most ambitious social scheme yet, called the Unique Identification, or UID, project.

Planned as the world's largest ID database, it would issue every Indian citizen a twelve-digit unique identification number linked to their biometrics—fingerprints and an iris scan. This 'Aadhaar' number would smooth the passage of benefits from sarkar to citizens. As debates raged in Delhi over the Indian state's right to surveil its citizens, and whether cash transfers could actually wipe out middlemen and fix leakages, 'Aadhaar centres' started cropping up across the hinterland.

In 2012, the same government made it mandatory to have an Aadhaar card in order to receive some state benefits, starting with wages under MGNREGA. It led to considerable commotion in many villages. To apply for an Aadhaar card, you needed proof of your address—a bank statement, driving licence, ration card, electricity bill, passport. These documents all presume a standard of living difficult to achieve in a remote village. But for every hurdle sarkar throws in its citizens' path, a way around it can be found. A village panchayat could give you an application form that turned into a legitimate proof of address if you filled in your address, stuck on a passport photograph, and got the village council chief to sign it. The passport photograph was no longer a square-framed reproduction of one's face but a game-changing talisman. 'My brother, my father, I, all of us took photos day and night for weeks,' Prasad told me. By the end of it, he had made ₹1 lakh, a princely sum.

* * *

It wasn't easy to get him to tell me his story. Over three years of regular visits to the block, I couldn't once get him to sit in front of me and utter more than two sentences. Prasad had a sharp understanding of what his life stood for; he just didn't have any time to dwell on the details. Time was money in his 'business'. He usually answered my questions in the middle of doing something or the other—taking thumbprints, writing reports, running between offices. '*Arré, kya batayein, bahut kaam hai aaj kal* (What can I say, there is so much work to do these days!),' he said every time I teased him about his packed schedule.

Of the two usual categories of *mofussil* (rural) players—those who do nothing whatsoever other than their job, and those who see a job in everything that needs to be done—he belonged to the latter. There was indeed more to be done in the block than anyone could wrap their heads around. Officially, my sister's job comprised a set of duties—developing physical infrastructure, collecting taxes, holding panchayat elections—but the trickiest matters she had to deal with fell outside of this purview. She was responsible for maintaining calm in the area in the fateful event of inter-religious elopement. It was equally her problem if a herd of elephants decided to tramp through a village on their way to a forest (a junior officer once reminded her of a traditional belief in the area, according to which the elephants only backed off after being fed a banana from the hand of the BDO herself). Her success would be measured not only by the government schemes she executed or the number of elections she conducted, but also her ability to cultivate loyalties or maintain her image.

And if you were clever, you read the newspapers closely, because no one is considered less reliable in a block than the local correspondent: His only commitment is to his own interests. You hear stories of people who go into that

line of work as a cover for their more dodgy vocations—an
unlicensed alcohol plant, perhaps, or even an extortion racket.
The logic is simple: You know too much—corruption, affairs,
scandals—for anyone to dare cross you. But the reason Prasad
became a stringer was simpler: to act as a fixer.

By 2008, he was already selling subscriptions to a regional
daily, so when the paper advertised an opening for a stringer
in his block, he offered his own services. He loved to read
and write, and had published a few articles in a local magazine
published in Sadri, the regional dialect. He would be paid
₹3000 a month. Added to the steady income from the photo
studio, it was not a bad deal. But more importantly, the job
guaranteed a close association with the block officers. He could
loiter in their offices to collect the day's news—of meetings,
announcements, special programmes—and follow them on
their district tours—inaugurations, inspections, general stock-
taking. Over the three years of my sister's posting in the block,
he wrote dozens of reports tracking her actions and movements,
from field inspection to flag hoisting. In charge of producing
enough content to fill a whole page of the newspaper, he also
reported on events of note from six villages under the block. In
Karanj, a subzonal commander of the People's Liberation Front
of India—a home-grown Maoist outfit—shot and killed his
relatives over an old family feud. In Marasili, another subzonal
commander of the PLFI shot a member of a voluntary peace
force working in the village. In Bedo, the deputy chief minister
said at a local event that the state's youth needed to pick up
books instead of guns, and face up to reality.

Mineral-rich Jharkhand, carved out of its parent state
of Bihar in 2000 to do right by its native tribal population, is
dealing with a widespread Maoist insurgency. It may have been
provoked originally by ideological disgust with the plunder of
tribal land, forests and mineral reserves by the government and

multinational corporations, but the movement soon atomized, with splinter groups fighting turf wars all over the state. The police believe that young men increasingly join these groups to settle personal scores. More cynical local observers claim that the government's policy of rewarding surrendering Maoists with cash and additional support may have something to do with the sudden popularity of Maoism as a career choice.

Other reports from Prasad were no more uplifting. A villager crushed the head of his panchayat president with a stone for ignoring his request to be enrolled in a food security scheme. Across the block, he reported, middlemen were demanding a 1500-rupee bribe in return for 'facilitating' a ₹15,000 loan from the government-run Bank of India. The police were hunting two youngsters who had fallen in love over 'missed calls' and run away from home to marry each other; the girl's family, Muslims, had charged the boy, a Hindu, with abduction and sexual abuse.

I read most of these articles on Facebook where he posted links every other day. He had no idea how many people followed his reports in the district, but he knew a sizeable number of his 1000-plus Facebook friends—a mix of local contacts and complete strangers—did. For someone who'd hardly left his village, his articles were travelling far and wide through the internet. In our conversations on journalism (he'd asked for a subscription to the English-language magazine I worked for and read the articles by typing each line into Google Translate), he stressed the 'power of the pen'. Six years into the newspaper job, Prasad was a crucial link between the various forces competing to exert influence over the block's affairs: administration, private stakeholders, police, politicians and 'unwanted elements'.

* * *

The forces clash regularly and violently. Some of these clashes stand out in local memory. In 2012, the headmaster and a teacher of a government-funded middle school were kidnapped and brutally murdered by a local gang that called itself the New Tiger Army. The demand for a ransom, a standard cut from government funds for the school, stayed on the walls of a new building being built on the school premises for a good two weeks. In 2014, seven members of Shanti Sena (Peace Army), a government-supported organization of ex-Maoists, were killed by the reigning guerrillas. In 2015, two men rode into the block headquarters and shot a middleman over an internal feud for a government contract.

I dropped by my sister's office one day soon after that last incident to find two police officers sitting across the table, smiling. They were asking her if she had her suspicions about the murderer and his motives. Unblinkingly, she told them she knew what they knew. After a brief period of panic and paranoia through the block, things were back to normal and people busier than ever. By this time, Prasad had much more to do than gather news. In 2009, the state government appointed him a VLE, or a village-level entrepreneur. His office—he called it 'dukaan' (shop)—served as photo studio, news bureau and Pragya Kendra. A Pragya Kendra, or common service centre, is a way to get someone with a computer and a working internet connection to ensure the village-level delivery of government—and private-sector—services. A VLE doesn't earn a fixed income, but gets a commission, a few thousand rupees, from the government or a private company on enabling a fixed number of service deliveries. To become a VLE, one needs to know how to work a computer and use the internet, show 'entrepreneurial ability and networking skills', and be able to invest ₹75,000 in setting up the centre—Prasad, naturally, was found to be an eligible candidate for a cluster of villages around his own.

The villagers started to line up outside his house instead of going to the block office, often arriving before the sun. Prasad didn't emerge from the house until 8 a.m., though. If he attended to them right away, he explained, no one was going to take him seriously. To mark his elevated status, he covered his revolving chair with a white towel, a familiar symbol of official authority, first cotton then faux fur. The job gave him a great deal of authority: the ability to issue caste and income certificates, to open bank accounts and make transactions, to dispense state pensions to old women, widows and the disabled, to pay wages for work under the rural employment guarantee scheme, to book train tickets, and to prepay mobile phone charges. Most of his new agency was contained in a piece of equipment resembling a credit card swiping machine, called a micro-ATM. The machine scanned fingerprints to verify the twelve-digit Aadhaar number of a beneficiary, and used the data service on the VLE's SIM card to route it through a complex network of servers to make any transaction under a welfare scheme, be it employment-guarantee wages or an old-age pension. Prasad would pay the villagers in cash from a set amount allotted to him by the government. One didn't need to make several trips to the block office any more, and bow in supplication before the constellation of abbreviations that represented the local power of the sarkar.

Since then, Prasad has made most of his daily income sitting in a small, 50-square-foot room in a partially completed house in his village, a ten-minute drive from the block headquarters. You can identify the turn-off on the state highway from a painted noticeboard that points inward, calling village residents forth to work their permitted 100 days of manual labour a year for the ₹120 a day mandated

by the MGNREGA. Still, to get to it you must pass a long
stretch of village scenery—farmers bent over their fields
of aubergine and wild gourd, sloping huts, loitering cows,
men playing cards in a tea shop, a dysfunctional solar panel.
Eventually, you get to Prasad's envy-of-the-neighbours
house, a two-storey structure painted powder pink, as if
blushing on account of its singular beauty. Most visitors to
the house don't enter via the main door. They are expected
in Prasad's office, a glass-fronted unit attached to the main
building.

Painted on the glass in bright red is a list of services he
offers. Prasad is as much a new-age entrepreneur as Moin
Khan or Vinay Singhal. If Khan uses English and Vinay Singhal
the internet to court success and influence, Pankaj Prasad uses
every form of technology, from camera to computer, available
to him to the same end. He is, in fact, the shrewdest of the
lot; his grasp of his clients' needs is the sharpest and their
dependence on him almost primitive. He not only created a
field of opportunity for himself, he became the king of his
domain.

The first time I arrived in his village, he led me straight
to the living room of his blushing-pink house. On my way
down a long corridor, I stepped around workmen fitting white
marble tiles on to the cemented floor. Prasad had bought the
tiles only the previous week, he said, ticking another thing
off his long list of self-assigned life goals. As I sat in a plastic
chair running my eyes around the living room—a box-framed
television set on a wheel-fitted stand, framed photos of the
family on the walls, the plate of salted biscuits on a plastic
table before me—he asked me, sitting on a wooden cot across
the table, what I thought of the house. I told him it looked
great. He was far from pleased. The day was a disaster, he
later told me—his father roamed the house in a lungi and vest

instead of a clean shirt and tailored trousers as instructed; his mother had gone to wash in the village pond even though he had recently got a shower fitted in the bathroom; everyone was talking to me in dialect instead of Hindi; children were peeking in from behind doors instead of coming in and saying their namastes. As he dropped me back to the block office, he said he understood it would take time for his family to adjust to its changing status. It wouldn't be long, we both knew.

* * *

Power rarely comes without its seductions in the sinuous networks that comprise the government of India. Within the first ten years of the creation of Jharkhand, a number of the state's ministers had been investigated, even arrested, for owning 'disproportionate assets'. Income tax raids on houses of senior government officials were no longer front-page news. And one of the state's seemingly endless parade of chief ministers was in jail for a mining scam amounting to thousands of crores of rupees; he was said to have allotted iron and coal-mining licences to corporations at artificially low rates. Among the things he allegedly bought with public money was a mine in Liberia worth $1.7 million.

No government scheme in India is free of everyday corruption. A large proportion of the foodgrain allocated for public distribution does not reach the poor; only about half of the houses commissioned under the rural housing project are actually built, and perhaps hundreds of crores are mislaid in the MGNREGA, which is overrun with fudged muster rolls and fake job cards. The corruption is not always about money alone. In the male-dominated world of mofussil administration, for instance, the inability to make more than one's official income is seen as a kind of weakness, a sign of professional impotence, and the ability to be corrupt is a badge of daring. Once in a while, Prasad's visitors handed him a fifty or a hundred-rupee note after he issued a caste certificate or enabled a bank transaction. The first time it happened, he told me, he didn't know how to react. Then he got over it. The villagers weren't used to getting anything from sarkar for free.

To Prasad, it wasn't corruption but conformity. Why should he feel guilty for taking an occasional bribe of ₹50 when the people running the state were rolling around in millions? All he wanted to make, in comparison, was ₹500 above his official daily income.

In June 2014, reaching the apex in his career as a sarkari fixer, Prasad became a registered Aadhaar operator, a man authorized by the government to receive application forms, record biometric details and issue Aadhaar cards. It would bring him another ₹4000 a month. Being a registered Aadhaar operator meant he had his own small office in the block headquarters now, a dark room in an old building in which the elaborate Aadhaar equipment was set up. For a few hours every day, Prasad had to sit behind it scanning irises and double-checking names and addresses. An identical machine was installed in his home office, now a photo studio, news bureau, Pragya Kendra and Aadhaar centre. It had to fit in whatever space was left by all the rest of the paraphernalia of a local fixer: desktop computer, laptop, printer, scanner, micro-ATM, digital camera, printing paper, and a framed and garlanded photograph of the god-man Sai Baba, to whose blessings he credits all his success. The UID authority mandated the use of a white background for Aadhaar photographs, so a white dhoti now covered the middle of the blue felt board used for passport-sized photos.

The crowd outside his office grew bigger and arrived earlier. It also seemed more desperate. Prasad's is the only common service centre for five villages; large numbers of locals walk a few kilometres to get there, clutching plastic bags in which they have put in every piece of paper that could conceivably certify claim to an identity. On a day shortly after the upgrade to his portfolio, I walked in to see him being mobbed by a group of villagers fighting for his attention while he crouched in his chair with a heap of applications in his lap. He waited in this pose for a few seconds before he jumped out of his chair, spread out his arms, swept the crowd out of the door, and shut it on their shocked faces. Prasad then organized the forms into a pile, went through the one on the top, opened the door, and called for Suko Devi. In came a woman bent over from the waist, using her walking stick to edge past the press of people blocking the entry. Suko Devi was eighty years old, had travelled 5 kilometres, and needed an Aadhaar card made in order to receive her old-age pension: ₹600 a month. After making her sit upright on a plastic stool placed in front of the white dhoti background, Prasad held a web camera to her terrified face, checked the reflection on the computer and clicked the 'submit' box at the bottom of the online application page. Then he grabbed her hands, rubbing the fingertips on a wet towel and pressing them against the transparent top surface of a box-shaped fingerprint scanner. The equipment failed to register any input. Dirt had settled too deep into the cracked skin of her palms. Frustrated, Suko Devi asked Prasad if that wasn't the natural texture for the skin of someone who worked with cow dung all day.

Just a few weeks into the launch of the UID project, the Indian government realized that many of the most needy people it wanted to help had hands too roughened by labour to mark a clear impression. It was nothing, the sarkar felt, a little dab of Vaseline couldn't solve. Prasad was going to go with water instead. He wet the towel again, swept it over

Suko Devi's fingers a few more times, and pressed them to the scanner. Five attempts and the job was done. Devi was back on the stool and staring, wide-eyed, into a telescope-like iris scanner, one enlarged eye at a time. It took only three attempts. Prasad took her thumb impression on the form and slipped it into a bulging folder. Suko Devi quietly gathered her things and walked out.

Prasad moved on to the other 'customers': sixty-seven-year-old Patras Bek who wanted an account opened with Bank of India; twenty-year-old Sanu Kumar, a mobile phone shop owner, who wanted to withdraw ₹1000 from his bank account; a woman in a bright sari and braided hair who came in to get passport photos made. As they left, some of these people gave Prasad money, anything from ₹30 to ₹100, that he slipped into a drawer. He explained, more to himself than to me, that it was money he was going to use to give them a better service, such as laminating Aadhaar cards he printed off the website. He had to be more careful about it, though, he said. He couldn't just take money every time someone offered it or from anyone who offered it. He was watching his back, he told me. There were people who wanted to bring him down, none more so than his so-called colleagues.

* * *

One day in September, Prasad woke up to find himself 'exposed' in the local edition of a rival newspaper. The blow had been landed treacherously, by a fellow stringer. The report quoted a man as saying he had paid Prasad ₹100 after receiving an Aadhaar card at his block office. Prasad was summoned to the CO's office, along with the man quoted in the report. The man was asked if he gave Prasad money. He said yes. Prasad was asked if he had taken it. He nodded in confession. 'I asked the officer then if it was unfair to accept a little money from someone for earnestly doing his work,' Prasad told me over the phone. The officer thought about it, said Prasad, then let him go. She also told him he couldn't use the block headquarters for the Aadhaar work any more.

Prasad told me he wasn't going to let the incident affect him 'even a little bit'. He took on so much work that there was no time to think about anything else. In his free time Prasad, who carried around a digital camera, took photographs for the beneficiaries of Indira Awaas Yojana, a state housing scheme; under it, the government released ₹75,000 to a villager in three equal instalments, at the beginning, halfway through the construction, and at completion. A beneficiary needed to show work-in-progress photographs to get the last two instalments. Prasad charged a total of ₹500 to shoot the two stages. For ₹2000 or ₹3000, he would digitize survey data for the district administration. While he was waiting for an officer to show up, he would pull out a phone and type reports as dictated to him on another phone by semi-literate stringers who were still his friends.

What was the rush, I often asked him. 'Kya karein, jeevan sangharsh hai (What to do, life is a struggle),' he said, making a long face. He still saw himself as a small man struggling against a big and unfair world.

On 15 August, Independence Day, Prasad called me in Delhi to say that the real freedom for India would be freedom from corruption. As he saw it, the difference between him and the people hunched outside his house was only that he understood the system and used it for survival whereas they lived their lives first in ignorance and then fear of it. If he didn't, his family would still be living without electricity and running water in the one-room house that he once pointed out on the way to his two-storey. On most days I saw him, he worked twelve hours a day. Unlike many in India's cities, he has no easy mode of winding down—hitting the gym or ordering a comfort meal, or a round of drinks with friends or colleagues. But he has access to the best tool for chilling known to his generation: Facebook. He accesses the website on one of his five mobile phones, three of which have high-speed internet. It's there that he spends any time he has to spare over the day: posting, liking, commenting, sharing. 'It takes so little,' he said. 'Whenever someone posts something, I immediately like it. If it's a photo, I comment "beautiful face". If I don't understand something someone has written as an update, I know it must be serious. I don't just like it, but also immediately share it.' Most of his status updates are either links to his articles ('proposal to build a new road cleared') or motivational quotes (*Only those who work make mistakes—the jobless waste their lives finding faults in others.*) There is a new selfie every few days, and sometimes, posted in the middle of the night, are lines from sad love songs.

Music is all he consumes as entertainment. 'Movies are too long for me. Waste of time. I only watch things that are up to seven minutes long.' The only film for which he sacrificed three precious business hours was Bollywood's biopic of Mahendra Singh Dhoni, the small-town boy from Ranchi who became the captain of the Indian cricket team. On most nights after he closes his office, eats his dinner and goes to bed, Prasad pulls out his phone and searches YouTube for song videos. His favourite songs are invariably romantic. When I last spoke to him, he was addicted to a chart-busting song about lovers who have fought against fate to be with each other. He didn't only like the song but also the singer—light-skinned, round-faced, deep-dimpled, curly-haired—who starred in the video herself. He had never found anyone so beautiful, he said, not even the fashionable Bollywood heroines.

In his own life, he has no time for love, he claimed. Every time I asked him if he had a girlfriend, he said girls were a waste of time. I wondered if he listened to the songs about break-ups and betrayal to prepare himself to live without love. But one day, when he was in the mood, he took me to see a 'special friend', a girl from a tribal community who lived in a neighbouring village and was training to be a nurse. They first met a few years ago in a computer coaching class, and had been chatting over the phone for a year now. They avoided seeing each other in person as it would complicate things; since marriage was out of the question, there was no point getting any closer. On this day, too, the 'meeting' was kept short: We drove past her village and she came outside her house and waved at us.

Prasad is extremely clear about the kind of girl he'll marry when the time comes. She must belong to the same subcaste of banias, a merchant community ('Otherwise I will have no respect in society'), should ideally have grown up in a city ('Are you crazy—I will never marry someone from this village!'), and come from a family that can afford to pay him a deserving dowry, not because he would need their money, but purely to validate his status. The only condition on which he would waive his dowry is if he found the girl drop-dead beautiful. 'But chances are low. Last time I went to see a girl, she was the opposite of what she looked like in her photos. All Photoshop. *Dekhne ke saath bukhaar aane laga* (The moment I saw her, I became feverish).'

I offered to create a profile for him on one of the matrimonial websites where he could choose from a wider pool of girls, even within his caste. But he'd rather not cast the net wider than Jharkhand's boundary: 'Arré, please don't do that. God knows where the matches will start showing up—Kanpur, Lucknow.' And in no scenario was I ever to suggest a match, however fitting, from Delhi. '*Sasur mar gaya toh Rajdhani mein 4000 ka ticket le ke jaana padega* (It would cost ₹4000 to go to Delhi in a train if my father-in-law were to die),' he said, with his usual air of deep concern.

He had every intention of visiting the capital once he felt he could buy an air ticket without guilt. He had no wish, however, to stay there longer than it took to see the sights. Prasad doesn't doubt for a second that he will find work in Delhi if he goes there, but he has no interest in slaving away as an insurance salesman or pizza delivery boy for a quarter of what he earns now. He is going to live in the same place and do the work he has discovered for himself. However damned the system, he is now hanging on to its edges.

Men like Pankaj Prasad cannot afford to indulge in lofty ideas about changing the country or the world. Unlike Moin Khan or Vinay Singhal, Prasad didn't turn around his fortunes by sharply exiting where he came from. He did exactly the opposite. If you ask what he thinks of the political scenario, he'll tell you that he has no time to think about it. His clients aren't American internet users or aspiring English speakers; they are people whose immediate well-being depends on how fast Prasad can process an application. Because he works so close to the system, he realizes that at their core, governments are the same. He's fine with the Congress, and he doesn't mind the BJP. He thinks Rahul Gandhi should try harder, but he isn't a blind fan of Narendra Modi. No matter who claims power in Delhi, Prasad knows that back in his village he is the only one in charge of his life.

* * *

The moment dust settled on the scandal, Prasad was back in his block office scanning fingerprints and irises. The villagers too resumed their waiting position under the neem tree outside. They'd been waiting for hours one day when Prasad rode past them on a new motorbike, parking it in style by the side of the building. Juggling bundles of application forms on his desk a few seconds later, he appeared more businesslike than I'd ever seen him: yelling at his clients for incomplete information, throwing them out for jumping the queue. I asked him if he was going to change his game. 'Nothing is going to change,' he said, shrugging his shoulders, *'Kamane waala kamayega, usko koi mai ka lal rok nahin sakta* (If someone has to make money, he will make money. No one can stop him.)' It was nobody's business to teach him the acceptable way of making money or spending it. He was becoming equally brazen about the latter. He realized that buying things gave him an immediate rush of power. When he wasn't buying shirts, jeans or dark glasses for himself, he splurged on items of home decor such as curtains, cushion covers or saris and jewellery for the women in his family. He bought most of these things from Ranchi's biggest shops and never asked for a discount.

In late 2015, he arranged his brother's marriage for a dowry that reflected the family's new status—₹1 lakh in cash and a motorbike for himself—and threw a feast on a scale the village had never seen before: a three-day party, 100 kilos of goat meat, and a proportionate supply of *daaru*. On the second day of the celebrations, he gave me a tour of his canopied backyard where a sizeable workforce toiled to make the evening a success—pounding masala, chopping onions, skinning goats.

His family had accepted his status as their guardian. His father and brother took his orders, and his mother and sister followed his rules. A family patriarch at the age of twenty-five, it's Prasad who got to decide the right time for his sister to drop her studies and for his brother to get married.

Back in his sitting room, where his brother and his bride sat in gilded chairs receiving gifts, there was a new addition to the room's decor. Leaning against the wall beside the television stand was a bicycle with a blue-green seat and matching handlebars. I asked him what he needed a bicycle for now that he went everywhere on a motorbike. 'It is my old bicycle from when I used to go house to house selling newspaper subscriptions,' he said. The point of the relic was to remind his visitors of the distance he has travelled in his life—the same reason that Santosh Thakur held on to his father's bicycle from his working-class days. I wondered how many such bicycles stand in how many living rooms in India, as symbols of a young Indian man's journey to self-determination.

Given the rate at which he was moving up now, not even a motorbike was deemed suitable as a personal vehicle. A month after his brother's wedding, he bought himself a brand-new Bolero SUV, the biggest symbol of his power yet: down payment—₹2.60 lakh, EMI ₹11,000 for forty-four months. I asked him if he was going to hire a driving instructor. 'I will learn myself by driving. Maximum one week it will take.' And in a few weeks, he'd driven the SUV—a sleek, shapely, mud-brown machine—all the way to Ranchi, stopping at our house to let me admire its beauty and speed. It wasn't entirely a rash impulse, though, he explained later. As someone who could spend ₹8,44,000 on a car, his value in the marriage market would stand at ₹6 lakh, at least. It fitted into the larger plan.

Within a month, however, he had to drive the vehicle away from its glorious place outside his door to a secret location, out of sight of the villagers. Like all objects symbolic of untimely or unfair fortune, the SUV had brought upon him the curse of *nazar*. Three weeks after he'd stationed the majestic beast outside his two-storey, the villagers had compiled a fat dossier of written complaints against his 'method of working' and submitted it at the block headquarters. I heard about it from my sister who I had called from Delhi for the usual chit-chat. 'It's serious this time,' she said. Prasad himself sounded no more hopeful when I called him later: 'The villagers—they couldn't stand the sight of the Bolero.'

I couldn't return to the block for several months after the incident. And just as I had expected, normality had been restored. My sister had, as always, a completely new set of things to worry about. There was, for one, the problem of food rations not reaching the neediest of beneficiaries marked for the food security scheme. Villagers had come in their dozens to a public hearing organized at the block offices to complain about being left out of their quota of free rice, wheat, sugar, salt and kerosene. Grabbing the mike from a volunteer in the middle of lengthy recitations of survey data, a young man in the crowd bellowed in the direction of the food supply officer: 'Give us our food or we will take up the gun!'

The crisis was made worse by the ongoing drought. The country was experiencing one of the most severe droughts in recorded history, affecting a quarter of its population and crippling agricultural life. Over 100 Indian farmers had killed themselves in the first three months of 2016. Jharkhand was one of the states on 'red alert'. The Central government had ordered the construction of five farm ponds in every village before the onset of the monsoon; for my sister, it meant 546 ponds through her block in three weeks. At the time of my return, she had to have 300 ponds built in one week. I spent a good part of my remaining time in the block following my sister through stone-and-mud cellars as she inspected the state of food distribution in the block. Entering a government-approved ration shop, she took a keen

look around, ordered her assistants to count the sacks of grain
and tubs of kerosene kept in the cellar, did the math in her
notebook ('Amount of grain supposed to be in the shop: 25
kilos or nearly three sacks [10 kilos to a sack, weight of a sack:
1 kilo'], number of sacks in the shop: 6. Extra grain in the
shop: 30 kilos), and asked the dealers to explain the leaks.

The answers veered from the comical to the bizarre. At
one shop, a newly appointed dealer, a young woman just
learning the ropes, explained, tears flooding her large eyes, that
she thought it normal procedure to save for one's own family
half a kilo of grain from every bag. At another shop, an old
man in the business for twenty-five years, told her, his hands
folded, that his cellar was stuffed with grain in the middle
of the month because the villagers were too lazy to come to
claim their ration. In the cat-and-mouse game of block work
inspection, it seemed to me, the biggest players are those who
view truth as highly subjective. At a farm pond inspection later
that day, the truth hung somewhere between the markings of
a twig. Seven feet, my sister had said the moment she bent
down for a look. Eight feet, said her driver and a local insider.
Ten feet, said the young construction supervisor in the most
earnest tone possible, not one inch less than the dimensions
handed him by the government. A long twig was then brought
from somewhere in the farm and made to stand in whatever
little water had collected at the bottom. With tacit knowledge
of the distance between the markings, the group bent over
again for a review. No one budged from their positions.

As always, Prasad had learnt from the past only that he
needed to move quicker to achieve his ambitions. The Bolero
was moved out of sight and business resumed. The office
had been revamped. A wall-to-wall desk was placed along
the entrance; apart from acting as an elaborate workstation, it
doubled up as a 'reception', literally turning the office into a

shop, and—more importantly—marking out a physical barrier
between the applicant and the authority. A young assistant sat
behind it sorting applications. Prasad had a lot of money to
make, and not much time left. He knew he needed to slow
down, but every time he thought of taking a break, large sums
of imaginary losses bounced in his head until it began to hurt.
'*Paisa chod ke jaane ka man nahin karta hai* (I don't want to leave
the side of money.) The more I make, the more I want to
make.'

He was probably making more than ₹500 above his official
income now. He was also becoming keener to live the life of
a man who had lakhs of rupees in his bank account. He had
yet to step outside Jharkhand, but he had decided that he was
going to travel only by air. 'Wherever I go, I will go in a flight.'
₹6 lakh is what he had agreed to pay in dowry—flat-screen
television, fridge and motorbike—to the man he had chosen
for his sister. 'The more we send her off with, the higher her
value will be to his family.' Her trousseau was bought from
the best shops in Ranchi and delivered to her new home weeks
in advance. In mid-2016, he married his sister off in another
lavish ceremony that employed half of the area's daily-wage
labour force, and was attended by the entire village council.
Prasad was back at work at 6 a.m. the next morning, because
'business is more important than anything'.

By November, the year was almost over for most people
in other businesses. Not for Prasad. On 8 November 2016,
Narendra Modi appeared on national television to announce
his government's overnight ban on India's highest-value bills:
500- and 1000-rupee notes. The prime minister explained this
as being part of a war on corruption and black money. It would
be the end of paper currency, argued his supporters, if 1.2
billion people could be persuaded to use digital applications
to pay and receive money. Panic seized the country as the

government imposed harsh withdrawal limits while new bills were being printed. Even with the currency printing presses running day and night, the lines outside ATMs grew longer and the people standing in them grew angrier.

India's cities might have been exploding in outrage. The villages were in far greater trouble, though. Not everyone in a village had a bank account and few families had more than one. Most of their unspent money lay beneath their mattresses, in 500- and 1000-rupee denominated bills. The villagers didn't just risk losing their life's savings; they were also being forced to walk dozens of miles to a bank to withdraw a small, state-approved amount of cash from an already small pile in their accounts.

The villages were the real test for Modi's grand experiment. If poor, unconnected people could operate without cash, then India would have something to teach the world. 'Experience tells us that ordinary citizens are always ready to make the sacrifices and face difficulties for the benefit of the nation,' the leader had said in a televised appeal.

Prasad was overworked. Between November and December, he ran bank transactions totalling ₹40 lakh through his home office. As one of the twelve specially appointed 'business correspondents' in the block for the period of the experiment, his job was to provide the services of a bank as well as goad his clients into going digital. 'It was simple,' he said, with his usual confidence. 'Customer comes, you ask him to log into this Jan Dhan account through this Aadhaar-linked micro ATM. Fill in the amount, say ₹5000. The machine will ask for his thumbprint. Then the thumbprint of the agent. Once both are verified, you can deposit money, take out money, do what you do at a bank. Every day, I was doing transactions of about ₹1 lakh for people from all over the block.' Once a transaction was done,

Prasad asked his visitors to check out the government's app for digital payments and to sign up for a state-issued debit card. By the end of December, he had convinced 3000 people in the block to either download the app or apply for a debit card. 'I told them even if they took out the new ₹2000 note, they would have to go around trying to get it broken. Why not just use their phone as a wallet?'

Prasad no longer works for the newspaper. 'I have no time left. There is too much running around, too little money.' All he does all day is expand his business. 'This is the best job. Who wants a government job? I make ₹30,000 to ₹40,000 every month.' I asked him if he's aware of his critical contribution to the prime minister's most ambitious idea. '*Dilli door hai* (My destination if still far off),' he said. As usual, he wasn't interested in talking himself up.

He did remember to log into a government website and enter the name and address of every person he had enabled to go digital. On 1 January 2017, the BJP government in Jharkhand organized in Ranchi a celebration of Modi's vision of 'digital wealth'. The plan, said the chief minister after lighting the ceremonial lamp, couldn't have been executed without the enthusiastic participation of villagers. The government had decided to award the work of notable facilitators. Prasad was the fourth to go up on the stage to collect his prize. It was a new biometric machine, painted as red as the rising sun.

Part II: 'I Am Ready For A Fight'

I SPENT ALMOST three years mostly listening to young men rant. They essentially complained about the same things: that they have no future in this country, and it has no future in the world. The instincts that drove them to take charge of their lives were the same as those that drove their politics—mainly anger and anxiety. Most of these men considered India's seventy-year journey since Independence wasted. Can a nation really call itself free, they argued, if it curtails the dreams of its youth? There was no shortage, in their opinion, of people who deserved blame for the state of things. The charge sheet began with foreigners, from Mughal emperors to British masters, who destroyed everything they believe made their country the crowning glory of early civilization—gurukul education, Hindu kingdoms, treasures of gold and silver. Was India once the richest country in the world? They not only believed it was, but threw a litany of figures at me that 'proved' it was, squeezed out of the alt-history blogs that flood young Indians' corner of the internet.

India was the largest economy in the world until the seventeenth century AD.
India and China controlled 50 per cent of the world's GDP until the late 1700s.

India had 32 per cent share of the world's GDP in the first millennium and 28 per cent to 24 per cent in the second millennium until 1700.

They swiftly move on to political parties and leaders who took over from the British. They blame Gandhi and Jawaharlal Nehru, India's first prime minister, who, they believe, knew what a newly independent India needed—economic revival, military muscle, cultural healing—but spent the nation's energies instead on abstract ideals of secularism, democracy and social inclusion.

Nehru ruined the country in its most critical time, when our country desperately needed a leader who can create a solid foundation for future generations to follow.

He missed nearly every step that could have made this country a respected, patriotic and cultured country in its foundation period.

If left to him, he would have decommissioned the entire army. Because he wanted to fly the pigeons of peace around the world in the name of foreign policy.

I don't really hate Gandhi ji, but some of his decisions were really pathetic, like setting up Nehru-Gandhi dynasty, reservation in the name of caste, concessions to Muslims in the name of morality.

And decade after blasted decade, they told me, the political party dominated by Nehru's descendants and subscribing to his vision pushed India further and further from its promise: 'Dynasty rule, gut-wrenching poverty, corruption, populism and minority appeasement . . .' They can go on at length about the damage the Congress party—the party that governed the country for the longest time since Independence—has done to the Indian dream. They said every time they stood up to be seen, a Congress government thrust in their faces someone

with a better claim on the state's attention—someone poorer
or from a lower caste or a marginalized religion. So they grew
up hating everyone they thought didn't have the right to stand
ahead of them in a queue stretching infinitely longer every
time they checked.

Hate comes easy if you happen to be a high-caste Hindu
man; you feel you have been cheated out of your rights in a
series of betrayals going as far back as the first conquest of the
country. You wish everyone else would see what you see—
that you *are* India and every blow to its ancient order has been
a blow to your place in it. You don't even have to stand in that
queue yourself to feel the anger. Irrespective of whether they
are rich or poor, young Hindu men I meet want the same
things: economic growth over social justice, majoritarian
democracy over liberal democracy, cultural nationalism over
secularism, boundary wars rather than friendly relations. It's
not just about things you want, but about things you earlier
didn't have to ask for, beginning with your status in your own
neighbourhood.

So what do these men do with their anger and
anxiety? Many of them turn to politics. Often, they find
an organization offering them an outlet for their anger
and anxiety without stepping out of their housing colony
or college. How these groups define themselves depends
on how far they will go to feed this anger and anxiety:
Hindu nationalist, Hindu supremacist, Hindu extremist,
or simply an organization working for Hindu interests.
They may fight elections, like the BJP (Bharatiya Janata
Party) or operate behind the scenes like the RSS (Rashtriya
Swayamsevak Sangh). They may either channel the Hindu
male rage within specific contexts—the Akhil Bharatiya
Vidyarthi Parishad (ABVP) for colleges or Bajrang Dal
for localities—or towards specific goals, like guarding the

symbols of Hindu honour: cows, tradition, women. And so it would have remained had not Narendra Modi swooped into view and swung it around. Someone had to see the gap in the market for the aspirational vote bank. What do young Hindu men feel other than the frustration of being held down? The hunger to move up. Modi spoke to their frustrations:

> *My dear young friends,*
> *You are our competitive advantage, our biggest strength. In your success lies the success of the nation. Yet not enough attention is given to your needs and constraints. Even if you manage to get education, jobs are difficult to come by. Weak infrastructure and poor public services have trapped you in cycles of inefficiency, indignity, and poor quality of life. The nation seems stuck in the past, while you are straining at the leash to leap into the future. This needs to change.*

And he spoke to their hunger. All Modi had to do was speak in motivational punchlines and his politics of 'Hindus First' became the politics of upward mobility. He used not only their language but their mode of communication—open letters, Facebook videos, Twitter.

> *Dream to do something and not to become someone.*
> *The glass is full—half with water, half with air.*
> *The youth of this country can rule the world with a finger on the mouse.*

They saw in him one of their own, a self-starter who imagined his life as a project and himself as the project manager. They cared little for his ability to create jobs or fix corruption as long as he kept their blood hot with chants of 'India will rule' and 'youth is power'. Led by his rhetoric of coming, the BJP has won nearly every majo[r] contested since the party swept to the Cent[r] BJP isn't the only political entity to rise i[n] every organization dedicated to the cause of Hindu men has too. Since he took charge of the nation, the ABVP has seized control of campuses, the Bajrang Dal of residential colonies, and hundreds of self-styled armies have spread through the country's highways hunting for stolen cows. The young men I met across middle India were driven either by anger or the desire for upward mobility; most of them were attracted to the politics of Narendra Modi and the new Hindu nationalism.

Where did that leave the *others*? I put the question to every angry or upwardly mobile man I met who wasn't a high-caste Hindu. I asked Shahnawaz Chaudhary, a young Muslim who couldn't be angrier or more upwardly mobile, if he saw any space for himself in India's politics. He said he believed in Modi's message. But what about his government's official and unofficial limits on the individual liberties of Muslims, from what they eat to who they love? He avoided my question. I asked Moin Khan, who sometimes quoted Narendra Modi in class, the same question. He said if your one goal in life is to move up, then you just shut up and carry on. They may not personally like Modi, but I knew they were afraid to tell me—a high-caste Hindu journalist—that as people whose job, like Modi's, was to sell aspiration, they were scared to be seen on the other side of the money.

How do India's young women feel about the country and the world? Do they feel angry? Yes. Do they want upward mobility? Certainly. But I saw few of them participate in local politics. It's too male, they said in their defence. Too unsafe. They find themselves blamed for the anger of young men around them, who see their desire to move up as a further ıreat to their status, and are wary of entering their drama of reclamation and revenge. Enough young women are drawn to politics to fill the female wings of the BJP and the RSS, but you don't walk into a college or a neighbourhood in a small town and find a woman burning with rage about India's lost civilization. And yet the young women I met saw politics in its barest essence: as power. What happens when one of them gets in the mood for it? Can a lone woman's battle for political power go any other way than expected? I was about to find out.

4

The Angry Young Men

VIKAS THAKUR WAS twenty-nine years old when I first met him in 2014. He had given himself five years to win an election. You couldn't tell that just by looking at him. Thakur had none of the trappings of a young north Indian politician: no kurta-pyjamas, no moustache, no aviators and no henchmen. In his graphic-art T-shirts (sometimes rolled up to reveal a trippy Shiva tattoo), lived-in jeans and beach sandals, he looked more like a software engineer on a Saturday.

I was curious why a convent school-educated, English-speaking man from a middle-class family would chase constituencies rather than cubicles. I found Thakur on Facebook; like most young Indians who had something to sell to other young Indians, Thakur plied his trade on social media. He had landed an important job at an interesting time. As the convener of the BJP's first social media war room in Jharkhand, Thakur was in charge of shaping the political perception of every one of the state's half a million internet users. Having secured an almost outright majority in the national election, the BJP was keen to repeat the winning formula across the states. It included the social media war room, where young,

internet-savvy members of the party would sit in front
of computers and create 'content'—status updates, jokes,
memes—catchy enough for smartphone users to share.

At the time I met Vikas Thakur, he had just six months
to 'build the buzz' around the BJP in Jharkhand. Thakur
maintained a high level of secrecy around the location and
workings of this war room. All he talked about at our long
conversations over coffee was his political *vision*. 'It's based
on the stalagmite theory,' he pronounced one day. 'Drop by
drop,' he said, fixing his gaze on me for emphasis, 'the ideas
will trickle down to the masses.' Thakur takes pride in his
self-image of a thinking man. He has spent, he told me, every
sentient moment of his life thinking about big issues: the
meaning of life, the history of India, the future of politics. At
some point as an anxious teenager Thakur concluded there
was something fundamentally wrong with the world. In spite
of a massive historical head start, India wasn't valued in the
world, and Hindus weren't in India. He believed there were a
number of things to be blamed for the imbalances of power,
but none as much as the priorities of the Indian state. For
someone born shortly before India opened itself to the world
in 1991, Thakur was disappointed by where the country stood
when he took note the first time. Who could he blame but
the people who set its priorities: the Congress party, which
governed India from 2004, when he was nineteen, to 2014,
when he turned twenty-nine.

From Thakur's perspective, the party was the embodiment
of everything that was holding back a country on the brink
of awesomeness. It was controlled by a set of people too
weighed down with colonial baggage to pick the country
up by its collar and drive it to glory. Theirs was a politics of
cowardice, its policies defined by words that made him sick to
the bone: 'subsidies' to the poor, 'appeasement' of minorities,

employment and education 'quotas' for the backward castes, 'dialogue' with its enemies. There was nothing in it for a teenage boy with the restless anger of a budding dictator. Thakur told me he first banded with the Leftists—Marxists, Leninists, Maoists—when he was still in school. It didn't work for him for too long. He related to their call for radical action, but his idea of a class war was different. Thakur aimed to restore his family's lost privilege. In our conversations, he often brought up a feudal estate in Uttar Pradesh his grandparents had had to give up as part of the newly independent India's socialist move to redistribute land. 'We moved to Purnia, on the border with Bihar. My family's new house was next to a Muslim *basti* (slum). The area was notorious for armed robberies in wealthy Hindu households. The Muslims were always up to something. We were Thakurs so we used to respond in the Thakur way.'

He didn't explain how Thakurs respond when someone messes with them—or when they assume it. He didn't need to. I had grown up hearing stories of Ranvir Sena murders in Bihar. Through the 1990s, the Sena, a private army of Thakurs (a powerful caste of landowners) out to deal with a Maoist-led class war in Bihar, killed over 300 Dalits (people right at the bottom of the caste hierarchy) in a series of massacres to set things straight. The Thakurs of Bihar were used to being the boss. They still owned most of the land—and the swagger necessary to keep it in their grasp, from the curl of their moustaches to the size of their guns. At first they didn't know how to adjust to the upheavals of the 1990s. There was on the one hand a new politics based on the promise of social justice, and on the other, a new language of aspiration set off by market-friendly reforms.

Thankfully for them, the decade had more to offer. On 6 December 1992, a mob of Hindu nationalists destroyed the

Babri Masjid, a Mughal-era mosque standing on a patch of land
in Ayodhya, in Uttar Pradesh, believed to be the birthplace of
Lord Ram. The Hindutva forces used the victory to power a
nationwide movement that enabled the BJP to win the central
elections in 1999. It was Hindutva's political success that
gave Thakur's family hope: 'It wasn't until the BJP came to
power in the centre that our family and community began
to feel better about their situation,' he told me. Between the
late 1980s and the early 2000s, the RSS opened thousands of
training units across the country. Starting at 5 a.m. every day,
Hindu boys aged ten and above assembled in the largest open
space available in a mohalla to train as soldiers in the battle for
Hindutva. 'One of the things I remember from my boyhood
in Purnia is the *shakhas* (training groups) the RSS ran in the
basti during that period.' Thakur didn't go to one. By the
time he was old enough for school, his family had moved to
Ranchi, where his father got a desk job in the state's health
department and went on to maintain what he calls 'a regular
middle-income household'. He was sent to one of the city's
wide range of missionary schools. He didn't like being there
very much—and he didn't bother to hide his feelings about
it, either. 'I used to wear a tilak, and holy threads around my
hand. One day, a Father told me I couldn't; he said the school
didn't believe in promoting any kind of religion. I asked him
why we had a church on the premises then, why we sing the
praises of Jesus Christ. He said he would have me thrown out.
I was thrown out soon after, but before leaving the school,
I went to his office and told him that if I could, I would
punch the hell out of him.' The following week, Thakur's
parents enrolled him in a school founded on the philosophy
of Swami Vivekananda. It was a philosophy that spoke to
Thakur's anxieties. Vivekananda wasn't simply a Hindu monk
who preached the tenets of Hinduism, after all. He was an

English-medium-educated boy from an upper-class family in cosmopolitan Calcutta who took it upon himself to convince the materialistic West of the inherent superiority of the spiritual East. He wore saffron and meditated under trees, but he also made speeches and wrote books—in English. He was the most powerful motivational speaker who ever spoke to young Indians—which is why his books sell as well as Paulo Coelho's.

Take up one idea. Make that one idea your life—think of it, dream of it, live on that idea.
Arise! Awake! and stop not until the goal is reached.
The world is the great gymnasium where we come to make ourselves strong.

Vivekananda persuaded Hindus to take pride in their Hinduness. He asked them to see their religion not as a set of arcane beliefs and practices but as the logical—even cool—answer to most of the world's unanswered questions. He asked Indians, then colonized by the British Raj for half a century, to take pride in their civilization. He offered them—'dumb millions awestruck by the all-conquering powers of the white races'—religion as a means of national reconstruction. Vivekananda gave Hindus a world view of their own: a timeless gift. It charged the Hindus listening to his speech at the Parliament of the World's Religions in Chicago in 1893 to challenge the Western narrative—and it charged a fourteen-year-old Thakur reading about it in 1999 to do the same. After he had finished reading the eight volumes of Vivekananda's thoughts, Thakur said he started to read anything and everything he could find on Indian history and Hindu philosophy. It's how, he told me, he began to build a personal trove of knowledge unsullied by the western-secular rewrite project. In college, Thakur chose to study communication. In the classroom, he learnt how to use information and rhetoric; in his free time, he wrote opinion pieces on politics for local newspapers. The other major decision he took in his first year of college was to join the ABVP, the student wing of the RSS and an aggressive force of Hindu domination across colleges and universities. In 2015, the organization claimed to have 3.2 million members—a million joined in the wake of the BJP's victory in 2014's national elections—and a presence in 20,000 colleges.

At the missionary college, Vikas Thakur was once again confronted with Christian authority; this time he wanted an eye for an eye. Vengeance is a good reason to join the ABVP, which draws to itself the angriest young Hindu men on any campus. The ABVP is a force to be feared—and not just by Christians in a Catholic institute—for its powers of dissent, often armed. 'I had reasons to join ABVP. It used to make me very angry to see the harassment of Hindu girls by the Muslim men from the ghettos around the college campus. No one dared say anything to them.' Through his years in college, Thakur basked in the machismo of the ABVP brand of politics. Chuckling, he told me about the many occasions on which he and his comrades had the pleasure of flattening their enemies. 'I have done everything you can imagine— *maar-peet, gundagardi* (fighting, bullying). We had contacts in the local police station and if I told them to, they would arrest anyone without a warrant and keep him hanging upside down for three days.'

I didn't always know how to react to these heroic stories young men told me about themselves. Should I have expressed awe, or looked suspicious, or kept smiling? I could clearly sense the exaggeration, even attribute it to their desire to impress me, yet I struggled to maintain a neutral face as they invented hurdles and multiplied enemies. Fortunately for me, Thakur was more interested in presenting himself as an ideological warrior. 'Earlier,' he said to me one day, 'politics was a polite term for *thekedari* (political fixing) and only a certain kind of person—rough, slimy—was drawn to it. But full-time politics is coming out of a crisis of youth indifference. We are learning about the country's past and present, about the power of narratives. We are coming up with our own findings.' This is what Swami Vivekananda advised as far back as the nineteenth century: 'Truth can be stated in a thousand different ways, yet each one can be true.' We were having this conversation a year before I met WittyFeed's Vinay Singhal; everything the patriotic CEO said to me about youth and nation would seem a repetition of this earlier conversation. A few years before Singhal started watching news channels and forming his opinion of India and the world, Thakur was spending his days buried in books and articles confirming his suspicions. He has a book to recommend for everything you need to know about the country's fall from glory: how Jawaharlal Nehru destroyed India, how the Congress party destroyed the Indian economy, how Western secularism is destroying Hinduism. Thakur's politics is the politics of anger. Thakur is neither poor nor desperate. He doesn't need any concessions from the government but he is angry because the government is giving concessions to people he thinks don't deserve them. Every time I met Thakur, I asked him why he wanted to be in politics. His answer remained the same: The nation needed him. 'When we think of the government, why do we think of vegetables or petrol prices? There's a lot we have to do to change that mindset.'

So it's not about Hindus versus others, I asked. 'I entered politics because I want to stand up for Hindus. I am not here to hurt anyone else's right to their identity. My politics is about standing up for my own,' he said. One day—we'd known each other for months by this time—he told me, 'I have to be in a position of power. Not for money. My family still has enough wealth left over. But for power itself.' His father would have liked him to get a government job. If his son couldn't lord over the fate of poor villagers like his forefathers, he could at least secure his own. "*Beta, sarkari naukri kar le* (Son, take up a government job)," he said when I was leaving college. I told him: "*Sarkari naukri kar li, toh sarkar kaun banega* (If I make do with a mere government job, who's going to be the government)?"' For a man preparing to fight an election in five years, Thakur had no backing on the ground. All he had going for him, as far as I could see, was 5000 followers on Facebook. 'You should see what happens when I post something political on Facebook and someone happens to disagree. Hundreds of my followers pounce on him at once.'

* * *

Who were these people and why were they so eager to pounce on anyone who might have a different idea of what it means to be an Indian? So far I had only engaged with the ideological soldiers of Hindutva, not the militant mobs. The armed warriors equally intrigued me, but it wasn't always easy to get one to sit across from me at a coffee shop and explain why he joined this battle. Then one of them finally came around.

On 14 February 2015, I met a nineteen-year-old man at a KFC outlet in a shopping mall in Meerut and asked him why he had tied an iron rod to the back of his motorbike as he left his house that morning. Arjun Kumar was short and skinny, his long, pale face dotted with pimples. He rarely looked at me during the six hours he sat across the table picking at his fried chicken. Seeing a teenager go through a whole conversation with a real person while looking at his phone didn't surprise me. What did startle me were the bloodshot eyes he fixed on my face every time I turned my attention to his two friends at the table. Kumar wasn't that pleased to meet me. He didn't hang out with women on principle. I was exactly the kind of woman he loved to hate: urban, independent, opinionated. But when one of his two friends at the table had called him in the morning to say they have got to meet someone from Delhi, he came along without thinking. So here he was, picking at a combo meal I had bought us, trying to find words to answer my question.

Finally, drawing circles on his plate with his fork, he said it: I hate couples.

His first instinct when he sees them around in public—in parks, shopping malls, fast-food joints—is to go flying at them with his iron rod. He isn't allowed to do that every day, so he looks forward to Valentine's Day for the rest of the year. It's when the boys of the Bajrang Dal get a free pass to do with young lovers as they please. It's the only day of the year when the world takes notice of them: Reporters follow them around and the police stand ready to control the damage caused. The boys plan their action days in advance, watching the movement of young couples and assigning stake-out positions. For years, Kumar tried to build an aura of fear in preparation for his first Valentine's Day; it's already his second. The whole of Meerut is his battleground on Valentine's Day and he a caped commander saving it from ruin. He is counting the minutes to dusk as he tells me about the various 'lovers' points' in the town. They are supposed to receive a call from their leader any moment, assigning positions for the evening. Kumar would have liked to calmly map his moves while he waits, but the scene around us was far from conducive to tactical planning. The restaurant had been filling up with couples

since morning. Kumar's eyes were no longer fixed on his
phone; they were closely examining the exchange of roses and
teddy bears around us. The rituals make him sick. 'I wish,
I just wish I could take a bat to each of their faces,' he said
to himself, his bony fingers thrumming with temptation.
However, he didn't have official permission yet.

Kumar joined the Bajrang Dal while he was still in fifth
standard. He was thirteen then. At that point, he says, it was
just about being cool in the neighbourhood. Growing up in
a mohalla crammed with men whose main occupation was to
somehow pass the time till the next festival, Kumar had noticed
the air of purpose bestowed by the battle for Hindutva. One
doesn't get to fight at its front line as a young teenager, though.
So what Kumar did in his early years as a teen soldier was
mostly stand outside the Bajrang Dal's local office with other
thirteen-year-olds and look aggressive. On days when there
was a meeting, he and his comrades arranged the plastic chairs
in straight lines and checked the mike for sound. His status
rose fast. Before he knew it, Kumar was using the Bajrang Dal's
badge to deal with situations as wide-ranging as poor school
attendance and street fights. Everyone backed off. Or as he saw
it: 'People give you izzat.' Kumar was a certified dude by the
time he joined the Chaudhary Charan Singh College in Meerut
as a seventeen-year-old. To make sure everyone understood it,
Kumar began by skipping classes. '*College mein apni chalti hai*
(It's my rule in the college).' How bad could it get, he asked
himself, if ever in doubt. The teacher would complain to the
principal and the principal would threaten to suspend him from
the college. But would the principal insist on taking action if
the president of the ABVP's college unit called him with gentle
advice that sounded like a warning about the consequences of
any such action? 'Mahamantri knows everyone in the police.
Whom will the college administration complain to?'

Gradually, Kumar moved into the next orbit of influence. His own attendance no longer mattered to anyone, so he upped his stake: organizing protests, damaging property, flattening enemies. In 2014, Kumar was angered to learn that the 'general-category' students of law—mostly upper-caste Hindus—had scored fewer marks in an internal exam than those who fell under 'reserved' categories. Kumar joined his ABVP colleagues in a series of violent demonstrations against the principal's 'partiality'. They wanted the man removed from his position. Later that year, Kumar said, in breathless bursts of words, the government in Uttar Pradesh decided to intervene. He told me it was he who went to meet with the governor of the state—'alone'—to let him know their demands. (The governor is an appointee of the Central government, which the BJP won in May 2014.) He said he has never felt more important in his life. 'You should have seen the security at his office. They shot a photo and video of me before I entered. Man, you can't even take a mobile phone inside.'

Kumar currently focuses his malevolent energy on one thing alone: fighting Muslims. Like most Hindu men of his age in Meerut, he grew up detesting them. A city of 42 per cent Muslims and 58 per cent Hindus, Meerut has long been classified as 'riot-prone'. Its first sectarian riot was well before Partition, in 1939, and its most recent in 2015. Hundreds of residents have died in the violence. News reports always pin the blame on a random incident—Hindu and Muslim college boys got into a scuffle; a Muslim man married a Hindu woman; Muslims encroached on Hindu property—but researchers have suggested the existence of an 'Institutionalized Riot System'. In a city where Hindus and Muslims are comparable in numbers as well as economic and political influence, Hindus find it harder to coexist with Muslims than elsewhere in India. In 1987, in a horrifying incident of sectarian violence,

a company of all-Hindu paramilitary men stormed into a
Muslim colony, picked up forty-five men, drove them to the
bank of a canal, lined them up, and shot them one by one.
Only three survived.

Sectarian hate is often the first strongly felt emotion for
a boy in Meerut. Kumar despised Muslims before he could
count to ten. He has felt furious every time a gang of Muslim
boys won a fight on his street. He has choked with frustration
every time a Muslim man bought a house in his colony. He has
burnt with anger every time a Hindu girl in his colony went
out with a Muslim boy. When the local chapter of the Bajrang
Dal vowed never to let another Muslim man woo a Hindu
woman again—they call it 'love jihad'—Kumar jumped right
in. Since then, Kumar and his gang receive an alert from head
office if a Hindu girl is sighted with a Muslim boy. His job
is to make sure they don't meet again. Fortunately, this is a
process that involves a degree of violence, since that is the bit
that Kumar likes best. Roaming the streets on his motorbike
every Valentine's Day, he keeps a special eye out for Hindu-
Muslim couples. 'Last year was fun. I had been watching this
guy for a month and it's on that day I finally see him with a
girl from Dharampuri walking hand in hand in Gandhi Park.
I was unstoppable.'

Today Kumar has what he hungered for as an adolescent
lining up for the Bajrang Dal's recruitment parade: izzat, or
status and honour. 'If I stand at any place in Dharampuri,
there will be a long line of men behind me in no time.' What
does a young man in Meerut desire after he has achieved that?
Kumar will be out of college in 2017, with a bachelor's degree
in commerce and no idea of what to do with it. Thousands
of other young men in Meerut will be in the same position.
Kumar already feels anxious about the future—he can't go
back to being irrelevant. There is only one way for him to

go and he knows it. 'I am thinking of politics,' he said, after a deep sigh of contemplation.

Arjun Kumar is what think pieces explaining the Trump and Brexit verdicts term a loser of globalization, one of the millions of leftover youths whose anger is transforming world politics. It's like the world swept past him while he was arranging chairs in the Bajrang Dal office. Kumar is not sure he will find a job he'd like or find a girl who'd like him. On an elemental level, he doesn't know if he matters to the world. There's only one way left for him to make that happen: punish everyone who's moved ahead of him in that queue. This is what he thinks politics is about. He knows only one party that will allow him to practise it.

Kumar has stopped going to college altogether. 'I divide my time between hanging out at the offices of the ABVP, BJP and VHP—two hours here, three hours there. It's how my days go.' Two months ago, when the BJP organized a mega convention in Meerut, Kumar did his best to be visible to the high and mighty of the Hindutva establishment. 'Twenty-five thousand people were there. Very important people—you can say celebrities.' Kumar spent his whole time there 'making connections'. He picked up his phone from the table and began to recite the names and numbers of people who 'personally know him' now. He wanted me to note down these details. He said all I had to do if I needed them to do something for me was drop his name. I felt a little sad for him, in spite of knowing that he would abandon this interview the moment he got a phone call telling him to go out on the streets. I asked him why politics. 'To serve the nation,' he said with a straight face. But one doesn't just become a politician, I said. He laughed his first laugh of the day. I shouldn't underestimate him, he said. He had a plan. It was to follow the track of a man whose plan had worked. Sangeet Som first won a state assembly seat as a BJP contestant from Meerut district in 2012. But that's not his claim to fame. In 2013, months before parliamentary elections in which the BJP eyed Uttar Pradesh, the young MLA circulated a fake video through mobile phone networks to spark off sectarian riots in western UP in which fifty people were killed and 50,000 displaced. The party, which won seventy-one of eighty seats in the elections that followed the riots, rewarded Som, a school dropout with no talent other than setting Hindus against Muslims, for fighting the good fight. He's been a role model for Meerut's young Hindu men ever since. 'I follow him around every time he comes to Meerut,' said Kumar.

There's another reason Kumar gets to observe the MLA at a close distance. Som has recently hired a personal tutor to teach him to speak English—the man happens to be Kumar's older brother. Why does a man who seems to have made a political career out of pitting Hindu boys against their Muslim neighbours need to speak English? For a simple reason, Kumar explained. Sangeet Som can use his success in politics as the shortcut to the good life he would otherwise have spent a lifetime chasing, but the world will still see him as a provincial wannabe unless he speaks the language of privilege. It's the language he will need to speak when he is travelling abroad, meeting dignitaries, mingling in high society. From the rumours Kumar has heard in Meerut, Som's long-term plan to develop his personality include getting an MBA degree from Australia. Kumar can't speak fluent English himself, but he isn't too bothered about it yet. He has more important things on his mind. Building his political image tops the agenda. The work has begun on the platform best suited to his needs: Facebook. Kumar has six Facebook accounts altogether, each targeted to a different audience, from his gang of boys in Meerut to the global soldiers fighting 'love jihad'. He keeps them active 24/7, often staying awake the whole night. I ask him if he has any time left for a personal life. He glares at me bewildered. Girls, I specify. 'Do you like girls?' Kumar tells me he likes to 'stay away from girls'. His friend almost snorts out his Coke. 'He had a girlfriend,' the friend explains, 'but she left him for another guy—a rich guy.'

'True?' I ask Kumar.

'Girls,' he says, his eyes on his phone screen once again, his mouth twitching, 'they are not worthy of trust.'

It's 5 p.m., but Kumar still hasn't received a call from the leader. By the time we say our goodbyes, it's clear the call isn't coming at all. There was a reason the Bajrang Dal cancelled its annual carnival of violence on that Valentine's Day. The bosses figured out couples wouldn't be crowding the streets and parks of Meerut. The lovers would stick to KFC and McDonald's like the previous year. Those who couldn't afford it would save up to spend the special day in the safety of the town's new shopping malls. Kumar's victims had sat around him all day—holding hands, exchanging teddy bears, sharing Coca-Colas—and all he could was glare. They were protected by the safe spaces created by that same globalization that had condemned Kumar to a place at the back of the queue. Life hadn't been fair to him, and as he rode his bike back to a neighbourhood empty of young men luckier in love than him, Kumar was officially tired of fighting it.

* * *

Girls came up again two years later, this time in Karnal, a town on the border of Delhi and Haryana. And again, I was asking a young man setting out on patrol to defend Hindu honour, why the rage? Like Arjun Kumar, Sachin Ahuja sees himself as a saviour. But what he's out to protect from the clutches of infidels—Muslims, Christians, Dalits—is not Hindu women, but cows. Ahuja is better prepared for life than Kumar on more than one level. For one, he's more outgoing. The twenty-six-year-old sees no reason to shrink into his smartphone every time someone asks him a question. He has the body of a wrestler and the attitude of a gangster. He also happens to hold a licence to kill. A state-sanctioned identity card certifies him as a member of the Cow Protection Army, Haryana's contribution to the nationwide movement to save the blessed bovine from everyone whose culture approves of its meat or its hide.

This evening, though, we are not talking about the war in the name of the cow mother. Not once in the conversation has any of us even mentioned Mohammad Ikhlaq, the old Muslim labourer who was rumoured to have a packet of beef in his refrigerator and was lynched for it by a Hindu mob in western Uttar Pradesh. We have also stayed away from Una, the town in Gujarat where a group of Dalits was tied to the back of a truck and beaten senseless by another Hindu mob for doing the job assigned to them by the caste system: skinning cattle carcasses. As the last vestige of daylight leaves this temple courtyard in the middle of Karnal, Sachin Ahuja is passionately debating with me how a woman should be. He starts with outlining, through three intriguingly specific examples, how a woman should *not* be.

1. Not like the nice girl in Karnal he knew and liked who went to Delhi to work and got mixed up in the big-city culture of short skirts and late nights.
2. Not like the wife of one of his best friends who walked out on him because she was bored staying at home and cooking for his family.

3. Not like the girl chosen for him by a local matchmaker who turned out, after an investigation by a friend of his who lived close to her, to have been with everyone in the neighbourhood.

'Look at you,' he points at my outfit—kurta and jeans—'you could have worn anything you fancied, but you see the value of dressing decently.' I argue that a woman isn't only what she wears. I try to be polite every time I disagree with Ahuja's views on the female character. *Gau rakshak*s are the most feared men in India today. The official logo of the Cow Protection Army is the gilded torso of a cow flanked first by a pair of swords and then AK-47s. Its slogan: 'We will keep the numbers of the cow mother intact with our corpses. It's going to be a fight our enemies will remember.' The army operates at the level of an independent republic. It has an anthem and a constitution. It also has a fleet of vehicles and a stockpile of arms and ammunition. Its commanders are elected through a three-tier voting process; foot soldiers are chosen through the submission of an application form. Dozens are filed every day by young men across Haryana. They are drawn to the thrill of violence, 'of taking the law in their hands', Yogendra Arya, founder of the militia, told me in his office in Rohtak.

At the age of twelve, Yogendra left his village and his family and joined a gurukul managed by the Arya Samaj, a sect of Hindu reformists. I asked Arya, wearing a white cotton dhoti and long black hair, what drove him away from a normal life. 'Otherwise,' he said, 'it would have been the same job-family-kids kind of life. One wants to do something uncommon.' Approaching early middle age, Arya does indeed have an uncommon life. He is single, lives in an ashram, and leads an army of 5000 soldiers. A chosen set live in the ashram at any point of time and follow its routine. 'Wake up at four, wash your clothes, join the prayers, lift weights in the gym, eat pure vegetarian food and drink milk,' said Parminder Arya, the senior Arya's secretary during the day and bodyguard at night. Leaving the ashram that evening, I asked him the same question. I reminded him that he could be going to college, dating a girl, hanging out at a bar. 'Any twenty-three-year-old can do that,' he said. Few of them, he reminded me, had access to his kind of nightlife. 'Car chases, gunfights—people see these things in movies, we live it.'

Sachin Ahuja became a gau rakshak because it makes him feel like a 'complete man'. Unlike Kumar, Ahuja's fight isn't driven by teenage angst. His moves follow a method. One of the things that make a man complete, he tells me, is the ability to manage his time. From 9 a.m. to 6 p.m., Ahuja sells insurance schemes; from 7 p.m. to 8 p.m., he pumps iron; and from 9 p.m. onwards, he responds to the call of the cow mother. He protects cows not only because he thinks they are tied to his Hindu identity, but because the position of a gau rakshak brings him what young men in his situation most crave: izzat. 'People listen to you,' he tells me, sounding not unlike Kumar or Thakur, 'you don't feel the lack of anything.'

And there's nothing Ahuja appreciates more at this phase in his life than the feeling that he matters to the world. Nothing around him is what it used to be. More precisely, he has nothing else that could make him feel important. Not family: He performs his duty as son and grandson and brother and brother-in-law, but it can no longer give him an edge over a man who doesn't. Not women: He knows better than to think he has any chance there. ('Since every girl in Karnal has a boyfriend, I doubt I will ever even be married.') Not work: He has neither the authority of a government servant nor the swagger of a farm owner. For eight hours every day, Ahuja sells insurance.

As proud as he is of working for himself, of expanding his circle of business every day, he knows no one cares. What they care about is the ID card he flips out of his back pocket every time someone takes him for just another guy—at traffic intersections, the local RSS office, the police station. The position earns him more than the ID card. It makes him the chief saviour of cows in a small pocket of the town, from one end of a railway line to the mouth of a canal. What he must do to maintain the privilege is constantly prove himself as a true gau rakshak. He wouldn't have to do that had a chain of reckless losers across India not posted on their WhatsApp groups selfies with cows they did not in fact rescue. ('All they do is show up at the very moment real gau rakshaks have rescued cows from smugglers and click their photos with the haul.')

People are no longer sure how seriously to take a gau rakshak. Not even their hero, Narendra Modi, who brought up the question of real vs fake gau rakshaks in a speech to the nation in 2016. Few would doubt Ahuja's dedication to the cause; the man is as fluent speaking about the place of cows in Hinduism as he is vigilant patrolling the streets for stolen cattle. But he knows better than to be smug. Everything is a test—even the speed at which the gau rakshaks drink the hot glass of milk before a big patrol—and everyone a judge. I wonder if Ahuja anticipated the question his boss swung at him one evening shortly after Modi's speech. As he walked about the temple premises passing orders, Sandeep Rana, the district president of the Cow Protection Army, shot a sharp look at Sachin Ahuja and asked him what happened to the two vials of cow urine he was handed the previous month. Ahuja was only lost for a second before saying he was halfway through them, mixing two drops of the liquid in his morning glass of water. Rana asked for a photo of the half-empty vials. Ahuja promised to send it through WhatsApp

later that night. It was going to be a while, though. This was
no ordinary night.

Not twenty-four hours earlier, Indian soldiers had stormed
across the disputed border in Kashmir and blown up a series
of militant camps on the Pakistani-controlled side. It was
Karnal's gau rakshaks' turn for some border action, although
their border lay only fifty miles away: the police outpost that
marked the official boundary between Haryana and Uttar
Pradesh. It's a separation more cultural than physical. The
latter state has a large population of Muslims and Dalits, the
former one a large number of Hindu vegetarians. Haryana
was governed by a political party committed to the interest of
Hindus; Uttar Pradesh, at the time, by one that depended on
the electoral support of Muslims. Cows make a safe prop for
the theatre of control. It's not the first time Hindus have used
the holy beast to put their imagined enemies in their places—
it has proved to be a handy mascot for over 100 years—and it
is unlikely to be the last.

The first person to ride out of the temple gates is Ahuja on
his bike. I sit in the car that follows him. There are five of us in
the vehicle—Rana and two others in the back seat, a young gau
rakshak at the wheel, and me. The rods and chains have been
thrown in the trunk. At least four other groups of gau rakshaks
on bikes and cars follow us on the highway. A long line of
transport vehicles is waiting just behind the police chowki
when we pull in outside. Prepared for the arrival of Rana and
company, the Haryana police have put up barricades and cut
off all traffic between the two states. Once the entire gang is
in, Rana assigns them different tasks for the night: searching
the vehicles, interrogating the drivers, receiving intelligence.
Over the next two hours, the gau rakshaks clamber on to a
procession of trucks jerking to a halt at the barricades and
perform the ritual of cow raid. Every lock is broken, every box

torn open. A great variety of things are being moved between Haryana and Uttar Pradesh on this night: apples, onions, soap bars, eggs, petrol. Sadly for Ahuja and his comrades, cows are not among them.

I watched the night unfold from the car. Rana refused to let me out on the pretext that I might get caught in a hail of bullets if things got out of control. He wasn't even sure I could keep myself safe inside the rolled-up windows of the Audi. As the self-appointed guardian of my life and honour, he left me in the care of our driver for the night, a gau rakshak of unparalleled passion. Vinod Suryavanshi is best described as a hater, a man capable of tenacious and overwhelming hate. Over the three hours we sat ensconced in the dark, Suryavanshi took me painstakingly through the list of things he loves to hate: Muslims, the Congress party, big-city culture, the liberal media. Until a few years ago, Suryavanshi used to frequently cross over to Uttar Pradesh with a group of Hindu radicals who spoke to Hindu students about the threats to their culture and identity. Since the arrival of the smartphone, he has moved the operation to social media. He currently manages six Facebook pages and 100 WhatsApp groups. 'From 7 a.m. to 7 p.m. I post Facebook updates about the agendas of Islam. Until 2.30 in the morning, I engage with WhatsApp conversations.' Like Kumar, Suryavanshi uses social media as a tool for political branding.

The more Facebook pages and WhatsApp groups they can 'manage', the better their ability to manage their political identities. They use each of these networks to build a different aspect of their political personality, from loving cows to bashing Bangladeshis. It's not only important to post stuff— news articles, personal views, photos in action—but to keep posting stuff all the time. I became used to receiving hundreds of WhatsApp messages through the day and receiving as many as six Facebook friend requests from a single man. 'So, which one of these is *you?*' I once asked one of them. He said he had a Facebook account for the real him and if I wanted he could send me a friend request as *himself*. I figured out in due course that this too was normal practice. You need a place to be yourself—to share selfies and songs, jokes and motivational quotes.

Like Ahuja, Suryavanshi is his own boss. He manages a lending agency he inherited from his father. 'What do I have to do? Give a loan if someone comes to ask for it; receive an instalment if someone pays it on an existing loan.' The rest of his time, he said, belongs to the nation. I nodded in awe. It was midnight by the time we wound up the list. He asked me if I was getting bored. I said yes. He told me he was going to play me a song on his cellphone—his favourite song from when he was a boy. It was a love song from a Bollywood film from the 1990s. '*Dil toh pagal hai, dil deewaana hai* (The heart is crazy, the heart is mad),' went the lines.

At midnight, Suryavanshi and Ahuja drove me to a petrol station from where I had arranged for a taxi to take me back to Delhi. Ahuja was disappointed I couldn't see him in action. I told him I would be back some other night. He smiled knowingly, as sure as me of the chances of my returning for another raid. He wanted me to believe in his cowboy swagger. For the rest of the ride he narrated dramatic accounts of the nights when he 'hung between life and death' to rescue the cow mother—the time a smuggler in an SUV drove his bike off the road and into a sharp ditch, the time when two trucks loaded with cows closed in on his scooter on either side. I wanted to tell him I believed him. But all I could manage as I got out of the car was a relieved smile.

* * *

I didn't think Arjun Kumar or Sachin Ahuja cared very much about the nation. They had offered me little reason to believe so. I was also sceptical of their claims of devotion to Hindutva. They have enrolled themselves in the battle to protect Hindu identity, but what they are really fighting for is their shot at any identity at all. What they wanted first of all is to be known in their towns: Kumar in Meerut, Ahuja in Karnal. Kumar had chosen to fight 'love jihad' because it appealed to the Hindus' fear of the attractive Muslim in Meerut. Ahuja had sworn to protect cows because it was the number one agenda of the BJP government in Haryana, the land of the cow mother. It was the same as editing your CV to suit the employer's interest. I didn't doubt the force of their hatred: for girls who were full of themselves, for the Muslim who had forgotten his place, for the world that is changing too fast for their comfort. But at its most basic, theirs is a rage against irrelevance. It's the rage of a man who has just been told his special pass no longer admits him to the coolest club in town. You have got to be a young man to feel their rage. No matter how hard they tried to help me put myself in their shoes—and they gave it their best—my feet were the wrong size.

Vikas Thakur was different. Our wide-ranging dialogue was one between equals: urbane, English-speaking, upwardly mobile, intellectually curious. We could have been friends. We grew up in the same city; many of my old friends live by his world view. We argued over meeting places, I pretended to find his jokes about the Congress party funny, and he promised to read articles written from the left-liberal position. Crucially, I continued to meet Thakur to see if there was any value in his shtick: that young men armed with facts and figures were going to change Indian politics.

In the politics Thakur dreamt about, there was no place for petty agendas. 'We have to wipe out the limited concept of nationalism floated by people with specific motives. The way we are shaping the youth, people who talk about cows, about love jihad, will be laughed at. Just because I am with the BJP, I am not sitting here to kill Muslims. What happened in Gujarat? Gujarat was the main ground for the Vishwa Hindu Parishad—made up of goons frustrated with life. All they wanted to play was the religion card. As Modi came to power there, the VHP retreated from Gujarat. *Kyun?* (Why?) Because of Modi's progressive politics, because of his government's inclusive development.'

Once again, Thakur chose to present the view of Narendra Modi's rule in Gujarat that most suited his rhetoric. I presented him with facts and figures questioning the 'Gujarat Model' that Modi had sold the country on in 2014, but he wasn't impressed. Nobody ever was: You had to admire Modi's ability to build political perception. Between 2002, when thousands of Muslims were killed in Gujarat in an organized riot early in his tenure as chief minister, and 2014, when he became the BJP's prime-ministerial candidate for the central elections, Narendra Modi fashioned an image as a leader who got things done: investments flowed, businesses profited, bureaucrats performed. He did it with a series of strategic moves such as getting media outlets to champion him and industrialists to endorse him. He put together spectacular events at which he sold himself to an escalating cast of VIPs—foreign dignitaries, corporate millionaires, spiritual leaders—as the man who could take India into the future. It worked. Hindus began to see in him a man who could keep Muslims down as well as get things moving again. Muslims saw him as a man to fear—but one who would get things done. Others, including investors from the rest of the world, simply saw him as a man who could get things done, never mind the rest.

His image as a performer hasn't gone unchallenged. Many observers have picked holes in his narrative. They have contrasted proposed investments with functional projects, pointed out his preference for certain businessmen over others, and counted the number of jobs created. None of this has made a difference. Since he became prime minister, Modi has tapped into every new channel of communication to brand and rebrand himself, from a stylish jet-setter to a 'servant of the people'. Two out of ten Indians listen to his Sunday monologue on the radio. Thirty million people follow him on Twitter, 40 million on Facebook, 5.8 million on Instagram, and 5,91,000 on YouTube, making him the most popular political leader on social media in the world.

Like Narendra Modi, Thakur wants to master the politics of perception. 'The public no longer cares about empty promotion of hoardings and ads. You have to connect with them on ideas and ideology. *Public prachar pe nahin jaati hai. Vichar ke star pe kaam karna hai* (The public doesn't care about publicity any more, you have to engage them with ideas.)' One day in late 2014, he finally took me to the party's social media war room. It was inside a new apartment building, the kind my parents had moved into some years ago. The living room was laboriously reimagined as an office space. It was safer to keep social media operations away from the party office, he explained. A six-member team sat inside executing the BJP's social media plan for the upcoming elections. None of them looked up from their computer screens as Thakur introduced me. Most of them were busy deciding a good way to juxtapose the faces of Narendra Modi and Arjun Munda, the chief minister hopeful in Jharkhand, against the BJP colours. There was the issue of the lotus—where should the party symbol be placed for maximum impact? In the middle of the two faces, on the top of the graphic, or in a corner? Scowling over the final image, Thakur ordered two corrections: toning down the saffron and green and ditching the lotus. When the image was finalized, a process that could take a whole day, it would be released to every official supporter of the BJP with internet access. 'This image will be circulated through WhatsApp to the 70,000 official BJP workers in the state. And put on Facebook through nearly 160 official and unofficial fronts for the BJP,' Thakur said, handing out cold drinks to his colleagues and me.

I went back to the house a number of times over the next couple of months. An average day in the war room was as exciting as one in a post office. Thakur's colleagues were a mix of young, IT-savvy recruits and middle-aged party workers. Most of the content they produced—a combination of text, pictures, sound and animation—drew on issues of everyday relevance to the average voter: roads, jobs, vegetable prices. On most days, the entire energy of the war room was concentrated on packaging as many insults about opposition parties as possible into one WhatsApp message. The first thing the team did in the morning was go through their Facebook feed and note things their friends were talking about: the rise of tribal politics in the state, reservations in entry-level government jobs, inflation. Their brief was to choose one topic every day, spin it into an appeal for votes, and keep it in circulation for at least twenty-four hours.

It wasn't a particularly challenging job. Thakur didn't really seem to care about it. 'Why not the bigger questions that will decide what India will be in the future: education, labour, industry, centre-state relations, federal economy?' he ranted during a coffee shop conversation. He was starting to realize that the BJP hadn't recruited him to set its agenda, but merely to circulate it. He looked forward to the evenings. At sundown, Thakur went to the top floor of the building, unlocked a door, placed a few bottles of whisky on a table, and called every major journalist on his phone. As someone in charge of the party's image, the evening addas were a part of his brief. Debating ideas of India was more suited to his interests than tweaking the lotus on Photoshop. 'You should join us sometime,' he once offered.

Thakur was as traditional a man as anyone else I was hanging out with. He never allowed me to pay the bill, for example. I was surprised to be invited by him to a room full of drunk men raving into the night. He would never have offered a local female journalist this exclusive access. Only my exposure to the world outside Ranchi could have qualified me for the honour; if you'd lived in Delhi, you'd seen everything. I let the offer lapse. As state elections approached, Thakur became increasingly detached from the everyday hustling. Instead, he used the time to build a political persona as a thinking politician. Every time I spoke to him in the following months, Thakur informed me of a new experiment with 'perception'. In October 2014, weeks before the first phase of the election, I walked into the war room to see him juggling two phone calls. He was organizing an event: an all-out debate between young voters and the chief ministerial candidates. He had drafted the outline for the debate himself. The students of the city's best colleges would be asking the candidates questions about skills development, economic policy, corruption and land policy. The idea seemed right out of the online polls Vinay Singhal posted on his nation-building website.

Q: Should rigorous imprisonment of up to a lifetime be given for the corrupt and the recovery of national losses made within two years?
- Yes
- No
- Don't know

Thakur said it was a good way to test the ground for his new non-profit firm for political branding. What he was doing over the phone calls was managing an event: fixing a venue, placing an announcement in the newspapers, allocating contracts for light and sound, transport, food and drinks. I asked him if his own party wouldn't have a problem with this inclusive exercise in the service of democracy. 'You don't understand the game, madam,' he said, bringing on his throaty neta-ji voice, 'Everyone will speak at the seminar, but the next day the newspapers will be full of things the BJP's candidate said.' The event was held at the largest stadium in the city. This is all one could say of its scale. Few students showed up and fewer were eager to grill the politicians on the stage. The contestants showed up late and once they did, mainly fought for longer time at the mike. The newspapers carried a report the next day, but it wasn't easy to spot it.

A month after the pre-election debate, Thakur told me he wanted to launch a newspaper or at least a news website. To make it big in politics, he said, you had to control the media in one way or the other. Two weeks later, Thakur had decided it would be a website of political news and analysis. He asked me what I thought of the idea. I asked him if it was going to be another digital publication acting as the unofficial voice of the BJP. 'No way.' He put away his phone and looked me in the eye. 'All that is crap. There is no original thinking, no dissent from the party line. What I have in mind is a space open to a larger debate, open to all points of view.'

I wondered if this would be as neutral a political exercise as his last event, but you couldn't get Thakur to interrogate his motives at this point. In his head, he was a visionary on a warpath. Every time I met him over the following months, he professed to be working on an idea bigger than the last: a chain of old-age homes and orphanages, an initiative to bring back missing children, investment in solar energy, adoption of a village. He seemed to have decided he was going to live the life of a public figure. I wasn't sure what he was doing. I couldn't see through to his real self.

* * *

I met Vikas Thakur far fewer times over the following year. He was rarely in Ranchi when I was. By the end of the BJP's campaign in Jharkhand, he may have figured things weren't going his way. The BJP's social media game was on, but the party hadn't exactly taken note of Thakur's leadership qualities. In December 2014, the BJP and its allies won forty-two of eighty-one assembly seats in Jharkhand. In a post-poll survey, people claimed to have voted for jobs, inflation—what Thakur refers to as 'vegetable prices'—and development: roads, electricity, hospitals. Fifty per cent of Jharkhand's Hindus had voted for the BJP. The media duly attributed the victory to the 'Narendra Modi wave'. The party's state unit was admired for its successful 'connect' with the region's young voters. The war room was going to stay. Thakur wasn't concerned with these developments. His man, Arjun Munda, a Tribal politician who served as the BJP's last chief minister, had lost his seat. It was a huge setback for the political career of the only party leader who had believed in his potential. Thakur felt good about the fact that Munda had come to his house. His family was proud of him for bringing back some of their lost privilege. Thakur feared his defeat would place caste back in the centre of the state's politics. Throughout the process of ticket distribution, Thakur had fretted about caste-based calculations of the parties in the fray. He'd wished for all of them to be proven wrong in the end. No matter what the people's verdict, he believed it would be foolish for his party to choose a non-Tribal to represent it in a state with a large tribal population. On 28 December, the BJP confirmed Thakur's fears by picking an obscure face from a backward caste, and not a member of one of the state's tribes, for chief minister. It signalled the end of the road for him. The only kind of world in which Thakur could win an election ticket was one where they were awarded on individual merit. But what exactly was his individual merit?

In October 2015, I met Thakur for the last time that year. We were sitting in the lobby of a big hotel. Thakur had showed up an hour late and needed to leave early. 'Important meetings,' he said, putting his two large-screen smartphones on the table. I brought up the election verdict. As he brooded over the future of Indian politics, I suggested that the BJP's decision could have been driven by upper-caste voters' fear of Tribals seizing power in the state. Munda may have efficiently run Jharkhand, but its middle class, including my parents, constantly brought up his complicity in corruption. In his signature style, Thakur cut me off to correct my narrow view of corruption. 'How do you define corruption?' Thakur asked me, putting down his glass of lemonade. 'See,' he said, holding up one of his cell phones, 'this mobile can be made at ₹90, but the MRP is ₹92. Whatever amount was needed to manufacture the phone has been put in. The product is fine. Other scenario is: The cost of the mobile is ₹90, price quoted is ₹90, ₹5 is distributed and instead of making a product that needed ₹90, you spend ₹85. Taking commission and doing corruption are two different things. First: I'll do your job and I'll take a commission. Second: The job is not done and the money is distributed.'

His relationship with the government is different from Pankaj Prasad's, but like the small-time fixer, Thakur can't imagine a system where work is done without any illegitimate transaction of money. I asked him about the option he would choose if he ever won political power. 'I will be corrupt, happily corrupt,' said Thakur, his voice booming across the hotel lobby. 'If you are not corrupt, you will be thrown away by the system. It won't be to make money for myself. It will only represent power.' He told me a number of wild and wonderful things that day. 'In the next five years,' he said, 'I would be an MP or an MLA.' He showed not the faintest interest in the future of his party in the state or at the Centre, however. 'What is there for a political worker to do after an election is over?' So, he'd decided to do gainful things with his time. His plans included expanding the services of his branding firm, setting up a factory for semiconductor devices, and going deeper into the realm of the unseen.

When he was in town, Thakur spent a lot of his time hunting ghosts. He has been a certified paranormal investigator since 2010. Since a metaphysical encounter at the age of fourteen, while he was at the Vivekananda mission school, he has been interested in what he called 'unnatural occurrences'. 'I could see things and hear sounds no one around me did,' he had told me the first time we met. While he was in college, attending classes in communication, he spent his nights decoding the mysteries of the universe with help from a centre for paranormal research in the American Midwest where he was enrolled online. In 2010, Thakur joined a group of paranormal researchers working in Mumbai who, when they weren't examining abandoned buildings, sold plot twists to the writers of cheesy horror films. Thakur hadn't been active in the field for a long time. He had put his political career before his spiritual quest. He was trying to reverse his priorities now.

There were developments in the paranormal world that could upset the power structure guiding the normal world, he predicted. There are times, he said, when the metaphysical world exerts itself in forms stronger than vibrations. We were going through one of those times, he said. There were more reports than ever, in the paranormal newsletter he received, of UFO sightings in India. He asked me if I was aware that an increased frequency of paranormal events always led states to tighten control over people. I stared into my lemonade. He said we need a new political ideology to deal with the incoming shifts in the structure of power in the universe.

At that time—I was months from meeting Vinay Singhal— I did not know how passionately young men with political ambition plotted the realigning of planetary forces. Thakur advised me again to start reading Vivekananda, all eight volumes. 'What he could achieve in philosophy, it would take Western philosophers another two hundred years to match.' It's only the illuminated who will be able to shape the politics of this new order. 'This,' he said sweeping his hands through the chilled air to gesture at the unknown, 'is just the beginning.'

5

The Angry Young Woman

RICHA SINGH WAS in her late twenties when she decided to
fight an election. She gave herself two weeks to win it. This
was one of the most important elections in Uttar Pradesh.
Not the one to the assembly in Lucknow or to the Parliament
in Delhi, but the election to the students' union of Allahabad
University. It doesn't just decide which student party gets to
call the shots in the campus—and by extension the city—but
is also known as the most reliable indicator of wider political
currents. Dozens of students fight for the five posts in the
students' union, with culture secretary at the bottom and
president on top, and thousands participate in the carnival
around it.

Richa Singh was going to contest the president's post.
For 100 years now, Allahabad University has been one of
the primary political battlegrounds in north India; and the
president of its students' union the ultimate boss. Students
fight the election driven not only by political ambition but a
lack of career options. A students' union post is more than a
political position—it's a lucrative career for the thousands of
young men who flock to the campus from towns and villages

across the Hindi-speaking region. If they can't get anything else out of slogging away for years at the university, like most students, they at least have the chance to join the heartland's economy of political protection.

To win a post in the students' union, though, one must have the ability to follow the formula. It begins with developing a good name for yourself. You identify a clutch of issues affecting students, such as hostel allocations, library hours, corruption in the admission process; make speeches promising to fight the administration; get contacts in local newspapers to publicize these events; cut out the clippings and read them out at your next set of speeches. You also need resources: first and foremost, money (₹2-3 lakh) to print campaign posters, pay for musclemen to lead your rallies, rent SUVs for yourself and your supporters, and pay local tea stalls and restaurants to distribute refreshments among potential voters on your behalf. You also need advisers, from among the previous student leaders and politicians with common ideological affiliation. Once you have a political strategy, you'll need a campaign manager to execute it. They must carry out a two-pronged process: mobilize members of your caste among the student population and make common-enemy alliances with the other groups. These deals must ideally be made over large amounts of meat and whisky.

Once you've got all of this in place, you need to put on the whitest of your kurta-pyjamas, throw in a pair of glamorous aviators, fold your hands in entreaty and stand on the seat of your open-top jeep. If you win, and become the president of the students' union, you can recover your investment in a month. If fixer is what you want to be, Allahabad is your ideal base. The leader of the students' union brokers every deal the university makes with a private party, including licences to small colleges to grant degrees in its name. He also gets a direct pass into the city's protection economy, collecting rents from everyone who wants to conduct business in the city—builders, shopkeepers, restaurateurs, coaching institutes—in exchange for safety from the harm rowdy students can inflict on their interests. These aren't men you want to end up on the wrong side of; once they are done with college politics, they will join either full-time crime or the state assembly—in that order. Most importantly, the students' union president can show up at any office—district magistrate, superintendent of police, political party chiefs—without an appointment. He is there to forward requests in exchange for suitable compensation. It takes a man to play this game, they say in Allahabad. There is a reason, after all, why no woman had dared to stand for the president of the students' union in the 127 years of the university. Allahabad was stunned, therefore, when on 21 September 2015, Richa Singh announced her intention to contest the post.

* * *

YOU HAVE TO be a little crazy to dare the boys of Allahabad University. They live to fight, it is alleged. Most news reports featuring Allahabad University revolve around the passion its young men have for mayhem: If the boys aren't creating a ruckus on the campus they may be found going on a rampage or, in their presumably gentler moments, indulging in violence. The range of their excesses is breathtaking: They break the windowpanes of their classrooms, vandalize the canteen, thrash hostel inmates, forcibly confine the vice chancellor, rough up his secretary and security guard, batter other students, hurl crude bombs, and occasionally set themselves on fire. Their taste for weaponry is similarly indiscriminate: Besides the bombs, they also wield stones, cricket bats, hockey sticks and handmade pistols. The university's vice chancellors keep a personal posse of security guards and have an emergency hideout. The city's police force usually has a couple of special battalions at the ready. The rest of the city, including the 2000 residents of the women's hostel, can do nothing but pray.

This wasn't always so. It wasn't, at least, the plan. In 1885, when the British colonial government set up Allahabad University, it aimed to build a very different kind of young Indian man. The university was to groom native men in cosmopolitan culture through an education in the best of Western law, classics, science and the fine arts, on the lines of Oxford or Cambridge. Supervised by Lord Macaulay—the architect of the colonial education system who inspires such fury in Moin Khan and Shahnawaz Chaudhary—its syllabus was designed to create a class of men who would be 'Indians in blood and colour but English in tastes and opinions'. Its building was the finest structure in the North-Western Provinces, meant to be second only to the Taj Mahal: majestic red-brick facade, vast courtyards, curving arcades, spiral staircases, carved stone pillars, pointed spires, stained glass ceilings and lush gardens. The teaching staff was drawn from the finest layer of the Imperial Education Board; and the first crop of students came from the Hindu and Muslim gentry across north and central India. The most mischievous thing the boys did was riff on the poems of Robert Frost. English, they say, was coded in the DNA of the institution. By the 1920s, the university had produced several batches of enlightened men who joined the corridors of Indian power as bureaucrats, political figures, scientists, academicians and writers.

Then everything changed. At some point during the peak of the independence movement, some of the students discovered politics. Between 1920 and 1925, every major leader of the freedom movement—Tilak, Gokhale, Malviya, Pal, Naidu and Gandhi himself—came to Allahabad and addressed them about resistance and revolution. Nehru spoke to them every week at his family residence in the city and his sisters went to their hostel rooms to distribute revolutionary badges. As the students became radicalized, so too did the students' union. The platform for intellectual dialogue became a platform for dissent. In December 1921, the union decided to boycott the Prince of Wales' visit to the university. In 1930, a student climbed the roof of the Allahabad Collectorate and hoisted the Indian tricolour on its flag mast. He was shot dead by the police. In protest, the students shut down the university. In the nearly hundred years since, the student politics of Allahabad university has mirrored the youth culture of provincial north India. It has defined how men should behave, what women should fear, what constitutes success and power, and what caste, class and community have to do with any of these.

* * *

I thought Ranchi held a distinction in filth and chaos until I got off the train at Allahabad station. Nowhere else in India I've been has the conflict between the past and present of a place resulted in a more disastrous outcome. The broken jam-packed roads, the half-finished buildings, the open drains and the thick haze of dust that greet you outside the station are the result of the same things that make the whole of second-tier India one giant pothole: crazy construction, overcrowding, civic collapse.

There is one feature from the city's glorious past, though, that still towers over its new cement-and-dust facade: the buildings of Allahabad University. The red has turned a rusty brown, but the colonnades still appear endless, the domes sit as big and round as the Taj's, and the spires still reach the skies. The other thing that has remained unaffected by time is the university's influence over the city's life and culture. I booked myself a room at the university's guest house, where the only evidence of change was a flat-screen television at the reception. A row of men in white kurta-pyjamas sat there watching breaking news ('Ruckus in State Assembly'). The guest house is run by a middle-aged Brahmin who rarely opened his mouth for fear of disturbing the position of the paan leaf he was chewing. Most of these men were there to lobby him to reserve rooms for their friends and well-wishers. A night's stay cost only ₹500, and the queue to get in was long.

I arrived in Allahabad at an interesting time. A shift was afoot in the power dynamics of youth politics across Indian universities. Its core remained the same. The interests of upper-caste Hindu men were directly opposed to those of everyone else out to challenge their privilege: Other Backward Castes, Scheduled Castes, Scheduled Tribes, Muslims, Christians, women. But its axis had turned. The 'others' were now equal in number and coming together. In 2006, the Indian government extended caste-based reservations in state-aided institutions of higher education. It raised the proportion of students across a range of disadvantaged groups—peasants, tribes, religious minorities, women—to nearly half of the total strength of major Indian universities. The subaltern now have an equal voice in university politics and they are using every occasion to assert it.

Every major Indian campus is a battleground today. And since 2014, the battle has centred on notions of what it means to be an Indian. Unlike the previous Congress-led coalition at the Centre, the BJP doesn't consider the conflict as something students should sort out between themselves. Pushed by the larger agenda of Hindu nationalism set by the RSS, the government has thrown its vast weight behind its campus army: the ABVP.

Four months before I entered the gracious campus of Allahabad University, a young man at the University of Hyderabad named Rohith Vemula had written an eloquent suicide note and then killed himself. He was a member of a Dalit-Muslim coalition whose candidate won the election to the president of the students' union in the university in 2014. That year, nearly 60 per cent of its students belonged to the reserved categories. The verdict pitted the Dalit students directly against the caste Hindus of the ABVP over the following months. In August 2015, the rival groups faced off over the ABVP's disruption of the screening of a documentary about the BJP's apparent orchestration of recent anti-Muslim riots in Uttar Pradesh—the incident in which Sangeet Som and his WhatsApp video message had played the leading part. Soon enough, the Ministry of Human Resources ordered an inquiry, which was followed by an immediate response to complaints of 'anti-national activities' on campus. In December 2015, five Dalit research scholars, including twenty-six-year-old Vemula, a research scholar of physics, were barred from entering the university's hostels and using common spaces in the campus. They were also barred from contesting elections. In January 2016, Vemula hanged himself from a fan in a hostel room.

Barely a month after Vemula's death, the Home Ministry ordered the arrest of the president of the students' union of Delhi's Jawaharlal Nehru University. The arrest was instigated by a complaint of anti-national behaviour from the ABVP. The supposed criminal was Kanhaiya Kumar, a young man from Bihar who had come to JNU through a reserved quota for applicants from backward districts. He was among those who participated in a march commemorating the death anniversary of Afzal Guru, a Kashmiri convicted of aiding an attack on the Indian Parliament in 2001 that killed nine. Guru was executed in 2013, after more than a decade in jail. His conviction and execution were contested to the end.

From Jammu to Kolkata, every big campus was caught in the fight between the politics of Hindu nationalism and secular liberalism after the BJP's ascent to power. Allahabad University, true to its roots, believed itself at the centre of the struggle.

* * *

The first question I asked Richa Singh was why she had decided to fight the election. We were sitting in her corner room in the university's women's hostel. Singh is short and slim and looked even smaller sitting cross-legged on her bed. She dresses exactly as you would expect a young, politically ambitious woman in India to do: kurta, jeans, sneakers, and a stole thrown around her neck. She has a small face with deep-set eyes gleaming behind black-rimmed glasses and straight, dark hair severely pulled back in a ponytail.

Singh told me she had been thinking about the students' union for a long time before she made the announcement. Power matters to her. She has been cultivating it since she was in school, first becoming class monitor and then house president. The students listened to her; so did the administration as a result. She continued to expand her influence in college. As an undergraduate student of economics at a women's-only college, Singh became involved with a gender-rights group. 'I had begun to understand the concept of women's rights. *Patriarchy samajh mein aane lagi*

(I began to understand patriarchy). I started to clearly see the place of women in small-town society,' she said. She found herself questioning the power dynamics within her own family, where her father and her brothers made decisions for her and her sisters: who to marry, where to live, what time to return home. Finally, as a postgraduate student in gender studies, she entered the Allahabad University and received the shock of her life. 'You didn't see girls around campus. Only in class. They came to college with their heads bowed and left college with their heads bowed. Not that it protected them from comments from boys.'

Singh responded to those comments with a few of her own. Things got worse. 'They would race with my scooter. I also raced—what was I supposed to do?' But the battle didn't have a foreseeable end. 'I then decided I will just respond with gestures. I will let them know that I see what they are trying to do and that I won't back down.' So while she raced with boys on the streets outside the university, she would keep one hand on the handlebar and the other free, opening and closing the fist in a loop. 'I wanted to let them know I am ready for a fight.' Her decision to take her fight to the union elections was about small things, she said. One of them was the matter of the tea shop outside the historic white stone building of the students' union. It's where she'd have liked to hang out with friends over a cup of chai, except few girls dared to even enter the premises of the students' union. Few of the university's 2000 women students had ever had tea at the famous shop at Lalajungi, the traffic intersection on the busy street circling the university. Like the lawns surrounding the union building, Lalajungi is male territory. So is everything that could be called public space in Allahabad: streets, parks, movie theatres. The only way a woman could access these spaces was with a man. Otherwise, anything could happen: She could be stared at, mocked, cornered or groped. So the first thing Singh wanted was the freedom for girls in Allahabad to move around as they liked.

Singh was also deeply irritated with the politics of muscle in the university. 'My problem was the students' union election is an exclusively male process. The girls made sure to shut themselves up in the hostel for the whole duration of the campaign. Or they went home. Because the way the male students let go of themselves around election time, anything could happen,' she said. During the union election of 2014, Richa Singh saw this traditional pageantry in all its gaudy detail from the balcony of her women's studies department, which has a view of the whole campus. 'Everything—the parade of SUVs, the tents, the feasts, the fights. That's when I decided to challenge this culture of muscle, money and caste.' From that day on, Singh made it a routine to go to the union chai shop and hang out alone. 'Gradually, three-four other girls started to come along. After some time, we began to make loud jokes about how girls were going to take over the union building.'

The date for 2015's election—29 September—was announced on 7 September. Singh first wanted to tell her family about her plan, but didn't know how to broach it. Just two weeks before, her father had coaxed her to visit a photo studio and pose for a matrimonial portrait. He was furious when he saw the photograph. 'He asked me, "Why the hell are you wearing sandals? Do you not have ladies' shoes?" I said I did not, as a matter of fact. I asked him why I wasn't sent studio portraits of the men.' Her father had saved up ₹40 lakh for her dowry; he wasn't going to be swayed by such repartee. There were also two older brothers to account for.

Her biggest worry, however, was one of resources. No matter how low scale you want to keep things, an election calls for cash: to print posters, put up a campaign office, arrange at least one meal a day for your campaign team. On 15 September, Singh woke up in her hostel room and did a series of things. She went to her university adviser to resign from her teaching fellowship. 'She was stunned,' said Singh of her adviser. 'She asked me, "Do you know what it means to contest a students' union election?" I said, "I don't, therefore I have decided to make it easier to understand."' The next stop was her bank. 'I realized I had saved up ₹80,000 from my salary so far. I decided to throw it all in.' She then went home and told her parents about her plan. 'My mother thought I had gone crazy. My father thought I was joking.' The last thing Singh did before she went to bed was call a meeting of her friends and well-wishers to break the news.

That done, Richa Singh took a view of the battlefield. These were, in order of influence, the parties: SFI (the student wing of the Communist Party of India), NSUI (the student wing of the Congress party), Pratiyogi Chhatra Morcha (PCM—an anti-quota right-wing group), SCM (the student wing of the Samajwadi Party), and ABVP. The next elections to the state assembly were only two years away at this point, and the stakes higher than ever before. Now that the BJP had conquered the centre, it aimed to go for the next big prize—with a fifth of India's population, Uttar Pradesh is demographic gold.

But the Samajwadi Party, in power in Lucknow, wasn't going to let go that easily: Before Mulayam Singh Yadav, leader of the Samajwadi Party, a powerful product of caste politics and muscle, contested his first election he used to be a professional wrestler. The party channels the aspirations of backward, mainly agricultural, castes and Muslims to keep returning to power. The electoral scenario boiled down to a simple resolution, which was obviously based on caste arithmetic: The caste Hindus would either vote ABVP (Brahmins and Kayasths) or PCM (Thakurs and Banias), and a mix of regional backward castes and Muslims would stick to the SCM. The parent organizations would provide the student bodies everything they need to win—money, muscle and strategy.

If Richa Singh were to enter this game, she would need to find people and issues left unaddressed. Luckily, she saw them all around her. 'No one was looking at the concerns of women. No one was looking at the concerns of the Scheduled Castes lying outside the vote bank of the Samajwadi Party. No one cared about people who belong to the Scheduled Tribes quota. But most importantly, no one had any idea what the needs of average university students even were.' The election manifesto Singh put together—a first for a students' union contestant—turned every leftover group on the campus into a unified constituency. 'It talked about the hypocrisy of imposing a curfew on girl students but not rebuilding a large stretch of the hostel's wall that's been missing since a collapse years ago—does that not put the girls in danger? It talked about the shamelessness of asking the SC-STs for votes when their hostel has not had a working water filter for years or chairs for them to sit on. It talked of specific issues faced by students who came from villages, who don't understand English or how to use computers as well as the others.' The fact that the students from Scheduled Castes and Scheduled Tribes lived in a separate hostel in far worse repair than the hostels for 'general' students seemed a fair indication of the priorities of previous students' union regimes.

On 18 September, Richa Singh announced she was going to contest as an independent candidate. Starting the next day, Singh and her team switched into full election mode. 'A number of friends contributed to a fund, which added up to

another ₹40,000. We put up a small tent inside the hostel to act
as a workspace. We needed a main campaign office with access
to male and female students. Someone suggested asking the
owner of this rubber factory nearby for permission to use his
porch. We put up another tent there. At some point, someone
made a Facebook page in my name.'

In the meantime, Singh went to a photo studio—once
again—and posed for a portrait. It was different this time.
The outfit of kurta-jeans-scarf-glasses that had failed every
classical standard of the matrimonial portrait was just perfect
on this occasion. The man behind the camera didn't even
ask her to smile. In the image the team got printed on the
posters, Singh's wearing a bright yellow kurta—minimum
promotion, maximum visibility—and looking straight into the
camera with an expression half hesitant and half earnest. On
19 September, her supporters took out a rally to inform the
whole of Allahabad of her decision. It had about forty people.
Two men walked in the front carrying a banner with Singh's
face. The women held up black placards with white slogans
that set the tone for Singh's challenge: *aadhi aabadi ka naara hai,
chhatra sangh hamara hai* (half the population has made up its
mind—the students' union will be ours.)

It was the wildest sight Allahabad had seen in a long
time. Singh received a series of phone calls the next day, each
more urgent than the last. Most of these were made by the
closed circle of influencers who control the students' union
elections, and by association, local power. They are known
as *Mathadhish*—literally, high priest; and what they do is
'manage' people and circumstances affecting the elections.
'Most of them said what I was expecting—you have no idea
what you are doing; you will be putting a lot at risk, from
character to career; you are going to regret this.' By the end of
the day, the tone of the calls had gone from 'concerned uncle'

to 'mafia lord'. Some of them went to her sister's house the next morning. 'They said to my brother-in-law, "She is a girl. Anything could happen to her." I was shaking with anger at the thought that people were trying to "manage" my family. I shot back at my brother-in-law, "If you guys can't support me," I said, "try at least not to support my enemies."'

Later that day, Richa Singh bought the nomination from a university office. She was expected to return to submit it the next day. One doesn't simply go and hand in one's nomination form, though. Before they turn into the university gate, the contestants drive around the city followed by hundreds of followers waving their banners and shouting their name. When Singh set out that day, she was followed by fifty girls. They completed a circuit of Bank Road and stopped, to a collective gasp of astonishment from bystanders, at Lalajungi to address the crowd. When Singh finally proceeded towards the university, she had around 100 people behind her, including a sizeable bunch of newspaper reporters. On the way, the procession stopped at rival camps and appealed to the students working the desks to vote for change.

Over the next four days, Singh walked class to class and opened her appeal with the same line: 'Don't decide to vote for me because I am a woman, but don't decide to not vote for me because I am a woman.' Four girls stopped by her campaign tent that evening. The next day, twelve of them offered to join her team in their all-night brainstorm session on campaign ideas. 'We were telling everyone who came by the same thing, starting with the fact that not one woman knew what it felt like to be union president. Then we told them the issues on which we will fight the election, such as the broken wall of the hostel, the visiting hours we are forced to maintain with our friends from outside the hostel. We spoke about the shame of having our voting choices dictated to us by our brothers and boyfriends. The idea worked.' Created by a mix of right-hand girls and new converts, Singh's campaign anthem was dropped on Facebook in the middle of the night. 'Friends,' the opening line said, 'let our lovers tell us who they want us to vote for, but let's vote for whom we want to'.

'Is our vote so cheap?' asked a campaign slogan formulated in the tent and released into the corridors of the six hostel buildings. It referred to the historic campaign tactic used by every man who has ever contested a post in the union. They typically show up at the gate of the hostel on the eve of the election and send in a bag of samosas through a loyalist to do the needful. The slogan ended with an answer: 'Let's eat everyone's samosa, but vote for whom we want to.' That year too, the male contestants appeared at the expected hour with jute bags stained with oozing oil, but as they snuck their head in to find a friendly volunteer, a posse of women at the gate asked them to read out their respective agendas. 'Every year,' some girls told their boyfriends during visiting hours, 'we vote per your direction. How about you listen to us this time?'

On the evening of 20 September, the university cancelled the nomination of the Samajwadi Party candidate because of a mistake in his nomination form. It left only two big contenders in the fray, both right wing. On 21 September, the Samajwadi Party offered its 'outside' support to Singh. After five days of thinking it over, Singh accepted. 'I told them, "I will neither take your funds nor any other resources." All I wanted was their share of votes.' On the morning of 27 September, she took out her first campaign rally. As Singh walked around the campus asking for votes, 200 women repeated her call. Once they were done for the day, Singh and her supporters walked up to the union building, sat in its lawns, and shouted in a chorus: *'Aadhi aabadi ka naara hai, chhatra sangh hamara hai* (The slogan of half the student population: the students' union is ours now).' Word spread through the city that girls had taken over the union building. 'The boys' hostels were rattled,' said Singh, 'and the campaign offices went totally quiet, perhaps to put their heads together.'

Singh's rally left the university at 5 p.m., but not to return to the hostel. 'We decided to go around the city, pausing at every major point to make a little speech.' At one point, they encountered a PCM contestant making a speech and decided to launch into their own across the road. 'There was a massive crowd listening to him, but we had girls speaking on this side, and some people were simply curious to know what's going on, so they drifted over. It was crazy: The PCM supporters across the road started throwing stones in our direction and when they still couldn't disperse the crowd, they pushed a bunch of cows through.'

Singh returned to her hostel room at 2 a.m. She spent the rest of her night crying. 'I kept thinking I may have made a huge mistake. I had staked my whole life on this election. When I woke up I would have to go up to the roof of the union building and make a qualifying speech making the point that I was the best candidate for union president. But that night I wasn't sure. I was running a high fever, had lost my voice, and at 8 a.m. I got an anonymous call from someone who threatened to rape me if I left the hostel.' Singh left the hostel at around ten in the morning, in the best outfit she could put together that morning: royal-blue kurta, white tights, white stole, and her usual sneakers. Her first destination was home. 'I told them it was a big day for me and I needed their blessings. By then they had come around to dealing with my insanity. "*Aisi hi hai, hum usse rok nahin sakte* (She is just like that; we can't stop her)," they had started saying to neighbours and relatives worried on my behalf.' Her father gave her his car for the remaining two days of the campaign. He wanted her to be safe.

Singh drove a car full of squealing cheerleaders to the union building, where a candidate for the vice president's post was making a passionate speech. She couldn't just walk to her spot on the rooftop. It seemed as if the whole of Allahabad was squeezed into the street outside; and the entire population of the university—students, teachers, staff—on the grounds inside. The city's police and paramilitary troops were stationed in and around the building for the day, and so was the media. The students' union election day is the biggest annual public event in Allahabad. The candidate who makes the best speech wins the election; and the candidate who wins the election wins the right to rule the campus. 'A single mistake can mean a huge setback,' said Singh. 'And there are people who want you to make that mistake. So, they make it difficult for you to get to the mike. It's common for someone to trip you as you are squeezing through the press or come face to face and punch you senseless. What can you do?' Before Singh got out of her car, her supporters—around 100 in number, both men and women—spread in two parallel lines from the gates to the steps and linked their hands. 'Another bunch of them pushed me along all the way through to the steps, where a contingent of police waited to take over.' Every candidate gets seven minutes to make their speech. The first to be invited was the presidential nominee from the PSM. He urged the people of Allahabad to forgive Richa Singh. 'She is like a younger sister to me,' he said, hand on his throat in a gesture of sincerity, 'misled by vested interests to fight this election.'

Singh was calm as a saint as she took the stage. She spoke about the students' union's glorious history and dreadful present. She spoke about the issues that didn't feature in her agenda: no Ram Mandir and certainly no rollback of quotas. She spoke about toilets for women, clean water for SC/ST students, longer library hours for everyone. At the end, Singh reminded her audience that she wasn't a younger sister to any man contesting the election.

When Singh left the union building, she had two more days to beg for votes. She spent every minute going from room to room in the boys' hostels. 'I went with a group of girls and we engaged the men in one-on-one discussions about what they wanted from their president.' In the early morning of voting day, Singh was woken up by a young supporter in a state of panic. The ABVP had struck back. 'They had made sure their female supporters tore off every poster with my face on the premises. We did the only thing we could do: take a stack of posters advertising random candidates for culture secretary and paste them on the face of the ABVP's candidate for the president. Two hours before 2000 residents of the hostel were to line up at the booth, a young woman cornered Singh and asked her if what the ABVP was saying about her was true: Would voting for her mean one was 'anti-men'?

Five hours later, every ballot box was sealed and sent to a vault in the administrative building. The counting began at 6 p.m. the next day. The people of Allahabad poured into the university's streets once more. The votes were supposed to be counted in a high-security meeting hall and the results broadcast on a massive screen tied to the top of the tallest tree by the boundary wall. The only people allowed in the meeting hall apart from the vice chancellor and the counting officer were the five fighting for the post of the president. Singh was the last to go in. She sat in the only seat left at the round table, between the presidential candidates of the ABVP and the PCM: her vilest enemies. 'The men turned their chairs towards me. They stared, I stared back. One of them slapped his thighs. I kept staring.'

The counting was over by 11 p.m. The street was tense with speculation. At the appointed hour the counting officer strode to the head of the table to take the microphone and announce the results. He read out the number of votes received for the posts of culture secretary, treasurer, general secretary and vice president. The ABVP had won them all. 'At last he came to votes for the president, going bottom to top. NSUI (700 votes), AISA (800 votes), ABVP (1400 votes). He took a break. It seemed to me to last forever. Finally, he cleared his throat and said, PCM: 2243. I had won, by eleven votes, 2254 in all. Nearly 100 paramilitary guards swooped in and surrounded me.' At 2 a.m. on 1 October 2015, Singh entered the women's hostel. The girls were all awake inside the hostel, dancing on the lawns. After another night of no sleep, Singh put on a dirty red kurta and blue jeans and started her now-famous walk towards the union building. 'The whole hostel came along, including the staff, the cooks, the sweepers.'

At 10 a.m., Richa Singh was back on the rooftop of the union building to take her oath as the first female president of the Allahabad University's Students' Union. One couldn't really hear what she was saying. Cries of 'Jai Shri Ram' rose from one side of the ground—the ABVP celebrating its majority in the union. The other side was taken over by women—hundreds of them—singing, dancing, beating drums, and generating an awful lot of noise. Her parents didn't come; they were too old to deal with the drama. They spent the day at home, answering phone calls and receiving neighbours. 'When I went home to see them, they told me they were feeling proud. My face was on the front page of every newspaper.' Too overwhelmed to say anything else, they repeated to her the common headline from that morning: 'Richa Singh makes history'.

Singh's victory meant big changes: for the politics of Allahabad University, the culture of Allahabad, and the possibilities for women in political cultures dominated by muscle. Singh made her first ride to the union as president on her scooter. It was her way of taking back the streets. Within days of Singh taking her place on the throne, a new slogan was circulating in the hostel corridors: *Aadhi aabadi ka naara hai,* Lalajungi *hamara hai* (If a girl can rule the students' union, who was to stop one from entering a tea shop?)

Singh's victory was a challenge to the defining politics—Hindu, male, aggressive—of the Modi era. It proved there was space for women—even those whose ideas threaten the core of the dominant politics—in the country's political landscape. Every time Richa Singh spoke of the young men she was up against, I was reminded of Vikas Thakur, whose politics was shaped by his time as an ABVP member, and the boys of the Bajrang Dal and the Cow Protection Army, who reacted with violence to everything that didn't sit well with their world view. Being a man was central to their politics. Perhaps a woman like Richa Singh was an even bigger challenge to their identity than a Muslim who ate beef and seduced Hindu women.

She certainly rattled the world of young men in Allahabad. Their first response was shock and anger. For a whole month after the announcement of the results, groups of men gathered outside the gate of the girls' hostel between midnight and 2 a.m., cleared their throats, and released a stream of abuse so lewd that the young women had to make their windows soundproof with tape. No one was surprised. The threat of sexual punishment had run as a thread through Singh's election campaign. It could be as subtle as 'You are a woman' and as crude as 'You will not be left worthy of showing your face'. It both scared her and made her scoff. It was hard not to take threats of sexual abuse seriously, but sometimes you saw through the swagger. The sight and sound of 100 men calling 2000 women 'sluts' in a chorus was as frightening as it was comical. And when the young women in the hostel weren't covering their ears at the memory, they were having a laugh about it.

Not every man in Allahabad University could possibly have hated Richa Singh. A sizeable percentage of her votes had come from outside the women's hostel, as she was sharply aware. But enough of them counted themselves as her enemies, notable among them the members of the ABVP. They had already made many compromises in the name of democratic decency. They had flanked her like flunkeys for the official photo session after the oath ceremony. They had stood and watched as she marched into her presidential office and sat down on a throne-like chair draped with the stately white towel that is the ubiquitous emblem of power in India. They had dragged themselves to meetings she called to keep track of the union's agendas. They had presumably done that hoping for an appropriate opportunity to restore order; it came soon enough. Just over a month after Singh took over the students' union, she faced her fiercest enemies in one of the bloodiest battles for power recorded in the university's recent history: the reason the world outside Allahabad came to know of Richa Singh.

* * *

On the morning of 10 November 2015, Singh's colleagues overturned union protocol—she was invited to join a meeting they had called to inform her of a union decision. They had decided who they wanted as chief guest at the ceremonial inauguration of the students' union. Singh first thought the men were teasing her. Yogi Adityanath was famous enough to be chief guest at the inauguration, but she couldn't believe the students' union would endorse the views that made him famous. An idol for Hindutva soldiers such as Arjun Kumar and Sachin Ahuja, Adityanath was a priest-turned-politician whose most memorable speeches talk of confronting Muslims and disciplining women. Singh had entered politics in anger against the ease with which a man like Adityanath could rise to power. In 1998, the twenty-six-year-old priest of a famous temple in Gorakhpur and one of the youngest BJP members of Parliament launched a cow protection group to consolidate his Hindu vote base. In 2002, just after the anti-Muslim riots in Narendra Modi's Gujarat, Yogi Adityanath renamed his militia the 'Hindu Yuva Vahini', literally a vehicle for young Hindus, and expanded its jurisdiction to every issue of Hindu interest. In the years since, he and his soldiers have been charged with a bouquet of criminal offences including 'murder, rioting, carrying deadly weapons, defiling a place of worship, trespassing on a Muslim graveyard, and promoting enmity between two religious groups'.

Singh told her colleagues they couldn't invite him to inaugurate the union without her approval. 'I said, "Yogi cannot inaugurate the students' union because the university doesn't only belong to students from one caste or religion."' They told her the invitation had been sent and accepted. 'They said it was either him or no one. They asked me what I was going to do about it.' Singh called a press conference the next day and told the reporters that she had nothing to do with the invitation cards sent around with her name at the bottom. She said there was nothing she was less likely to do than invite a sectarian rabble-rouser to inaugurate the democratically elected body. Her face was on the front page again the next day, this time next to the face of the man she had taken on. On 15 November, the ABVP caved in and sent out a new set of invitation cards without her name on them. 'They insisted that the programme will happen because they have the majority in the union,' Singh said. The university had already allotted them the space to put up a tent big enough to accommodate the thousands of Adityanath followers expected from all over Uttar Pradesh.

Singh walked past the tent, where dozens of ABVP volunteers fussed over floral decorations, on her way to the hostel. She took a blank sheet of paper and wrote out her statement of protest. 'I went to the VC and presented him with the paper.' On the morning of 17 November, the VC called a meeting with senior authorities and the students' union. A solution had to be found. Students were asking questions about the stand-off; the newspapers were carrying a story every day. 'Five of us were supposed to come for the talks. But there were over 100 men in the room when I went in, all supporters of the ABVP. When they saw me they hooted: "Madam president is protesting."' Singh felt sick—and scared. 'But I couldn't show it. I left the room. I told the VC, "Invite me if you are calling a meeting with the right protocol."' Richa Singh drove to the office of the district commissioner and told him about the event and her decision to protest it. 'I wrote down my intention, signed it, and handed it over to him.' By 18 November, classes had shut down in the university. The student parties had split into two sides. Singh was all over the campus, climbing walls to seize students' attention. 'There was no other way to convince them of my reason to protest. *Aapko apni baat pahunchane ke liye thoda uncha khada hona padega* (You have to find a high spot to get your message to people).'

The arrangements for the inauguration were completed by the morning of 19 November. Yogi Adityanath was expected to arrive at the university the following morning. At 7 p.m. that evening, Singh and her supporters sat down on the steps of the library, the building closest to the university's entrance, on a hunger strike. Stationed outside the walls were about 100 policemen sent by the district administration. 'The eight of us started raising slogans and singing songs of protest. At around 1.30 in the morning, around thirty people barged in the gates and pounced on us. I recognized some of them as members of the ABVP; the rest looked like hired bouncers.' Then, Singh said, she saw in the middle of the mob her own general secretary. 'He had a rod in his hand and he was about to strike me on the head with it when one of my friends swung in and took the impact—his face exploded right away.' The police couldn't enter the campus until authorized to do so by the university administration. 'I still took a chance and went out to appeal to them, but they said they couldn't break the rule. I had to do something myself—my friends were getting pulped in front of me—so I picked up a stick and jumped in.' Several things happened very quickly. 'I went and stood in front of a friend being pounded and was pushed off the scene with so much force that I broke an arm the moment my body hit the ground. The last thing I saw before fainting was the police coming in and breaking up the mayhem.'

Singh was back in her hostel room at 4 a.m. She had no intention to cede the premises to the ABVP, but she didn't have any of her people left. 'Also, my arm had begun to hurt—a lot. From 4 a.m. to 6 a.m., I made calls. To anyone and everyone in the city who could help keeping Yogi out of the gates.' Between 5 a.m. and 7 a.m., a marigold arch was erected outside the gates, a placard at its centre welcoming Yogi Adityanath to Allahabad University. 'Still pondering in my room, I thought what's the point of getting beaten up, getting molested—someone had snatched my dupatta and flung it into the wind in the middle of the mayhem—if I couldn't even stop Yogi at the end of it. I got up, took out from my cupboard a black dupatta, wrapped it around myself and set out for the campus. The police were spread out through the street. The ABVP guys were shocked to see me.' Singh climbed a wall and began to address them. 'I said, "You are deluded if you think you can carry on with the programme. I will not allow it to happen." They began chanting "Jai Shri Ram". I continued to speak over it.' By 9 a.m., a sizeable section of the city's civil society had gathered at the gates, followed by the district commissioner and the superintendent of police. The city administration proceeded to throw everyone out and lock the gates. They couldn't enter the campus without the vice chancellor's permission, but they had the power to stop Adityanath from disrupting law and order in Allahabad. At 11.30 a.m., news broke that the demagogue's caravan had been stopped from entering the city by town officials. 'Our supporters—we were nearly 150 now—were standing outside the gates. On the other side of the road was a crowd of BJP supporters from all over the state. They charged into us. We didn't back off.' At noon, curfew was imposed on the city. Two hours later, Singh sat surrounded by fangirls in her room, drinking orange juice to break her fast.

* * *

Richa Singh had won—once again. She saw this victory as harder-won than the last. She had defeated a powerful politician and a mob leader, not just young men driven by hate and hormones. I first heard of Singh's battles just after this incident and immediately felt they had a larger relevance. Over the following year, I repeatedly visited Allahabad to piece together the story of her journey from conversations with her and others, local news reports, photographs, and audio and video clips of the events between her decision to contest the election and her face-off with Yogi Adityanath.

By this point in her adventures, though, things were getting a little predictable. Protest was becoming her brand of politics and I wondered how far it would carry her. I wondered too if she had a talent for real politics. Could she win over opponents or even work with them? Could she handle a

situation not going her way? Could she strike a deal? If she did
have a future in Indian politics, what kind of politician would
she end up as? Was she more likely to go the way of UP's ex-
chief minister Mayawati, a canny, cold-blooded Dalit leader
as good with the rhetoric of justice as with caste calculations,
or West Bengal's current chief minister Mamata Banerjee, a
fulminating force of nature who remains driven by the same
transparent anger that pushed her into politics as a young
woman? More importantly, how long could Richa Singh last
in politics?

In May 2016, I went to the students' union for the first
time—on a scooter. In the driving seat was Asiya Baig, second-
year student of history and Richa Singh's de facto campaign
manager. She had been on the back seat when Singh drove
the scooter to the union to claim her throne. It was dark when
we got there, but I could see how the majestic building itself
could be reason enough to want to fight the messiest student
election in all of India.

Baig's story began a little differently from any other
student of Allahabad University. When she came to the
university from a town on the outskirts, all she wanted to do
was finish her course and leave. She first met Richa Singh in
the college canteen, and they became friends immediately.
In September 2015, when Singh decided to stand for union
president, Baig was one of those in Singh's close circle of
friends who couldn't believe her chutzpah. 'I told her I would
support her in whatever she had in mind,' said Baig, standing
in the middle of the union lawn. Baig is different from her
friend in many ways: younger, chirpier, girlier and not half
the expert Singh is on the theory and practice of politics. But
when Singh bought a nomination form from the university,
it fell to Baig to get the campaign rolling. Since then, the
twenty-year-old has put up tents, written campaign songs,

and sat on at least two hunger strikes. Everyone in Allahabad who knows Singh, knows Baig too. 'People recognize us wherever we go, from streets to shopping malls. They point at Richa ma'am and say, "that is the woman, Richa Singh, president of the students' union."'

Singh tends to be too busy for people to reach her on either of her two phones so it's Baig who often answers questions about where madam president is and when she will be available next. It is Baig I called the night I got on the train to Allahabad. Singh had never been busier: In September 2016, she officially joined the Samajwadi Party and took over its youth wing in Allahabad. I asked her why she did it. She said she chose the best option available to her as the next step. She couldn't have joined the BJP and none of the other rival parties, neither the Congress nor Mayawati's BSP, had made her an offer.

Singh's phone never stopped ringing in the time I spent following her after she entered the political mainstream. People stopped her for all sorts of things: a juice vendor seeking a kiosk inside the hostel, graduating students wanting to push back the date for the public service entrance test, random men lobbying for a seat in the Samajwadi panel for the next union elections. An armed guard from the Allahabad police shadows her day and night. Her parents still nag her about marriage, but she knows they know it is even harder now to send her off with a suitable man. They keep looking for one, though. 'I say to my father, "At least now you don't have to send them my photos."' At the end of the week, Singh and I both left town. I returned to Delhi and she headed to Lucknow, where the chief minister and Samajwadi Party heir, Akhilesh Yadav, had summoned her. Her term as president was set to end in October 2016. On 1 September, the university announced the next election season open. The fight would be between the SP and the ABVP this time, its political implications even bigger

than during the last hustings. On the same day, the Samajwadi
Party made Richa Singh the head of its campaign.

I was rooting for Richa Singh, in guilt and in bewilderment.
We had the same ideas, but I didn't have her idealism. I
didn't have her guts, either. The furthest I had gone in the
service of secularism was to politely debate its meaning with
a gau rakshak. Singh's fight against caste, communalism and
patriarchy—what she called 'muscle power'—voiced most of
my issues with the country's politics.

I was drawn to stories of women putting up a fight; reporting
and writing about their fight was almost a compensation for
not participating in it. Four months before I went to Allahabad
to meet Richa Singh, I had gone to Barabanki, a much smaller
town in central Uttar Pradesh, to meet a group of young Dalit
and Muslim women covering news you'd rarely see in a regular
newspaper: caste violence, ration leaks, female suicides. I had
jumped on to the back of a bicycle and let a twenty-six-year-
old Dalit woman take me around on a reporting trip. I had
clutched the rack with both my hands as she twisted the bike
through village lanes to ask a series of people—shopkeepers,
police officers, loitering men—for clues to a question no one
else was asking: What actually happened to the fifteen-year-
old Dalit girl found dead in the village well the night before?

Shraddha Bhaskar is brave in more ways than I had space
to elaborate on in the article I ended up writing. She is brave
enough to be a Dalit woman in a Thakur-dominated area to
roam the district hunting for truth, often at the cost of being
up against the highest holders of power. She is constantly
threatened by people: by Thakurs in her village who don't
like the idea of a Dalit woman who won't take their orders; by
government officers who don't like the idea of a Dalit woman
digging around for dirt; and by random men who don't like the
idea of a Dalit woman asking them questions. I was staggered

by her courage. She had set limits on her quest for justice, though. Seven hundred people subscribed to *Khabar Lahariya* (News Wave). That's a lot for a regional-language publication rooting for social equality, but few people outside of Barabanki had heard of it. Shraddha Bhaskar's was an intimate struggle. But university-level student politics was different: high risks, high rewards and high drama. And Richa Singh loved every aspect of it. When she recounted lines from her fiery speeches, she did it with a sense of pride. Even when she narrated her encounters with her worst enemies, you could hear the thrill in her voice. I was riveted by her story and so was she.

In September 2016, I returned to Allahabad, but it could have been an altogether different city. On my 5-kilometre cab ride from the railway station to the university guest house, I saw more faces on posters than I did on the streets. The university street looked like the front line of a war—one fought with paper. At least four layers of campaign pamphlets covered the ground and nearly as many crowded the walls. There would be more than paper as the week progressed. The newspapers from that morning were full of reports of things the police were seizing ahead of the elections: luxury cars, guns, briefcases of cash. There was nothing the BJP or the SP wouldn't provide the student leaders over the following week. The ABVP, it was said, would stop at nothing to win the post of the president. I wondered how far an SP unit led by Richa Singh would go. I would have enough opportunities to find out.

That evening Singh and I clambered into an SUV waiting for her outside the women's hostel. A young Samajwadi Party worker held the door for her while another two waited inside with frozen schoolboy smiles. We were headed to the first Samajwadi speech of the election week, to a neighbourhood crowded with university students slumming it in pay-by-the-day hostels.

Singh was going there as the star speaker of the evening. Her job was to introduce to this prime constituency the five Samajwadi contestants for the students' union. More importantly, she would have to tell her audience why they should vote for the man standing for president. The reason the party chose Ajit Yadav as its candidate was simple. 'I have taken the maximum number of beatings from the police fighting for rights of common students,' he would scream from a stage in just a while. He would point to the deep scar on the left side of his forehead. He would tell them he was fated to be their leader. It's not for nothing that his parents had added *vidhayak* (member of state assembly) to his name years ago. Dressed in a starched kurta-pyjama as white as daylight, he would remind them what student politics in Allahabad stands for: 'from the street to the Parliament'.

Ajit Singh 'Vidhayak' is as street as they come in this town, but everyone knew that wasn't enough to win this election. This is why we are racing towards Allapur at this point. The scene is totally set when we enter the mohalla. On the stage are five young men in white kurta-pyjamas, and on the ground 100 young men waving fat bundles of colourful pamphlets. Everyone is waiting for the evening to kick off for real—which would happen the moment Singh quite literally set foot there. A group of young Samajwadi volunteers rush to hold open the gate, poised and ready, watching her feet; they lunge for her feet even before they touch the ground. It is one of the funniest things I have seen, but Singh doesn't appear in the least amused.

I realize how the axis of power had shifted over the year. The Samajwadi beefcakes are relying on her star power to win this election; few in Allahabad could remember the last time the union had a president who could pull in such a crowd. She needs to show the boss in Lucknow that she is more than a one-time winner—her only means of advancing from street to Parliament. There are enough people who believe she won the election because of what she had to offer her voters. Sadly for her, though, there are also enough people who think her victory had nothing to do with her skill as a politician. A year from this night, I would sit in an all-male adda in neighbouring Rae Bareli and hear a veteran journalist, a local power broker, reveal the reality behind the myth of Richa Singh. 'She's nothing,' he would say, 'a nobody. The only reason she won is because she got the Samajwadi votes—Thakurs and Yadavs. The university is 60 per cent rural students from the OBC category now. Anyone using the Samajwadi platform would have won.' Everyone there would nod in agreement.

But this evening in Allapur is all about Singh's star power; the crowd of university students is exploding with excitement as she takes the microphone. She wears white too, a Samajwadi-red scarf showing off her new position. 'To all my friends here, my socialist revolutionary salute,' Singh begins with a bang. Then, as a light drizzle falls, haloing her face, she unfolds the paper in her hand to read a poem written for the occasion: 'We thunder like a storm / We rumble like an earthquake / Do not take us lightly, our enemies / We are Samajwadis, not your average politician.' Every man has his phone out to capture Richa Singh in her element. The photos were posted on Facebook as soon as they were taken and 'liked' just as quickly.

This is the most attention Singh will have tonight—it's time for her to come to the point. 'Vote for these five men,' she says, hands folded in request. 'You have my word.' She wasn't a member of the party when she became the president, but she tells them that everything she did for students over the year was based on socialist principles: free bus rides through the city, free Wi-Fi on campus, a vigorous fight against English-language imposition in the public service examination 'because socialism doesn't allow you to discriminate on the basis of language'. She reminds them that she stood at the same place last year, asking them to help her make history. This time, she wants them to help her change the course of the future. 'We cannot allow sectarian powers to enter the state. Only one kind of politics must rule UP, one based on equality and social justice.' Pamphlets shoot up into the falling rain, along with cries of 'Richa Singh Zindabad'. Singh doesn't pause this time. 'All you people do on Twitter and Facebook is demand a new politics for this country, but the only thing you think of when you go to vote is your own caste, your own religion. Not this time! This time, your vote must be a vote against their narrow idea of nationalism.'

The street is packed with men by the time Singh finishes her speech. So is the stage. As the only two women facing the night in Allapur, we are both vulnerable. Singh is more scared for me, an outsider, than for herself. She hasn't just ordered her bodyguard to stand by my side, but watches the situation from the stage. Later that night, sitting in her bed, she told me that the hardest part of her new life is balancing her routine with the middle-class idea of a woman's honour. There are few nights when she's not out in the streets asking for people to vote for the 'panel' of Samajwadi contestants, but she makes sure not to step into her own neighbourhood if it's too late. 'Papa says, "Don't be seen here if it's after 10 p.m. or our neighbours will talk."' She knew the unspoken condition when she accepted the offer to lead the election campaign. 'I will be setting the strategy for the campus, not for the street.'

What works on the street is not strategy but presence. It's what takes over after Richa Singh has made her speech and returned to the hostel. She was allowed to set new rules—'no wads of money, no big cars, no violence, final say in choosing candidates'—but three weeks into the campaign, what mattered wasn't rules but results. Singh didn't object when, at an emergency meeting called at the Samajwadi Party election camp the next morning, a group of party veterans over the age of sixty upheld the candidate mix—Yadav for president, Muslim for vice president—and persuaded the police to release the seized BMW. She laughed away the vice-presidential candidate's introduction of himself as a 'Muslim who reads his namaz after taking a dip in the holy Ganga'—an appeal to Brahmin voters. Richa Singh was not even there when the Samajwadi round table discussed the make-or-break statement of the previous night: Should Ajit Yadav 'Vidhayak' have said: 'Student unity is bigger than Yadav unity?' And how many votes could it cost the Samajwadis?

By midday on 21 September, as we left the election camp, the streets had turned into a carnival of masculinity. A dozen processions hit the university street at the same time: The candidates themselves were in the front rows, perched on the shoulders of their respective gangs; their followers rallied behind on motorbikes and SUVs—waving party flags and screaming slogans. It was less a show of strength than a call for battle. Only four kinds of people come out on the street on the day before the qualifying speech: candidates, supporters, journalists and police. Richa Singh was in the front row of the Samajwadi procession, her right hand locked with Yadav's, for support, and her left hand locked with mine, for safety. Singh had told me numerous stories to explain the insanity of the student elections, and I had noted down each detail, but it was finally now that I understood her point. Shoved by rows upon rows of men from behind and glared at by rows upon rows of them in front, I wondered if I should stick around for the rest of the week. I gave myself another day.

At dusk, Singh asked me if I wanted to come to the night's 'mike meeting'. I knew what it was in theory—an open debate between the various panels—but she told me the actual thing would be nothing like anything I had ever seen before. I would soon know. It's called a mike meeting because the various 'panels' for the union poll are supposed to face off each other armed with microphones. Sound is key to the ritual. The mikes are placed on stages built on opposite sides of a narrow road with a dead end. The two biggest student parties position themselves across the road, the small and harmless ones taking whatever spot is available. The SP and the ABVP faced off this time.

Even more important than mikes, it turns out, are speakers—massive, colourful, deafening, a set of four tied to each of the four poles holding together a stage. Behind each microphone stands a line of men organizing the party's election campaign, but not the candidates themselves. The candidates are parading down the aisle on the shoulders of their supporters. The space is packed with men. Those not carrying others are either waving banners or tossing around pamphlets. Everyone in the 500-metre space is speaking at the same time, including the three battalions of Allahabad police trained in riot control. Across the road, the opposing parties are screaming into their microphones, attempting to drown out their rivals.

It may seem a completely pointless exercise at first. No one can hear anything, but as I have already been told, that's not the point. What matters is that the rivals keep speaking without a break; the idea is not to be understood but to cancel out each other's noise. It's like a rap battle in the middle of a Kumbh Mela; more insults are exchanged across this aisle on election eve in Allahabad than during the rest of the campaign.

At the centre of the action this evening is the strip of
road between the stages of SP and ABVP. The Samajwadis
kicked off the session by accusing the ABVP of killing Rohith
Vemula ('You are murderers'). I know this mainly because I
was standing behind the speaker. Singh stands next to him,
smiling at the insults coming from the other side. On the stage
across the aisle are her colleagues from the union. It seems
she can tell what they are saying, or she knows everything
they could say. Midway through the evening, everyone
can see what's going on—on the ABVP stage, the men are
pointing at Singh and then the mike. Richa Singh takes it in
the middle of a deafening roar from the other side. Smiling,
she tells her colleagues what she's been meaning to say since
day one of the campaign: 'I didn't allow Yogi Adityanath into
the campus and I won't allow you to enter the students' union
again.' Surely no one can hear it, but it makes the ABVP stage
throb with rage. The moment the words leave her mouth, a
bomb explodes on our left. As I cover my ears and jump off
the collapsing stage, two more crudely assembled explosives
go off in quick succession. The police flood into the smoke-
covered street just as everyone else tries to leave it all together.
Like everybody there, I run for my life, except I don't know
where to go. By the time I find Singh in the stampede, I know
I am done with Allahabad.

I had never seen anything so out of control. I had seen a
bunch of young men build a straw effigy of China, drape it
with the flag of the enemy country, burn it in the middle of
a crowded market, and stomp on the ashes until every bit of
red in the flag of the People's Republic had turned to black.
I had seen another group of young men search 200 trucks
in one night for the slightest trace of a Muslim smuggling a
cow. Rare exceptions aside, my wide-ranging forays into the
madness of modern India boiled down to the same thing: the

anxieties of young men who no longer know their place in the world. What they find hardest to deal with are women who do. The young men can deal with me. I am there more to understand their masculinity than to threaten it. They have no idea how to deal with someone like Richa Singh.

But Richa Singh knows exactly how to deal with them: the argumentative Hindu, the gau rakshaks, the anti-Valentine's Day mobs. This is what makes the madness of the student elections different. The men thrusting their pelvises at her across the aisle are driven by an urgent need to assert their existence. So is she. She's rarely made a safe decision since the day she decided to fight the election; some of them could have killed her easily. The four-day hunger strike against a university order ranks high in that list, followed closely by the time she hurled herself at a bunch of drunk men waving cricket bats.

Now, as an official member of a political party built on the notion that 'boys will be boys', it was her job to lead a contingent of men who live by these words. Every second of this scenario was fraught with tension. It was hard to tell if she was winning or losing. One week into the election cycle, I knew better than to look for clear answers. I focused on things I could see clearly. And what was clear to me in the aftermath of the mike meeting, as the Samajwadi brigade assembled in its camp to take stock, was that this night marked a climax. There wasn't a single man in the compound who didn't want an eye for an eye. Every face burnt with insult, whether it was Singh's security guard's, her senior advisers', or her young colleagues'. All of them wanted the same thing: revenge. Finally, a young man standing in a large circle of party members faced his seniors and said it. 'Give us one order and we will respond to bombs with bombs.' It was a veteran student leader who answered, his eyes fixed on Singh: 'No. Let's respond with our work.'

I left Allahabad the next day. I didn't stop following Singh, though. On 1 October, she posted on Facebook a solemn update on the election results: The ABVP had won the president's post. It was also through Facebook that I learnt of the next big milestone on her journey. On 17 January 2017, Richa Singh posted an update thanking the chief minister of Uttar Pradesh, the Samajwadi Party heir, for giving her the biggest opportunity of her life. She had been chosen as a Samajwadi Party candidate for the elections to the state assembly—and from the neighbourhood where she grew up. Richa Singh would have to return to the photo studio one more time.

Part III: 'Nothing Is What It Looks Like'

So LET'S SUPPOSE you are a young Indian who has pushed himself past the most important obstacle: You have told yourself you were born to be big. No one else sees it, but you don't blame them—they are too busy getting by. Now, you start thinking strategy. You know you are going to be rich and famous, but you have got to do something to get there. Then one day someone offers you an A-Z plan to change your life. You are told that there is a world out there in which someone like you, with no qualification other than a burning desire to become successful, can succeed if he follows simple instructions. You take the bait. You go all the way, do everything you are told. You change how you look, how you walk, how you talk. You memorize the answer to every question you may be asked and the names of everyone who may be asking the questions. And then, bracing for glory or nothing, you dive into your dream world.

But you are tied to the spot where you landed. You think of all the things that no one told you, beginning with the fact that you weren't the only one diving in. The place is swarming with people who seem no different than you. They look like you, walk like you and talk like you. You wonder if they too have memorized the same answers to the same questions. But this isn't the worst omission of truth. It's not half as bad as figuring out that simply following the instructions wasn't enough. You can't take a single step forward without producing a special pass. You could go back and acquire it, except no one will tell you what it looks like. It's at this point that you realize your worst mistake. You chose the wrong world to chase your dream in; it isn't run by the usual formulas of nothing-to-everything success. This is not like launching a start-up or selling English. In this gated wonderland, no matter how hard you chase your dream, it's always someone else who decides if it will come true. You wonder if you wouldn't have been better off guarding a gate rather than begging to be allowed inside. It seems to be the only way to make money and have influence in this place.

But you've already paid for the plan. There is no going back.

* * *

You don't even have to be a dreamer to end up in the same place. You could be a basic guy who wants basic things: a job, a house, a car. But you have to start with a job to move on to other things. Turns out it's not easy. You could have it easier just dreaming of treasures and trophies.

You don't understand why. You think you are ripe for the market. You have got some education—'high school with 64 per cent, bachelor's in commerce with 56 per cent'—you have learnt some skills—'spoken English, computers'—you have even put together a CV. You may have paid someone else to write the words, but you truly want to 'work in a challenging environment that provides generous opportunities for learning'. You promise to 'work hard with full determination and dedication to achieve organizational as well as personal goals and become a good professional'. It's not that you don't dream of a farmhouse and an Audi, but for now you'd settle for a monthly salary. You have left home, you have counted your savings, and you have about a month to go before hitting rock-bottom. One day you meet someone who offers you a salary, and you thank the gods. He doesn't discuss the nature of the work and you don't dwell on it either. You hope what you are entering is a real world, but you don't really care if it's make-believe. You dive in, and this time you land in the centre of this dreamworld. You are in control this time. You are the one who is creating the illusion and laughing at those who fall for it. You don't want to do this forever, but you have already rented a house and applied for a car loan. You don't think what you do is fair, but you have begun to doubt the world functions on fairness. If it did, would you have found yourself here?

This is the story of the young Indians prepared to play the game even if the rules are rigged against them.

6

The Star

ONE LONG AFTERNOON in Ranchi, I walked into a beauty contest. Mr and Miss Jharkhand seemed like a big event if you went by the size of the hoardings all over the city. The newspapers had been full of details for days leading up to the pageant: The largest banquet hall in Ranchi's biggest hotel had been booked; a handful of contestants had been chosen from a pool 100 times larger; and numerous calls had been received from people seeking front-row seats. In the middle of the dark banquet hall, a plywood stage throbbed with multicoloured light. I entered the room in the middle of the 'ethnic round'. Up on the stage, girls and boys walked back and forth wearing a variety of traditional wear in very bright colours. Party songs blasted forth from the DJ console. The contestants—ten male and ten female—had already gone through four rounds of appraisal by a panel seated to the left of the stage. They would go through another six over the rest of the evening, each highlighting a different with-it theme: 'modern', 'funky', 'casual', etc.

One of them was eliminated after every other round for reasons not immediately obvious to an audience mostly made

up of their friends and family. Ten of them made it to the Q &
A round. Dressed in their glittering best, they stand along the
length of the stage awaiting the question that would make or
break their dream. The questions are the usual: Who are you?
Why do you want the title? What will you do with it? The
answers don't seem to be moving the jury. The last person to
be interrogated is a tall young man wearing an embroidered
black sherwani and a gunslinger beard. The crowd likes him—
he's greeted them with a throaty *as-salaam-alaikum* before the
jury throws its question to him. He has no blazing answer to
who he really is or what he will do with the honour. What he
tells them, loud and clear, is why he wants to become the first
man to be crowned Mr Jharkhand. He has had the answer in
his head for a long time: 'Because I have everything one needs
to be a star.' The line leaves his mouth like he has been saying
it in front of the mirror for years. The applause is loud enough
to seal the night. The trophy perfectly matches his outfit; he
probably chose black for precisely this moment.

Mr Jharkhand, Mohammad Azhar, spends a large part of
every morning planning his look for the day. He may repeat his
clothes, but never his look. He has a thousand ways to make a
look stand out: a goatee with streaks of brown, a *gamcha*-print
scarf worn like a cravat, a single black earring, a stick-on tattoo,
a turned-up shirt collar, ankle boots, imitation Ray-Bans with
blue lenses. His hair changes its shape and size faster than it
takes most people to comb theirs. It's mostly cut close to his
head—but sometimes he shaves the sides to a fuzz, or rakes
sharp furrows on either side of his head, or raises it all up in
spikes, the colour rarely even through the crop. That kind of
vanity has got to turn you a little crazy. Azhar constantly scans
his surroundings for reflective surfaces and talks in the tone
of someone surrounded by cameras. '*Mera height aur personality
Allah ka shukr tha* (My height and personality were gifts from

God),' Azhar said after he had scrunched his six-foot frame into a chair at a Café Coffee Day in Ranchi's main shopping street. 'My dreams were unique in every way, from the beginning,' he said, explaining his attraction to glamour and fame. 'I always wanted to do something that would make me popular. Something different. Something that would bring glory to the place where I was born.'

Azhar was born in Chanho, a Muslim-majority ghetto just outside Ranchi city limits. If the place is ever in the news, it's because of incidents of sectarian tension, never the achievements of its young men. Azhar grew up in a two-bedroom house with nine other siblings, the family getting by on the salary his father made as a labour supervisor at an electrical factory. All Azhar knew, running between a crowded house and an empty school, was that he had to get out. He was convinced that the only way he could leave Chanho was by doing something so big that no one in the 'hood would know what to do with him. *'Tu jaa modelling kar* (You go and become a model)!' a friend once taunted him about his fussing over his face. So Azhar decided to become a model. He reasoned it was the best way to use his gift from god to get rich and famous. He threw himself into the grind: watching videos of models walking the ramp on YouTube ('even though my phone screen didn't allow for zooming in'), turning a corner of his room into an exercise zone ('hands-free push-ups, yoga, everything'), having himself shot in various poses and posting the photos on Facebook for 'feedback'. At the age of nineteen, when he entered Ranchi's show business, he felt ready. He even took on a surname that he deemed worthy of his new self: 'Khan', like half the superstars of Hindi film. 'Look at me,' he said leaning away from the table to allow me a view of his towering torso, 'do you not see a Khan?'

What I saw was another young man who didn't like the look of the life he was fated for. By September 2014, when I called him to ask if I could buy him coffee, Azhar Khan had taken the biggest step of his life. He wasn't the first man in Chanho to leave. Young men leave the ghetto in hordes every year to work in the kind of places that don't fuss over qualifications: courier companies in Ranchi, factories in Mumbai, restaurants in Dubai. He had taken an even bigger risk.

Ranchi was ready for Azhar Khan when he barged in. The city had a scene it loved to show off: Cafes offered house lattes, hotel bars threw Saturday night parties, and local markets touted the latest trends from foreign ramps. There was enough disposable income going around to sustain an interest in fine living. The new middle class had shed the baggage of judgement. People were no longer surprised by other people holidaying abroad, eating at fancy restaurants, slimming at wellness centres. 'Tell me all about it,' I said to the editor of Ranchi's first lifestyle magazine—called *Ranchi Lifestyle*—one day at his barely furnished office in Lalpur Road. In 2010, twenty-five-year-old Shivam Aggarwal had left his corporate job in Gurugram and returned to spin his father's printing business into a city magazine. I'd been seeing it around a lot—at the airport, in hotel lounges, at beauty salons. 'The scene is exploding,' said Aggarwal. He swivelled his MacBook and asked me to observe the details of his wife's last 'girls' night out'. She posed at the centre of a long row of girlfriends in a fancy restaurant, each dressed in a little black dress. 'The theme was LBD,' Aggarwal informed me, turning the computer back. 'Each of their parties has a theme—beach, masquerade, bridesmaid.' Enough happens in the city for him to fill the pages of his magazine month after month: hookah hang-outs, pool parties, rock concerts. And fashion shows: to launch gyms and car showrooms, announce surplus sales and craft exhibitions, mark cultural programmes and company galas. And yet, when Azhar Khan started hunting for a platform to announce his arrival on the scene, he felt lost.

'Once I had made up my mind to become a model,' Azhar told me, 'everywhere I went in the village, people would say, "Azhar, you have everything one needs to become a model. *Tu deserve karta hai* (You deserve it)." But how could I have become a model without participating in a fashion show? And how could I even have known of fashion shows before they happened? I only saw the photos the next day in the newspapers. The well-wishers who kept telling me I deserved to be a model had no idea what a fashion show was or what walking the ramp was all about.' He did what he could: scan the news reports for names of organizers—and, if he was lucky enough to find any, look them up on Google, note their phone numbers and addresses and hunt them down. 'The lady at the reception would tell me to leave my portfolio and wait for a call, so I would give her an envelope of photos and keep waiting.' The photos were a careful selection from his album of profile photos on Facebook, each presenting a different look: tough, brooding, sexy.

One day in early 2012, he noticed an audition call in a local newspaper. When he got to the location—a university parking lot—at the specified time, a bunch of boys and girls stood there in a long line. *Pyaar Mein Kabhi Kabhi Aisa Ho Jaata Hai* was only supposed to be a local, low-budget film, but Khan had heard the producer was in talks with a Bollywood actor for an appearance. The murmur had passed through the restless queue of contenders for the lead roles, quickening heartbeats. Khan didn't think he did that well at the audition, so he jumped off the bed next day when someone called to tell him he had been selected for the lead role. So were all the other young men who had auditioned, he found out eventually. As they rushed to the same place for a meeting with the director, each of them was asked to deposit ₹20,000 for things to move ahead. It was a fair bargain, said the man across the table, for the faith they were putting in a nobody. 'None of us had the money, so all of us backed out,' Khan said. There were some—there always are—who'd later change their minds and sell a motorcycle or a watch, but there was no one to hand the money over to. The phone numbers of the producer and the director had long become unavailable.

However perverse, the system made sense. If one man's aspiration was another man's money, then why stop at promises that could be delivered? I regularly encountered people who had placed themselves between young Indians and their dreams in order to fulfil their own, be it Moin Khan or Vinay Singhal or Shahnawaz Chaudhary. Not everyone was fair and honest about it. And most of these people chose to intercept young people who had decided to strive for fame. It's a scam as old as the idea of stardom. It makes Mumbai as much the city of deception as the city of dreams, a trap stretching out from its crowded railway stations to Bollywood studios. But now you don't have to arrive in Mumbai to enter this trap. If Ranchi is a good place to chase money and influence, then why not stardom? And where there is a dream, there is a scam; where there are dreamers, there are scammers.

The incident didn't break Azhar's heart, but now he understood that his journey to stardom wasn't going to be easy. Things weren't what they seemed to be, but there was not much to go back to. 'I met a guy at the audition who was doing a bit of modelling in the city and he said he would get me into the next fashion show he was doing. So it turned out not to be a total waste.' Three weeks later, Khan was rehearsing his walk at *Zila Maidan*, the district's official exhibition ground, for a fashion show to be organized by a design institute. 'Until then, my idea of the ramp walk was what I had seen on YouTube. All I knew was that you maintained eye contact with the audience. I walked the ramp the way Salman Khan walks in his movies.' Now, Azhar gave himself over to his 'seniors' to be trained: '"Your feet," they told me, "should fall straight to the ground. Your shoulders shouldn't move as you walk. Your arms will be stiff above the biceps and moving below it. The eyes should always be fixed at the crowd—you will pretend that you are looking at them but in reality you will be seeing no one." Azhar now boarded the daily bus from Chanho carrying the building blocks for his new life in his backpack: 'Shirt and pants for formal look, torn jeans and T-shirt for funky look, shades, make-up.'

Azhar Khan was finally 'launched' in the business in an event called 'Jalwa: Season 4'. It was an 'all-in-one show': singing, dancing, modelling. Khan did well at the auditions; he'd even slipped in ₹300 to the selection team when they gestured for a 'fee'. The audience clapped when he strode down the ramp—feet falling straight, eyes looking at everyone but not seeing anyone—in the clothes he had bought and styled himself. A friend made a video on his phone when, at the end of it, Azhar was being presented with a trophy by a local businessman. He felt on top of the world that night, at least until he realized he had missed the last bus to Chanho. 'I roamed the streets for three-four hours then, until it was time for the press vehicles to leave the city carrying newspapers.' Squeezed between other young men who had made arrangements with the press vans to go home to their villages, Azhar Khan looked out of the back of the van as the city fell away, and felt a surge of relief.

* * *

His life soon clicked into a pattern. It started with auditions. The standard fee was ₹300; no event manager wanted to appear cheaper or pricier than any other since they were all drawing from the same pool. To the aspiring superstars, the fee seemed more or less fair. The event managers, who probably have to pay 'fees' to all sorts of people to put together events, needed to make something at the end of the day. Besides, ₹300 was nothing compared to what 'strugglers' paid in big cities as an entry charge. You also had to buy your clothes and accessories for the fashion shows. Thankfully, every fashion show featured the same 'looks' on the ramp—formal, funky, western and ethnic, remember—but one knew better than to repeat the same collection more than twice. It was a far bigger investment than the audition fee, and those who couldn't afford it kept dropping off the strugglers' stream.

By his third fashion show, Azhar Khan's savings were a quarter of what they had been. 'The ordinary man has festivals—Durga Puja, Diwali or Eid, Chaand Raat—he has to go shopping before these occasions. I had fashion shows, I had to go to the market to buy clothes before every one of them.' You even knew the broad categories of judges and chief guests. It could be, depending on the event manager's budget and connections, a bank manager, the head of the fashion department of the women's college, the owner of a car showroom, or a small-time politician. Once he had figured out the drill, he set out to ace it. Tackling the problem of introduction took him days. 'I had convinced myself *ki apna dar nikalna hoga* (I will get rid of my fear). I tried to get more comfortable with English by chatting with friends on the phone. I could understand what was said in English but speaking was far more difficult. Anyhow, I rehearsed the response to "Why do you want to become a model?"' His set answer, delivered without losing eye contact with the judges, was: 'Height, personality, good looks, photogenic face.'

The first and most important rule was, of course, to take anything that came your way. Every show, Khan explained, was an opportunity to get another. Mr and Ms Popular led to the Republic Day-special show at an amusement park and onward to two college farewell shows and finally to his first 'designer' show at a trade fair. His earnings at the end of a whole season: 'zero'. This, in Khan's own poetic telling, was his life as a model: '*Show khatam hua, memento mila, press gaadi mein baitha, ghar gaya* (The show finished, I got a memento, got on the press van and went home).' Azhar Khan wants the same things as everyone else I was following: money or influence or both. And like Moin Khan or Richa Singh, he knew only he could help himself. He tries at his dream as hard as any of them—working on everything that will bring him closer to the end, from his body to his looks, from his walk to his spoken English. The only thing different about his quest is that he seeks success in a world where no one has yet found a formula for success.

* * *

Azhar Khan first heard of Mr and Miss Jharkhand in the month of Ramzan, two years after he had entered the business. Everything about it screamed glamour. The programme would feature 'fashion shows, beauty pageant, Russian belly dancers, Page Three parties, an exclusive DJ from Mumbai and a Sufi lounge'. The designers, drawn from the fashion design department of local colleges, were going to make copies of clothes showcased in the latest Fashion Week in Mumbai. Models would be selected through auditions in four cities. The audience would be a selection of the city's elite— doctors, IAS officers, industrialists.

Getting in would be hard, though. Whoever got through the auditions, which cost ₹300, would need to deposit another ₹2500 to actually participate in the show. The amount, they were told, would be spent on their grooming. For the first time, said the event manager, hired 'experts' would work on them, from their walk to their spoken English, as they breathed the sanitized air of a three-star hotel. Khan didn't have the money, but he knew he had to get it—this was do or die. If he won the title, he would never have to beg for work or work for free. If he won the title, he could stride through the ramps in Mumbai or breeze into Bollywood. If he became Mr Jharkhand, his life would be made. From the very first day of training, he decided to put on his best show. 'With the help of a friend who filed a bank loan application on my behalf, I bought a motorcycle so I could travel back and forth easily. I chose the brand "glamour"—it suited the world I was moving into.'

He put together a compelling introduction and then practised it on tape a thousand times: 'Hello, dear friends, as-salaam alaikum to all of you. My name is Azhar Khan . . . Meri hobbies cricket khelna, fashion shows karna aur bike chalana hai. Dream hai ki main ek successful model banoon jis se mera aur mere area ka naam roshan ho (My hobbies are playing cricket, participating in fashion shows and riding the motorcycle. My dream is to become a successful model so that I can bring glory to myself and my area).' He had watched enough talent competitions on television to know that contestants were judged on a number of things besides the supposed talent. He put every tip to use. 'Everyone else would slack off before and after the rehearsals but I never let myself slip. I made sure to make an effort with my looks every day—showing the judges my range. I would also treat them respectfully: saying my salaams when I came in, waving goodbyes when I was off.' When the two-day contest finally began, Khan seemed to have an edge from the very start. He was picked by the better designers, the judges shot looks of approval when he entered the stage, and not one but two female contestants said he looked all right. 'I had a feeling that I was going to win. Even before the announcement was made on the stage, a reporter from a channel rushed into the green room and asked me about how I was feeling. I said I was feeling on top of the world.' After the official announcement was made by the esteemed jury to the sound of a blazing horn, Azhar Khan shook hands with the chief guest, the wife of a former chief minister, and received from her the most glittering trophy of his life.

* * *

Surrounded by slavish assistants, Tabrez Khan looked like the head of a drug cartel. He would have done so even without them: His short build, thickening in the middle, is made menacing by a camouflage T-shirt with sleeves rolled up to his beefy biceps, black jeans and big black leather shoes with chunky heels. His face is round and wide, clean-shaven except for a goatee, and his hair stringy. Had he not spoken, I wouldn't have believed him to have the tinkling voice and the child's laugh that emerged. He had to speak, however; he didn't trust anyone else to tell his story. At twenty-nine years of age, Tabrez Khan is the owner of an event empire in the making. Plastered with photographs of him standing next to celebrities, the walls of his office outline his journey from being just another guy to hosting the state's first fashion week and beauty pageant.

I first met him a few weeks after he appeared on the front pages of local newspaper supplements. Flanked by the

winners of the contest and various other dignitaries, his face
had shone in the reflected glow of their glory. The story I
was tracking was very important, he said. Event managers,
he agreed, were redefining life in small towns. 'I started
with zero paisa,' Khan said, the standard opening line of the
self-made man. He is from an average middle-class family
where men brought in fixed salaries every month. Khan
made his first blow against the tradition by dropping out
of college, a step straight out of Shahnawaz Chaudhary's
rule book. You didn't need a college education to capture
the hottest opening in the market. 'Everywhere you looked
in Ranchi, you saw an event. People had too much money
in the city thanks to the abundance of mines and minerals
all around and no way to spend it except to travel to the
big cities. Then they started throwing big parties at home.
There were birthdays, wedding celebrations, silver jubilee
celebrations and golden jubilee celebrations. All you needed
to arrange was golden chairs, golden-themed stage, golden-
themed guest costumes, golden-themed entertainment
programme, a mix of old and new songs. The first call
I got was from an auto dealer. It was their annual party,
and they needed a dance floor and anchors. I put it all
together. They paid me ₹2500 as coordination charge.' In
2007, convinced this was his true calling, he set up an event
management company called 'Ramp': 'See, you need models
for everything in the city. It could be the launch of a car
showroom or the distributor meet of a cement company—
everyone wants you to put up something glamorous. If
nothing is coming your way, you organize your own fashion
show. Ask the models to pay a certain amount to participate,
ask the designers for a certain amount, invite the wife of a
politician as a chief guest. What's my profit in this? Nothing
but brand building.'

In three years, the entrepreneur had expanded his company's portfolio and changed its name to Dream Merchant. 'Then I started thinking: Mumbai has its fashion week, so do Delhi and Kolkata. Why don't we in Ranchi have our own fashion week? So I organized one.' All he had to do was convince people: first the owner of a textile company, that for ₹15 lakh, he would get all the visibility he wanted for his brand; then fashion design students that for just ₹1500 they could present their clothes before people looking for ways to spend their money ('It takes no less than ₹1 lakh to participate in a Lakme Fashion Week'); then starry-eyed youngsters that ₹3000 was all that stood between obscurity and fame ('They could only have dreamt of getting the chance to walk the ramp at a five-star hotel'); and finally the wife of an ex-chief minister that handing out trophies at a high-profile fashion show was exactly the push she needed at that point. Tabrez Khan had hit upon a formula.

* * *

When Azhar walked back home with his towering trophy, at the head of a procession of relatives, friends and neighbours, it was his mother he saw first. 'She kept crying.' And then he saw the men, five of them, to whom he owed money. 'Somehow rumour had spread that I had won ₹5 lakh as part of winning the title and they had come to demand the 1 lakh that I owed them altogether.'

The ₹1 lakh was debt from his years in 'business'. You see, before Azhar Khan threw himself into the pursuit of fame, he had tried his hand at riches.

'Papa had a private job as a factory supervisor. He had a lot of knowledge of the field, but everywhere he went, he

was exploited. He worked hard for little money all his life.
And then he wasn't able to. He was getting old: his body
gave up—his hands and feet refused to cooperate. He was
forced to retire. The household had run on just his salary
until then—nine of us and my mother. And we were used
to living well in spite of not having a lot of money. I was in
a fix. My older brother had finished a part-time course in
engineering and was still waiting for placement. It fell to me
to do something.'

So in his final year of high school, Azhar had become an
entrepreneur. It began with a Chinese restaurant.

'It was a small food joint: chilli chicken, chow mein,
momos, spring rolls. It wasn't going to take any major
investment—only ₹10,000 to ₹15,000: All you needed was a
couple of plastic tables and chairs, plates and spoons. I took a
small room on rent in our locality. *Uss mein do table adjust kiya,
decorations kiya, poora restro-bar feel daala* (I put in two tables,
did the decorations, gave it the feel of a restro-bar). I found
a good chef. The opening was spectacular—everything we
cooked was sold. Things remained that way for some time.
If I spent ₹1000 a week, I made ₹4000. I ran the house for
five-six months. Everyone was so happy. And then the cook
ran away. I tried to bring in others, but no one could match
the original taste and the customers slowly stopped coming.
We started making losses—at some point I was unable to pay
the cook his daily ₹200. Finally we shut up shop and took the
tables and chairs home.'

Next came hardware marketing.

'One day, I met a guy who worked in hardware
marketing. *Sabse plus cheez iss mein yeh hai woh bola ki "no
boss, no time limit"* (The best thing about this is "no boss,
no time limit"). You do the number of hours you want to
and amount of work you can. I felt this was ideal. If he was

picking up material for ₹10 he would sell it to me for ₹12, and I to the shopkeeper for ₹15. The material was regular stuff that goes into making doors and windows: latch, bolt, doorstopper . . . You dropped the sample in your bag and set off for the day. I made a list of potential shops in my diary and went to each one of them—some of the owners asked me to come back with the samples. I started doing well in this line; I was able to convince people to buy stuff. If I sold material worth ₹50,000 in a month, I easily made ₹5000-6000 myself. Eventually even ₹10,000 or ₹15,000 depending on how the month went. It covered all our household expenses.'

Then, since 'one shouldn't rely on just one source of income', he started selling men's shirts on the side.

'I moved to Ranchi and rented a room just below a factory that made shirts. I went up to the man who owned it and told him that I could sell his shirts like hot cakes. He signed me up. If a shirt cost ₹300, he used to give it to me for a concession of ₹50. For every shirt I sold to a shop, I made ₹50, then. I would sometimes even give the shopkeepers a discount of ₹5–10 and sacrifice my share of profit just to earn their trust. The orders started streaming in. At the peak of the business, I was selling shirts worth ₹1 lakh a month. In the month of Eid that year—it was 2011—I sold shirts worth ₹2 lakh and made a 20 per cent profit. My family had never shopped more lavishly for Eid. We spent all of the ₹20,000. Our fate was finally turning.'

And then he set up his own shop.

'Marketing, I slowly realized, was a risky business. You never got paid on time and sometimes not at all. I thought: Wouldn't it be better if I set up a shop? I would buy shirts directly from the manufacturers, sell them at the shop and give them back the profit. So, one year on Eid, I put up my own shop at the chowk near our house. It began doing well almost immediately. But the thing I hadn't realized before rushing into this business was that people bought new clothes only during festivals—so the shop was only selling shirts from Ramzan to Ramzan. One of my younger brothers would sit there all day without selling a single shirt. Thankfully, around that time, my older brother finally got a job. Reliance Communications. He was offered enough money for our family to survive on. I took this chance to shut the shop down. I still owed several people money, altogether nearly ₹1 lakh. I kept dodging them with excuses. My family had no idea about any of this, until the creditors showed up at home to demand their due the day I came back home with the trophy.'

* * *

By the time I met Azhar Khan, he had a few days left to come up with ₹1 lakh. There was nothing he hadn't tried already. He had gone to Tabrez Khan first, the man who was partly responsible for the mess. 'I said, help me in some way, at least give me a show where I would be paid a decent amount.' He said he wanted to help me but there was little he could do for someone so raw. He said I should first invest in getting a professional portfolio made and then come to him.' Khan then spent days chasing everyone in the market who owed him money, even ₹1000. No luck there, either.

Finally, he turned to the government. Advised by friends who had more 'experience', he applied to a state-run bank for a loan under an employment scheme. He was going to keep bees. Honeybee units are one of the 'small-scale enterprises' for which the government provides loans on easy terms. The first instalment of the loan would be ₹2 lakh—₹1.5 lakh after taxes—roughly enough to solve all his problems. But what about the honeybees, I asked him. He said there were people who would rent him the whole set-up on short notice in the event of an inspection. I was suspicious of his ability to keep up deceptions, but there seemed to be no other way for him at this point. If things went well, he said he could make an honest attempt at honeybees with the second instalment.

Khan was dying to get out of this situation and begin the life meant for him. Every time I met him between the end of 2014 and mid-2015, he presented a new plan to *fix* his life. On one of those days, we sat at our regular table at the Café Coffee Day, started my laptop, and pulled up the application form for the real, nationwide Mr India contest. He made me fill out the details and attach his favourite photographs, including the one from the night of the pageant in which he was dressed in a black sherwani and bent over in the traditional *aadab* greeting. If he won the title, he said, nothing could come between him and his dream. He never got the phone call. There even came a phase when he would call me an hour before we were due to meet and say he didn't have the money to buy petrol for his bike. He talked desolately of friends who had made it. One of them had featured in a music album recently; in the video he posted on Facebook, he wore a polka-dotted shirt and danced around trees with a beautiful girl. One day we went to a shopping mall to see the producer and director of that music video. When we entered the tiny office, Riteish Kumar was staring into a cup of tea in front of him. He wore a denim vest over a loose white T-shirt. His face looked haggard but striking, with bulging eyes and dark, curly hair. Kumar sat surrounded by evidence of his showbiz access: stills from music video shoots, portraits of actors he claimed to have 'made', newspaper clippings. It wasn't his full-time job, he explained, as we settled down to yet more tea. His main occupation was 'business'—I can't remember if it was cement or cooking gas—but he took regular breaks to help clueless kids deal with the 'glamour world'. He had experience: In 1992, he had worked as an assistant cameraman on the sets of a mythological television show. More than thirty years on, Kumar had positioned himself, like many others with 'experience', at the gates between strugglers and stardom. Like every showbiz fixer, he had his own formula for easy and assured profit.

'There are aspiring singers, they get their songs recorded by themselves and need to promote them. There are aspiring actors looking for some acting experience for their portfolio before they head to Bombay. I help them find each other and invest in a music video that will showcase both their talents. The investment is all theirs; I only do the technical stuff—getting the shooting licence, shooting the video. If one were to get a music video shot in Bombay, the licence to shoot at the forest department's resort would cost ₹16,000 for a day; here it costs ₹16. In one day, you can shoot eight songs.'

I asked him what happened to the video after it's made. 'You put it on YouTube, promote it online, take the royalty home.' It was all about the kids, he stressed. I asked him what it would cost Khan to get a music video made. '*Woh toh yeh khud sochenge* (That he will have to think of by himself),' he said, looking impatiently at Khan. 'It depends on you to decide the way in which you want to build your career.' The little room grew tense with insinuation. 'It's not like I am asking for money for my own sake', Kumar finally said, pushing back his chair. 'Look at her,' he ordered me to look at the wall behind him, 'This is an ex-Miss India contestant. Now, if this guy wants her as his co-star, that alone will cost at least ₹2500.' I realized Kumar wasn't going to quote his 'fee' in front of me so I left after making an excuse. When I called up Azhar later in the evening, he said Kumar had quoted him ₹10,000 as a flat fee. He had left without a word.

Azhar was coming to think it was not his fault things weren't working out. It was all because of the place he was in. He had to get out; one small role in a minor ad film and he would come back and pay off everyone. He started to scour the newspapers for audition calls from Delhi, Mumbai and Kolkata. It wasn't hard to find them. The format was always the same: WANTED male and female, age 18–25, good face and personality, role in ad/TV serial/Bollywood film. Send photos and biodata to the number below. He called all the numbers again and again every day. He would tell the people on the phone, representing production companies with familiar-sounding names, that he had sent over his photos and biodata as advised. Perfect, they would say. He had been shortlisted, in fact, they would add, for a side role in a crime show or an ad film for a motorbike brand. He should start packing for a two-week shooting schedule in Mumbai. He would start thanking them for the great opportunity, when they would interrupt. 'Wait,' they would butt in, 'there is only one small formality to go over: Could you note down this bank account number and deposit ₹6000 in it that we'd need to make your artist card?' Sometimes he called me in Delhi and asked me to find out if these people were real. I would call the numbers and ask the people on the line for anything that might settle their identity—an actual address for the production house, a website, a Facebook page even. They appeared, not entirely to my surprise, always to be moving location or in the process of building a website.

Khan was not giving up yet, though. Going through the newspaper one morning, he saw an advertisement for an acting school in Delhi that seemed as real as it got in the business. There was a real address, including directions from the nearest interstate bus terminal. There was even a landline number and a functioning website loaded with videos of film shoots. Their offer: Attend our acting course and win a guaranteed acting role. A friend offered him a place to stay, and he started putting together a plan. He'd have to convince his family to let him go and his creditors to keep their trust in him. He'd also need to raise a small contingency fund.

Meanwhile, I made a trip to the acting school. The C.L. Balani School of Acting was a small room in a dark basement in an overcrowded Delhi locality. The lane leading to it was festooned with tangled electrical wires hanging so low you were forced to walk in hunched. The man in charge, C.L. Balani himself, was middle-aged with a weathered face, sharp—almost suspicious—eyes, and floppy hair he dyed jet black. He sat at a desk littered with odd artefacts from a previous era, including a battered briefcase. On the wall behind him was a steamy poster of a film in which he had starred as a cop under layers of chalk-white make-up, waving a revolver with one hand and holding the heroine's waist with another. I asked him if this space was the school. 'We don't have a space as such. I prefer holding classes in real locations—it could be a village, a market, whatever the requirement of the script we are acting along.' Acting, Balani said, was all about instinct. The first thing he tells his students is to take what they are offered. 'I tell them I'll give you an acting role, however small. And I keep my word. It could be a five-second advertisement on a religious channel. It could be the advertisement for our own school on a news channel, but they all get to say their lines on television, even if it is "Want to be an actor? Come to C.L. Balani acting school."' Over the past fifteen years, he has trained about fifty or sixty students. Not all of them have ended up as actors. 'Not all children who leave a school do well. I make sure I give them all a start. If they went straight to Bombay, they would be cheated out of everything the moment

they get off the train on the spot. There are kids who have gone to
Bombay after my classes and still haven't faced the camera there
even after six or seven years.' Some of them, he added after some
rumination, hadn't done so badly for themselves. 'Four months
ago, I got a call from a student. He said he had done a course with
me eight years ago. He has been living in Bombay for seven years
now with his brother. He makes his money hanging around
Film City and bagging any small role that comes by, mostly a
man in a crowd. You get ₹700 to ₹750 for a day's work. Ten
days of work a month and life's set.' So, when does the next set
of classes begin, I asked. 'Any time someone walks in,' he said.
Balani had recently found a more profitable way to run an acting
school: 'The kids come here. They live with me, I take care of
their food. I teach them the basics. And I give them a CD that is
a crash course in acting over three hours. Altogether the package
costs only ₹12,000.'

Azhar Khan was chasing success in a world that revealed
itself to be more make-believe with each passing day. It seemed
much easier to become successful feeding on other people's
dreams than following your own. In the three years I spent
following Azhar Khan, I didn't see one aspiring superstar in his
network make it, not even the friend who had starred in his
own music video production. Someone somewhere must make
it, though, for there's always someone from a place no one has
heard of bursting into Bollywood. But for the thousands who
set off on this journey not knowing where it will end, every step
is crazier than the last. By the time I saw Khan next, I didn't need
to tell him about my meeting with Balani. He told me he'd got
the loan. It was the first time I had seen him not worried about
anything: money, career, family. It was a sign, he said as I got up
to leave, that his life was going to change.

* * *

Two months later, I arrived at a banquet hall of a railway station hotel in Ranchi to find Azhar Khan seated behind a long bench covered with a white tablecloth festooned with golden ribbons. Placed in front of him was a sealed bottle of mineral water and a notebook-and-pen set. He was dressed, for the first time, to ooze success: crisp white shirt, plain blue jeans, pointed black shoes. It was the audition for the next edition of 'Mr and Miss Jharkhand'; as the previous winner of the title, Azhar Khan had been invited to be on the panel of judges. The panel was a mix of people Tabrez Khan trusted never to challenge his decisions, such as his office assistant and a visibly distracted friend. As I made my way over to the row of contestants seated along a side wall, Tabrez Khan shouted my name and asked me to join him on the panel, which was still short of three dignitaries. It was perfect that I showed up, he said. I could use my English-speaking skill in judging the mental strength of the contestants; the rest of the panel would focus on the physical aspects. I quietly slipped into the seat next to him. Having waited for hours for the panel to be assembled, the contestants—around twenty young men and women in their fanciest outfits—and their friends, siblings and parents had started to fidget. Unperturbed, Khan had called for another round of coffee and sandwiches for the panel.

The first person to get up from the row of contestants and sashay down the hall was a young woman, a nineteen-year-old college student wearing a shimmery black dress she'd designed herself. After she had bowed and sat down on a stool for the 'interview', Khan asked her where she was from. She named a remote village. He expressed surprise she'd come so far for the contest. 'It has always been my dream to be famous,' she said right back. Khan signalled that it was my turn to interrogate her. The girl turned towards me, her eyes pleading for kindness. I asked her what had inspired her to contest the title. She said it was simply that nothing else had ever interested her. Watching videos of fashion shows on the internet since she was ten, she'd figured she could do this. It was a chance for her to escape the boring life otherwise waiting for her. He couldn't promise she would make it to the next stage, Khan pronounced, seizing control of the matter, but her chances were strong. Her walk needed finesse but it had character. He said it was her face that needed more work. The chubby cheeks had to go before the pageant.

Between delivering Simon Cowellesque 'honesty' to the rest of the contestants about their height, weight, teeth and acne, Khan leaned in to me and continued the story of his life. The way he saw his own journey, he was an underdog like none other. These kids, he said, they won't understand the courage it took for him, a college dropout, to tell his family he wanted to do something different. For them, he said, it was more an empty adventure than real ambition. Real ambition is what *he* had, driving him to pursue things beyond the imagination of the salaried middle class—money, connections and the power to make and break lives. It wasn't over yet, not until he had acquired the last set of things he associated with luxury: a farmhouse and an Audi.

Tabrez Khan saved his worst taunts for men in whom he saw his younger self. His question to a young man in a waistcoat and a French beard who had strutted up to him was why he was late to the audition. Making a sorry face, the contestant said he had to first drop his father off to work. Khan asked him if he had told his father he wanted to be a star. Not yet, he said, he hadn't had the courage to, but he would if he made it to the pageant. Khan's verdict: 'I don't think you are ready. Have you heard yourself speak? You talk like someone right out of the village. Work on your personality, your English. Come back next year.' Walking out of the hotel in the next break, I ran into Azhar who was busy appraising himself in a mirrored column in the lobby. He told me he was honoured to be invited as a judge. He had also been asked by the organizers to mentor the finalists in their walk and 'presentation'. It felt really nice, he said, to be acknowledged for his talent. Things were moving ahead for him.

* * *

'I am done being used,' Khan said, looking through the glass from our usual spot in Café Coffee Day. It had been a couple of months since I met him at the auditions. He now lived full-time in Ranchi, renting a room in a seedy lodge with four other friends. 'There is only exploitation in what I am doing. I was told I would get paid walking the ramp at Tabrez's Fashion Week. I did that. I did another show for him to launch a showroom. What did I get? ₹2000. If they had any decency, they would have given me a cheque for ₹5000. On top of that, I was being told they were doing me a favour.' At some point over these two months, he had also got a taste of life on the other side. 'My friend got an offer from a new hotel to organize its launch function. We worked together. We got a budget of ₹50,000. From that we arranged everything—a few girls to dress up and receive the chief guest at the entry, a DJ, flower garlands, lighting—and managed to save ₹20,000. ₹10,000 for each of us!' For most of his life he'd believed that a man could achieve anything if he chased it hard enough. Now he looked at it as the biggest lie he'd been fed: 'All those guys who had invested in getting their own music videos shot, not even one of them have been released. I am done with all that.' Khan had decided to run the show himself. He was going to launch his own event company and run his own fashion show. 'I have been to other cities for small programmes. The young people there, they are very interested in this sort of thing. There is a lot of hunger in them. I have a friend who will be my partner. It will be a combination of beauty pageant and fashion week, but we'll do a better job.' He'd done his research. 'I'll first need to print posters announcing the audition and stick them around. If the two of us put in ₹10,000 each, it's all we need. Then, sponsorship. We need at least ₹1 lakh for the main sponsor to arrange for the basics. Then we need a few smaller sponsors for this and that. We need the support of a local politician. We need permissions from the police. All of this will take money. We'll need to make a website, a Facebook page. The plan is to save ₹1 lakh each for us two partners.' He had sought this meeting with me to ask me for a name for the company. I suggested 'Starmakerz'. He said he would discuss it with his partner. But what about Bombay, I asked him? 'Bom-bay,' he stretched out the syllables as if to remind himself of the sound of the word, 'that will have to wait.'

* * *

The next time I met Azhar, we were sitting on plastic chairs in the middle of a suburban slum in Mumbai, hardening ourselves against a sudden blast of light and sound. Around us, a large and eager crowd was spilling out of the passageway and clambering on to any surface with a view of the makeshift stage at its front end: window ledges, balcony rails, stacked-up asbestos sheets. It was the evening of 26 January 2016, India's Republic Day, and we were all waiting for the special festival event to begin. Azhar looked different. He had grown a beard and he had, of course, changed how he styled his hair—a close crop, now, with two rows of slightly longer and spiked hair at the centre.

He also looked older. For someone so obsessed with himself, he now seemed intensely aware of things around him. As we negotiated the notorious filth of the Mumbai slums to locate our address, he turned to me and said the place felt familiar to him: 'This feels just like Mira Road'—the dirty and crowded suburb at the end of municipal limits where he, like hordes of other do-or-die migrants, spent his first few weeks in Mumbai.

'*Haar gaya tha* (I felt defeated),' he had said earlier that day at a coffee shop in Andheri, trying to explain why he left Ranchi. We were surrounded by young men and women dressed up like film stars and looking into their coffee. This is what passes for daily activity for the thousands of wannabe heroes and heroines who live in the area and drive a local economy premised on *waiting*. What you needed for this routine was enough money to buy endless cups of expensive coffee day after day in the hope of being 'spotted'. Unfortunately, Azhar Khan didn't have any. He'd left Ranchi because all his plans of making a fortune had crashed. His event company had remained a dream because neither he nor his partner could arrange a sponsor. The first instalment of the honeybee loan was gone too. ('My brother decided to invest it all in stocks whose values crashed right after.') He'd even tried his luck in the lottery business. 'There were four-five of us. The plan was to organize a weekly jackpot for two months, make ₹2 lakh, and chase our dreams. Everything was set. It's an illegal enterprise so we were paying the local police station a fixed amount every week for letting us carry on. We had all invested ₹30,000 each. The way it worked was that everyone who bought a ticket would get ₹100 at the time of announcement of results. The winner would get a motorcycle. It went well for two weeks. But on the third week, the crowd broke into a riot. The police were forced to come after us. We had to run.'

Since I first met him, Azhar was either being cheated by someone or plotting to cheat someone—first, the government with the beekeeping loan; then hapless drunks with his lottery scheme; and people like him with his event company. He had tried his luck at honest work, from running a momo shop to selling door handles, but only to fail harder every time. I couldn't blame him for thinking that cheating is essential to success; he didn't know a single person who became rich without cheating his way up. So, no matter how long I spent telling him otherwise, I suspected it was only a matter of time before he went back to the routine. He dealt with his last failure by running away from everything: the lottery crowd, that old bunch of creditors, bank loan inspectors, family problems. He'd boarded a train to Mumbai. Once he landed here with all his belongings—bedsheet, pillow, clothes, school certificate, passport—he'd followed the standard route of Bollywood strugglers. He'd rented a small room in Mira Road with two young men from Uttar Pradesh who were trying to break into playback singing. He'd signed up with an employment agency and secured two fake certificates confirming work experience; Azhar Khan was now highly recommended by a hardware store in Lucknow as 'store supervisor' and a catering outfit in Kolkata as 'catering supervisor'. Soon after, he'd started working at a brand outlet as a store boy for a salary of ₹15,000, enough to pay rent and other expenses. And while he settled down in the city, he spent all his free time looking up phone numbers of casting agents and calling them in a loop. At the end of his first month in the city, Azhar was homeless ('both the guys gave up trying and went back home'), broke ('I left the job in two weeks. They expected you to stand in a place for ten hours without even a lunch break'), and tired ('the casting agents—they are always saying they will call back, but they never do. *Yahan pe log ghumaate bahut jyada hain* [In Mumbai, people keep you hanging].') He could go back home like his room-mates, of course, but as shameful as it is to run away to Mumbai, to run away *from* Mumbai is the ultimate defeat. So, he had asked his younger brother to wire ₹1000 to his bank account and sat down to map out a new Mumbai strategy. 'I called some of my friends back home to see if there was someone they knew who was already settled here. They gave me the names of a group of guys who worked and stayed together in Kandivali. I told them I didn't know any of these people, how could I expect them to accommodate me? My friend laughed at me. He said I might not know their names but all of them knew mine. They'd all added me as a friend on Facebook after I became Mr Jharkhand and like every photo of mine I post on my page. They would do anything for me, he said.'

Thus started his new life in Mumbai. By the time I met Azhar in Mumbai, he'd been living with four other young men from Chanho in a two-room apartment in the industrial suburb of Kandivali. All of them worked as craftsmen in a local bangle factory. Every year, it turns out, dozens of young men come to Mumbai from his village to work at the same factory, owned by a man who came to Mumbai from the same village as a young man. An old-fashioned businessman, he liked to work with his own people. Azhar's new room-mates adored him. 'They have a wholly different idea of me. They think of me as someone who has come from the same small place but wants to become something big. They have followed my life in modelling through Facebook, they feel proud of my title, and encourage me to follow my dream without any worries. I tell them I am a nobody here, I offer to help with cooking and cleaning, but they won't even let me serve my own food.' Through the same village network, he found a new source of income. 'I offered to help the factory to market bangles, since I'm good at selling things. Travelling on the local train, I would ask people, people who looked like me, about the big local markets around. I noted down the places: Virar, Vasai, Dahisar.' So, every morning now, he picks up a few sets of bangles from the factory and gets on the train for a day of business. 'These are metal bangles, six different designs in total, twelve pieces in a box. I sell them to retailers in these markets. The deal isn't bad. If I make a profit of ₹5 on a bangle, it adds up to ₹60 for one box,' he explained, showing me photographs of shiny bangles on his cell phone.

* * *

Several hours later, when we parted the curtain leading to the green room of Byculla chawl, things were just starting to get serious. The cultural event was to begin in five minutes and the eight performers of Amit Kumar Dance Group jostled for their inch of space in a cupboard-sized *kholi* examining their faces in plastic hand mirrors. The programme for the evening was simple: The women would dance to the popular songs of the year and the men would imitate male superstars from different eras of Bollywood. There were five of these lookalikes, or 'juniors'. Most of them were middle-aged, or plain old; some of them copied actors long dead. With visible desperation, they tried to squeeze their chests and bellies into costumes now several sizes too small and put on wigs that refused to sit in place. Rushed by the organizer to be ready for their cue, they looked into their mirrors and rehearsed the mannerisms of those they were emulating: a head tilt, a boyish grin, a smouldering stare. It worked as well as muscle memory. They knew it wasn't for them that the audience was going wild outside. The roar of impatience was meant for the youngest man in the room—the hottest junior to hit the town in a long time.

Standing amid this graveyard of the Bombay Dream, Shan Ghosh, aka Junior Salman Khan, radiated hope and promise. Ghosh was dressed in Mumbai's reigning superstar's most popular on-screen costume: a police uniform. Every bit of his face and body evoked Salman Khan this evening: the thin black moustache on a clean-shaven face, the dopey eyes, the curve of biceps spilling out of short sleeves. When Ghosh went on stage at the end of the evening, the slum audience, who'd been whining about the endless parade of faded juniors and overweight dancers, rose from their positions at once and ran towards him with a cry of 'Salman'. Over the next ten minutes, Ghosh combined Khan's most popular lines and dance moves into a performance they'd remember until their next Republic Day. As he swaggered back to the green room, children fell over each other trying to shake his hand, the evening's host made repeated pleas for order, and his fellow performers brooded behind the curtain. Borrowed or not, this was fame with all its trappings, and Shan Ghosh seemed to be enjoying every second of it.

Ghosh had first became famous two years before that night. In early 2014, he appeared as the central character in a documentary, *Being Bhaijaan*, which investigated the effect of Salman Khan's screen image on young men in small towns. Khan is bhaijaan to these young fans notorious for ripping open their shirts the moment he appears on the screen in decrepit cinema halls. Ghosh and his gang weren't merely fans of Salman Khan; they lived their lives according to the value system promoted by Khan's characters. Members of a Facebook group meant to bring together Khan's followers in the small town of Chhindwara in Madhya Pradesh, these men internalized every trait of Salman Khan's movie persona: physical strength, moral purity and respect for traditional values. Ghosh was their leader. Not only did he follow the

Bhaijaan code of conduct to a fault—which included a vow of celibacy to preserve physical stamina and moral character—he happened to look a little like his idol. The moment Ghosh realized this as a high-school student, he began to mould his face and body to mimic Khan's. He spent hours at the gym shaping his muscles; stayed awake at nights to enhance the droopiness of his eyes; and invested in knock-offs of clothes and accessories Khan's characters wore in the movies. By the time most young men in Chhindwara were filling up application forms for jobs in banks and railways, Shan Ghosh was rocking weddings and birthday parties with punchy lines and pelvic thrusts.

This was a brilliant escape plan from middle-class prison. Ghosh now didn't have to end up like his father, who had worked in the district's electricity board for most of his life, or his younger brother, who came out of an MBA programme and went straight into married life. If he didn't look like Salman Khan, Ghosh said in the documentary, he would have ended up like any other man in Chhindwara, 'with a paunch, a small business, an ordinary life'. Like Azhar Khan, Shan Ghosh saw himself as the architect of his story. Dancing at cultural events wasn't his only way to make money, however. He also invested in real estate and dabbled in jewellery design, Ghosh had revealed. 'Warren Buffett said that one must have five sources of income, so that there are always backups.'

A year after the first screening of the film, Shan Ghosh left his backups behind and came to Mumbai. With friends from home, he rented a house in Andheri and fixed his droopy eyes on Bollywood. He would begin by performing as a 'duplicate' of Salman Khan and leverage the money and connections accrued in the process towards an acting career as Shan Ghosh. I first met Ghosh when he was a few months into this plan, in the waiting room of a railway station in Delhi from where he was taking a train back to Mumbai. He wasn't only performing as a junior in Mumbai, he explained, but invited to cultural events in places as distant and obscure as Meerut and Indore. In Delhi, he had performed at a three-star hotel with a troupe of juniors brought in from Mumbai. ₹20,000 for fifteen minutes of playing Salman Khan. Not bad at all. He had movie offers—two of them, in fact. He would play a Salman Khan duplicate in one and in the other, he would be launched, as a bargain deal offered by the same producer, as an independent hero. I called him shortly after arriving in Mumbai and asked him if the plan was still working. More or less, he said. He was flooded with invitations to perform as junior Salman. Bollywood was more difficult though. Film shoots, he explained, take a lot of time to materialize. He was still waiting to be called for one. Ghosh was thirty-three at this time and had every hope of ending up as a real Bollywood star. I asked him if he could watch over Azhar, who had just turned twenty-two, as he stumbled around in the struggler terrain. Absolutely, Ghosh said. And later that day, as we shook hands with him in the green room, Ghosh gave Azhar the big-brotherly once-over and asked him to 'connect over Facebook'.

Azhar was anguished through most of the evening. He was shocked at the shoddiness of the stage—two wooden beds pressed together and draped with cheap, colourful fabric—the garishness of the make-up and costumes, and the rowdiness of the slum audience. He pitied the dancers and the duplicates for their desperation. He was enchanted by the sight of Shan Ghosh, though; how he had made himself look like Bollywood's hottest star, how well he walked, spoke, danced. On the way back from Byculla, he slipped into reflection. 'Perhaps they are right—my face is not ready,' he said. Azhar had gone to some film auditions since he settled into the Kandivali life, but every producer and casting agent had told him the same thing. '*Uss layak main abhi tak nahin hoon* (I am not ready yet for that).' His face lacked something. Give it a few years, some had suggested. 'Maybe it's best to wait for two or three years, join a gym, join acting classes, let my face achieve the quality of a hero,' he said, looking out the window of our cab. 'Some people will say I gave up. This friend of mine was just telling me that my struggle is nothing compared to most others. He slept on the railway platform for two weeks after he arrived here. He tells me unless you have slogged in that way, you don't become successful here. But I don't believe in that idea. As I have been telling you for a long time, one has to be prepared before entering this field.' He had a new plan actually, he said. He would go to the Persian Gulf and join its thriving labour market. He had even gone to one of the visa agencies operating around the central railway station and submitted his passport and application. He didn't care where he was sent and what he was asked to do. He could be a catering manager in Saudi Arabia or a shift supervisor in a Dubai mall. Anything was fine. In two years, he estimated, he would have enough money to pull his family back into the middle class and jump to the Andheri life of cafes, gyms and theatre workshops. If you have money, he said, nothing can stop you from storming into the industry. 'Once I'm back, I'm going to show everyone my talent.'

The Scammer

IN MID-2017, A few months after I had returned to Delhi to work for a national newspaper, I began to browse jobs websites. I had been thinking about the young people I had met in the past three years—not the ones I'd chased, but those I'd lost touch with because their lives hadn't exactly been going anywhere. All they had talked about was their long, never-ending quest for survival—in other words, for a real job, the sort Shan Ghosh so despised.

Every other day, a news report underlines the gap between jobs and jobseekers. In 2016, 19,000 people applied for 114 jobs at a municipality; among those who competed for the sweeper's position were thousands of college graduates, some armed with engineering and MBA degrees. Over the same year, 17,00,000 applied for 1500 jobs with a state-owned bank; 92,00,000 wrote entrance exams for fewer than 1,00,000 jobs in the railways; and 70,00,000 crossed their fingers for 8300 entry-level jobs in the public sector. Private-sector jobs in a country with few powerful unions are poorly paid and have punishing hours; the state is the first hope of a jobseeker at the bottom of the food chain. Regardless of their point of entry, from a driver to a teacher, government workers are paid better than private-sector workers, other than receiving a host of other benefits. Only a section of 'qualified' or 'highly skilled' Indians choose a job in the private sector. Unfortunately for the rest, even a Narendra Modi-led government can only offer them under 10,000 jobs a month. What are they going to do? Many turn to rioting. Within months of returning to full-time reporting, I had already covered two youth revolts, in which entire cities had been shut down to demand quotas in education and jobs, because these young people from agricultural castes wanted to work in offices and not farms. I wondered what other options were open to them. Then, one day browsing a jobs website, I saw the ads: a mix of keywords that seemed designed to hit the spot.

- MNC job
- International BPO
- 0 years' experience
- 10th, 12th pass. Backlogs may also apply
- 40 per cent ENGLISH required
- ONE-DAY training
- Salary ₹25,000 to ₹30,000
- UNLIMITED incentives
- Fast CAREER growth—a LIFE is what you make
- Willing to SUCCEED in any situation

This was too good to be true. If well-paying companies were calling out to jobseekers with minimum qualifications but maximum aspiration, then things didn't look that bad for the future of India's youth. Unlike at WittyFeed, a company with a similar hiring philosophy, these novices with '40 per cent English' weren't going to be required to create viral content but simply make and take calls.

A call centre job in 2017 (at a BPO, or 'business process outsourcing' company) doesn't have half the appeal it did back in 2004—the BPO industry has lost much of its value over the years because of poor oversight and competing markets such as the Philippines and jails in the United States. But it's still a job. At the bottom of each of these ads is the name and number of an 'HR', who is not, in fact, a human resource professional but a middleman between a jobseeker and a placement agency.

One day a colleague and I called one of them. HR Amit was curt on the phone. He wasn't interested in knowing anything about us, not even our names. He said to expect a text message on our cell phones right after the call and asked us to follow the instructions. The automated SMS was even more indifferent, calling us to an interview at a recruitment centre in west Delhi where we were supposed to hand in the code at the bottom of the message. The next morning, we went to Rajendra Place, a business centre in an unfashionable part of Delhi where a maze of commercial towers provide a wide range of consumer services, and found that the recruitment centre we were looking for was just one of many. Each offers a better call centre job than the next: closer to our location, more salary, less English needed. At a commercial tower whose roof was midway to collapse, one of the two functioning offices in the building was a recruitment centre. In it, a young fixer offered us a call centre job within 50 metres of wherever we lived. We said we had an appointment at a different centre, one across the street. He said we needn't wander around looking for another address when he was offering us a job on the spot.

We crossed the street anyway. The location of our fixed interview wasn't very different. Up endless narrow, dark and stinky flights of stairs was a recruitment centre where a pimply young man at the reception paused a game on his mobile phone to look at the text message and sent us into one of the two rooms for our interview. I was a high-school graduate from Uttar Pradesh for the day and my colleague was posing as an equally qualified cousin. Our interviewer across the table—a dusky woman wearing a sequinned green kurta, streaked hair, dark brown lipstick and long, brightly painted nails—wasn't interested in the details of our lives, either. Introduce yourself, she said to us one by one, and we obliged in our best '40 per cent English'. She asked us how much success mattered to us. We said our lives depended on it. She said we weren't ideal candidates—she expressed her dissatisfaction with both our English and our confidence— but she was going to offer us jobs anyway. Using the back of one of our fake résumés, she wrote down a jumble of words that followed up on the promise of the job ad: 'International exposure, night shift, ₹20,000 salary, 30 per cent increment every three months, promotion in six months.' She even gave us a slip of paper confirming our jobs: 'We are pleased to inform you that you are hereby selected for C.C.E. (Customer Care Executive) in the BPO department of our organization.' Unlike most jobseekers who leave these agencies, we pushed our interviewer for the name and details of the company we had been hired by. Irritated after a while, she blurted out a name, but nothing else. When can we join the company, we asked. Next week, she said. But before that, we had to go to a different place in Delhi for a one-day training—details would be sent in another text message—and before we left the room, we were to give her ₹500 each for coming this far along.

The text message came in as promised and directed us to an even more obscure address in south-east Delhi for the 'training'. Uttam Nagar is a hub of coaching centres—medical, government service, engineering colleges, MBA—not unlike Ranchi's Lalpur Road, except twice as wide and four times as packed. It's also a hub of everything else: auto-repair shops, ATMs, mango carts, etc. Our destination was a neighbourhood school tucked deep in its peri-urban mess. Dozens of backpack-bearing youngsters were trying to locate it at the same time. Everyone asked around for directions, and trained in this weekly ritual, locals pointed a finger down a lane without wasting effort on eye contact.

About 700 job aspirants undergo this call centre training every Sunday, and this is only one of many training locations across the city. Before we were herded into six or seven classrooms across three floors of the school, we were made to stand in one long queue stretching from the building's entrance to its top floor. Everyone paid ₹1000 to enter a classroom. In return, our slips from placement agencies got a stamp reading 'P.A.I.D.' After we took our seats, we were taken through a drill right out of a Moin Khan class. We were asked to introduce ourselves by our trainer, a young man wearing a snug T-shirt, loose jeans and spiked hair; he then critiqued our numerous flaws in speech and confidence. He gave us a formula for the perfect introduction—'your name, where you are from, where you live, your education, your experience, and your hobbies'—and the best way to end it: 'Thank you. That's all about me.' Spoken English is key to a call centre job, he reminded us. He informed us that there was no word in English he couldn't pronounce: 'Zoo, Alpha, Nancy, pleasure, treasure, vision.' He went on and on: 'My father went to zoo and we saw green dinosaur. My favourite movie is Prince of Persia. It's my pleasure to have treasure.' When he was done showing off, the man took us through his personal journey from a village in Bihar to a call centre in Gurugram. 'It doesn't matter where you are from if you have a plan,' he said. Someone in the class asked him what his plan was. 'I work for money. Career should follow money.' I couldn't have been the only person in the class wondering why anyone would work at a call centre to make money.

Later, I would remember one of the first things he had said after entering the class. 'How many of you know the meaning of "manipulate"? Have you ever taken someone for a ride?' By the time he was done, most people in the class looked baffled by how little they had learnt about their jobs in spite of paying handsomely for the training. All they wanted was to start the jobs promised them in their slips. The day was hardly over, though. The moment we left the class, an army of coordinators led us to another floor where we were once again divided into groups and sent into different rooms for a fresh round of interviews. This time we faced actual representatives of companies interested in hiring us. My colleague and I asked a coordinator if there was anyone from the company whose name we had received at the placement agency. He pondered the name and sent us into a room where eight other jobseekers were lined up in front of a woman sitting at a desk and going through CVs. When it was my turn, I told her that I had already been hired by her company. She said she would still like to be sure of something. 'Sell me this phone,' she said, pointing at the mobile phone in my hand. I did my best to expound on its battery life and selfie camera in '40 per cent English'. After challenging my colleague to the same task, she said we should wait for a call from the company.

Many jobseekers leave the school with appointment letters asking them to report to work the next week. None of them mention the name or address of the company. Everyone is told to expect another text message with further details. Pradeep Saluja left the building thinking that he was about to start working in the customer service of Amazon. This is what the job ad on the internet had promised, he'd repeatedly reminded himself. So he went back home to Ludhiana, picked up his belongings, and come back to Delhi the next week to start work. I called him a month later to find out where he ended up. He told me it was a small office in Gurugram with a strange name where he was given a script to memorize and asked to get on the phone like the fifty other 'executives' his age in the room. The job itself was easy, he said. All he had to do was call people in the US off a list, introduce himself as Charles, and tell them that they were under federal investigation for tax evasion.

One out of ten people freaked out, he said. At the first hint of panic in their voice, Saluja told them he was going to transfer the call to a different department where one of his seniors would help them pay their taxes through an online money transfer. But he didn't like the company's work culture: the hours were long and the 'targets' insane. Saluja quit the company in three weeks and went back home. 'So you worked at a call centre scam,' I asked him. 'You could say that,' he said without the slightest change in his tone. Before he hung up, he told me it wasn't a terrible gig for someone truly in need of a job. He asked me if I had gotten a job yet. I said I hadn't. He said I should consider this company. I had a message from him within five minutes of ending the call, with the number of the company's HR.

Six months before I met Saluja, the police had raided a seven-storey call centre in a north-eastern suburb of Mumbai and arrested 700 youngsters for posing as officers of the Internal Revenue Service and cheating Americans of hundreds of millions of dollars. Two months before the raid, two employees of Phoenix 007 had called the Federal Trade Commission in Washington to tip them off. Nineteen-year-old Pawan Poojary, one of the two whistle-blowers, hadn't always hated his job, he told me on the phone. Unlike Saluja, he, in fact, joined the company knowing he was going to be a scammer. His parents ran a welding shop in a working-class suburb and Poojary, a college dropout, was looking for a way to make 'lots of money'. One day he got a call from an 'HR' who had seen his résumé on a jobs website and found his profile perfect for a job. He was called straight to the company's office in Mira Road—the same shifting migrant ghetto where Azhar Khan had shacked up after arriving in the city—for an interview. 'I was asked to introduce myself. I told him my name, my father's name, my mother's name, my elder sister's name. I told him my family belongs to a village in Karnataka. I told him I have passed twelfth. I said my hobbies are playing indoor and outdoor games.' The company found Poojary's English and confidence good enough to appoint him as a 'closer', the person to whom an 'opener' like Saluja passes on the call after introduction. The salary was ₹15,000 a month, apart from incentives. 'Whatever I made in dollars in one call, I would be paid twice the amount in rupees.' In other words, he kept less than one-thirtieth of the take. He was asked to come for the training the very next day. 'It was a big floor—at least a 100-seater. Everyone was on the phone. Five-six girls were in the HR section. Ten of us were taken into a room for the training.' The trainer kicked off the session by asking the new recruits if they had ever heard of the IRS. He spelled it out for them. Everyone shook their head in a no. 'Then he explained that we were going to call Americans as IRS. The moment he said this I knew something was wrong. I asked him, "Is it a scam?" He said it was and then he told us that if anyone had a problem, they could leave. Only two people left.' The remaining eight were handed over a six-page script. It went like this:

'My name is Paul Edward and I am with the department of legal affairs, with United States Treasury department.

My badge ID is IRD7613. We called to inform you about a legal case filed under your name by Internal Revenue Service under which you are listed as a Primary Suspect. Now I want you to grab a pen and a paper so that I can provide you with your case ID number: IRC7647. Now this is your case ID number and I even have a legal affidavit against you which is issued by Internal Revenue Service. If you allow me I can read the affidavit to you so that you will come to know what your case is all about.' Poojary read it out to me in his Paul Edward accent, a talent he had perfected by the end of his first week as a scammer. 'You speak to foreigners through the day; you just start speaking like them.'

Poojary insisted that I play along as a clueless American so he could remember the script—if I must say something at all. 'But when I read the affidavit to you please don't interrupt me in between because the lines on which we are right now are being federally monitored and recorded so if you have any doubts or any questions, ask me once I'm done reading your affidavit. So I can answer all your questions . . .' No matter what I said, Poojary had a ready-made response in the list of 'rebuttals' in the script, including the line that settled the matter once and for all: 'The police department along with our IRS investigation officer will be at your doorstep within thirty minutes.' While he said his piece, Poojary would look up the address of his victim on the white pages using first name, last name and zip code, details transferred by the opener. 'Many people started crying on the phone,' said Poojary, dropping his American accent. When that happened, Poojary would ask them to drive out to their nearest department store and buy an Apple gift card worth hundreds of dollars. He would then transfer the call to a senior who collected the code on the back of the card.

Poojary was loving it. 'Bahut maza aa raha tha (I was having so much fun),' he said. I believed him. He chuckled while telling me about fake federal departments ('EFTPS—nothing like that exists!') and procedures he had dropped into the middle of his script. He was good at the job. In just two months of joining the company, he had 'earned' $24,000 for the company in iTunes cards. He was informed of his achievement on 14 July 2016: his birthday. 'I felt so happy.' Poojary was thrilled at his ability to scam Americans, who, according to his friends and colleagues, considered themselves superior to the rest of the world. Like most young employees of the company, he wanted to live it up like the mastermind of the scam, a twenty-three-year-old man who rode luxury cars—Audi, BMW, Mercedes—owned big bungalows, travelled business class, and dated beautiful women. On his birthday, Poojary was given ₹50,000 in incentives. 'I blew it all away immediately.'

By the end of the same week, though, he decided he couldn't do this any longer. 'I was on the phone with an American lady. Her name was Regella, she was from California or Texas. I told her the script. She started crying. She said she had no money, that she was about to go to a food bank to get her son something to eat. I felt miserable. I was like "how would I feel if someone did this to my mother?"' Poojary put her on hold and told his supervisor he couldn't go through with that call. 'It didn't matter to him. He took the call over from me and carried on.' Two days later, Poojary and his best friend, who he had brought along with him to the company, started searching for phone numbers of federal investigative agencies. They quit the company two months before the bust. Poojary was offered three jobs within two weeks of leaving. 'So many call centre scams are running in Bombay cheating foreigners. There is tech support scam in Borivali, there is Viagra scam in Kandivali, there is loan scam in Jogeshwari. Two other companies are still running IRS scam.'

If Pawan Poojary ever wants to provide his service to Americans again, he won't be short of options. However messy his departure, the job at Phoenix 007 is the most exciting he'll ever have. For thousands like him who end up at con call centres across big cities—Mumbai, Delhi, Kolkata, Ahmedabad—impersonating tax officers, loan agents, Apple executives or cut-rate Viagra manufacturers, the job provides the same thrill as Lavanya Srivastav of WittyFeed felt when she first cracked the code to American emotions. In both cases, it's these young Indians' first dealing with foreigners—con call centres prefer to hire outsiders new to the big city—and their success at the workplaces depends on how well they understand the weakness of the people on the other side. Since I first saw the job ad calling out to the young and desperate, I have met dozens of current and previous call centre scammers. And between them, they gave me a range of insights into this American life.

> 'America is full of old people who live alone. They have no one to turn to if anything goes wrong.'
> 'In the US they don't like to fix anything by themselves. If they have any issue, they will call customer care. This dependence is their main problem.'
> 'In America, they are very particular about their privacy, their security, their individuality.'
> 'It's very easy to scam Americans. They are very gullible.'

This sociological wisdom powers a large chunk of the job economy in places like Noida and Gurugram, where entire sectors of the satellite cities' corporate layout are dedicated to call centre scams. 'The best part about these places,' said Vikas Tanwar, an ex-scammer, 'is that you can easily get a job.' In what other place, he argued, would someone like him—just

ιbseeker with a bachelor's degree from a college in
n Rajasthan receive a call from a company telling
ɔrfectly matches their requirement? Often, young
employees of these companies don't even have to leave the
building if they want a new job—or a new kind of job. I have
never felt as bewildered as I did going up and down corporate
towers along a 10-kilometre 'phase' of Gurugram trying to
tell real call centres from their scammer siblings, call centre
professionals from their confidence-trick twins. Some young
Indians navigate the maze of con jobs—travel scam to loan
scam to antivirus scam—for years, telling themselves they will
quit this world after just another month's salary. This is how
Abhishek Singh ended up spending two years honing his scam
skills after he arrived in Delhi with a degree in engineering
from Kanpur. 'Everywhere I went I found the same kind of
company, from Gurugram to Noida to Delhi.' He got his
first scamming job at a 20,000-square-foot call centre in a
corporate tower in Gurugram where 500 other people like him
participated in a tech support scam. It unfolds like a theatre
of horror. The scam begins with infecting a computer user's
web browser with a pop-up message that tells them that their
machine has been compromised, and the only way to save it
is to call the number flashing in the middle. Often, the pop-
up seizes the whole screen, locking down the device, at times
accompanied by a screeching siren. Once the user—American
or British or Australian or Canadian—calls the number, it's
picked up by someone like Singh or Tanwar, who worked
at the same company although not at the same time. On the
phone, they acted out a script they were taught in their first
week. They asked the panicking caller for remote access to
their computer, and once connected, took them through the
internal workflow of the machine to present regular files as
deadly threats. 'We also ran a fake software on the computer

to make up virus, trojan, malware. Then we tell them that if you don't buy our security products—$299 for a year, $399 for two years—the computer will become unusable,' said Tanwar, whose brief was to make $500 from every call. His incentive: ₹1000 for every $1000, or 1.5 per cent of the take. 'The moment you put on your headphones, your supervisor tells you, "You are scammers. *Aapko customer ko fasana hai, kuch bhi kar ke* . . . (You have to trap the customer, no matter how),"' he said.

Tanwar didn't mind the job that much, but he was enraged by the company's denial of incentives. For Abhishek Singh, too, the guilt came in much later. 'There would be nothing wrong with their computers. The whole thing was a scam: *poora farzi-wada.* You take remote and after taking remote you make up whatever stuff and charge $400-500. *Jitni unki maar lo, utna badhiya hai* (The more you fuck them over, the better). Most people who get pop-ups are doing something wrong— porn or illegal downloads. But what we did was wrong because the software we sold them is freely available on the internet by Microsoft and others.'

Two out of three people in the world experience a tech support scam within a year, according to a 2016 survey by Microsoft. Americans lose approximately $1.5 billion to tech support scams annually. Most of them—86 per cent— originate in India. Singh told himself he was going to quit the company after the second month's salary. And he did exactly that, but only to realize the only other job he could find was also a scam. 'This company takes calls on behalf of Facebook,' he wrote in an email to me, 'So a caller calls in saying he has issues with Facebook—for example, "forgot my password". The executive on the phone says he is a Facebook expert and will help the customer recover the password, and in order to do so he will need to gain remote access to his computer. Once he is in the computer, he goes ahead and does a diagnosis. LOL.'

Singh was trained to upgrade his scare skills at this company: 'Even the FBI was involved if the customer refused to pay, and as a final blow, we told them that Homeland Security, which monitors all internet activity, would be informed and their internet would be cut off and they would not get a connection anywhere in the US as they would be BLACKLISTED. The customer paid anywhere between $200 to $2000, sometimes through Apple gift cards.'

As in the case of Phoenix 007, it's a matter of time before the new recruits forget about their life goals and succumb to the thrill of pulling off a scam. The work vibe at many of these con call centres is set by the best of Hollywood's heist dramas. 'At this company, everyone thought they were characters from *The Wolf of Wall Street*,' said Singh. The film about a bunch of alpha male stock-market con men had released at about the same time as he entered the world of IT scams. 'People turned up at work high on weed. Everyone abused each other across the floor for not being able to cheat like a pro.' Like Pawan Poojary, most of these shop-floor scammers never even get to meet the masterminds, but Facebook photographs flaunting their lives—cars, parties, holidays, girls—act as a common inspiration.

And before they even know it, their idea of right and wrong becomes blurred. 'Whether it's fraud or not, depends on perspective,' as a young man who's spent his entire five-year career conjuring up viruses on normal computers said about his job. An ex-scammer, a man called Amit Singhal who can speak for hours about the trippy zone between black and white, once told me, 'If you go to a shop and you have a Samsung phone and the man scares you by saying this phone can explode any time, do one thing, give me 1000 bucks and whenever it explodes, I will give you a new phone free of cost. It is a lie that the phone is going to explode. He is scaring you so that you pay him the money. That's it. It's the same thing with tech support scams. It's not that they are stealing your money. People are willingly paying them because they got scared. No one put a gun to their heads.'

But none of this is as effective as the justification every scammer gives himself when torn between money and morality: As young men with no prospects, they are the biggest victims—and the whole world is a big scam.

'Americans complain of being scammed, but have they thought of people sitting on the other side of the call who sit around talking to them for hours for ₹30,000 a month?'
'Nothing seems wrong if you are getting a salary at the end of it.'
'Someone is paying you—it's all that matters.'

For some, the question of ethics had been settled the moment they decided against mediocrity. 'In Delhi, you can't become an important man without pulling some kind of fraud,' Sunil Kumar, a scam call centre recruiter, told me with a smile. I had met him posing as a jobseeker at the training centre in Uttam Nagar where he happened to be one of many 'HRs' matching candidates with companies. A lanky, long-haired twenty-six-year-old, Kumar moved from a village in Allahabad to Delhi eight years ago. A school dropout, he started his career supervising security at a shopping mall, but swiftly moved on to fixing low-level jobs for youngsters arriving in Delhi from his village. He has since become a veteran of the underground job placement business.

Kumar is an important man today by his own reckoning. He makes ₹1.5 lakh a month and employs eight people. His employees spend most of their working hours trawling CVs on popular jobs websites to identify anxious jobseekers they can lure. He pays them on the basis of the number of jobseekers they direct to the agency. If he is able to place even fifty in a month, he has met his target. 'I charge commission from companies: ₹2000 for placing one kid,' he said. Usually, he ends up placing more than fifty in a month. The city's wide network of scam call centres—in tech support, insurance, banking, and travel—depend on this shadowy hiring system for staffing. I asked him if he ever felt responsible for what the 'kids' are made to do. The margins of profit in his business are too big for anyone to care about what happens to the kids. If a hundred jobseekers walk into a placement agency over a day and pay ₹500 each, it adds up to ₹50,000. If 500 jobseekers turn up at a training centre over a day and pay ₹1000 each, it means ₹5 lakh. 'See, every call centre is engaged in one or the other kind of fraud. You can't do much,' he said, avoiding eye contact. Still, he has tried to think through the implications of helping to staff scamming groups, even if only to save his skin. 'If [jobseekers] call you and complain that they are made to take part in a scam, you say, "Is that so?" You try your best to act in their interest. You say, "Why don't you stick it out until the end of the month and get out after collecting the salary and join another company?"'

This way, he said, he can kill two birds with one stone. Not only has he shrugged off his own responsibility in the matter, he gets to keep a 'captive' pool of 'kids' to peddle. 'No one works at a [scam] call centre for more than a month,' he said. They either leave the job unable to meet the targets or learn enough in a month to launch their own scam. '*Unko fatoon chadh jaata hai* (A madness comes over them). They think, "This fraud money can come to me instead of going to the company.'" Kumar's business thrives on the fact that scam call centres are always short of employees. When we talked in June 2017, Kumar said he had 2500 to 3000 openings to fill.

We were sitting in a coffee shop in Noida and he was asking me to stop looking for a job and start thinking big. 'What's the point. *Naukri ya toh milti nahin hai, milti hai toh achchi nahin lagti* (You either don't get a job or don't like your job). My father worked the same job his whole life. When I recently went home I asked him, "Was it worth it?" I told him I don't work for anyone, but I can claim the respect of at least 500 people. I have izzat.' Kumar said he didn't even have to work any more to earn his income; the money just kept on coming. He devotes the free time he is thus left with to his two passions: dancing and playing cricket.

I was reminded of a YouTube clip the motivational speaker Santosh Dev Thakur once uploaded on Facebook in which he explains the difference between 'being rich and being wealthy'. Sitting in a hotel room with his dark glasses on, Thakur drops a piece of wisdom as old as humanity: 'If you have money, you are rich; if you have money and time, you are wealthy.' I wondered if Kumar's story would work as motivational material. It ticked every box except nobility; but most young Indians would ask exactly how far nobility would take someone who arrives in Delhi with nothing to their name but ambition. I was slowly discovering that the Indian market for motivation cut across moral divides. A week before I met Sunil Kumar in Noida, I had visited a placement centre that specializes in fake jobs whose walls were plastered with the words of every great man who has ever made an inspiring statement.

Take risk in your life. If you win, you can lead. If you lose, you can guide—Swami Vivekananda

All I ask is that today you do the best work of your entire life—Steve Jobs

Don't compare yourself with anyone in this world. If you do so, you are insulting yourself—Bill Gates

'*Kuch bada karna hai* (You want to do something big)?' Sunil Kumar suddenly asked me. I knew where this was going. Crossing his arms on the table, he proposed that I work for him. I could find him jobseekers to sell to call centres instead of hunting call centre jobs myself. He offered to make me a partner in his placement agency. He said he had seen a spark of outsize ambition in me; like him, I wasn't destined for an ordinary life. I did feel a little flattered.

* * *

My colleague and I had still not heard from the company we interviewed for at the training centre in Uttam Nagar. One day we searched for its name online. It did at least have a website; a slide show on top of the home page featured the skyline of Manhattan as well as smiling, confident Americans holding meetings and striking deals. In its description, the call centre kept things fashionably vague: 'a passion to create an environment . . . redefine perfection . . . inspiration . . . the moment has now arrived . . . exquisite product service delivery . . . timeless creation from the master of this craft.' There was no way you could tell what this 'exquisite product' or 'timeless creation' was, and to whom this service was delivered. The website also featured a list of the company's clients, although not one of the names was known to Google's indexes. But how could such petty details compare to the company's ultimate promise: 'If Perfection defines you then Experience is our definition.'

We decided to show up at the address and claim our right to a job for which we had already paid ₹1500 each. There was no signboard outside the four-storey building in the bowels of a marble market in north-west Delhi, but it was nevertheless easy to get there. All you had to do was say '*sheeshe-walla* (glass-walled) call centre' to any rickshaw driver at the Kirti Nagar Metro station, and they would hurtle down dusty by-lanes without a word. Where else in this maze of shops selling low-cost home decor—sofa sets, bathroom fittings, dirty grey marble blocks—could hordes of young men and women be headed every morning and evening? At the reception, a small space with lockers, a saggy black sofa and anti-drugs posters on the walls, we informed a security manager that we needed to see someone in the HR department. We were handed application forms and asked to wait for our interview calls. Unable to convince the man that we had been through the process before, we quietly filled in now-familiar invented details—education ('Government High School, Kanpur') objective ('to excel at every given opportunity'), reference ('Global Expert BPO, Rajendra Place')—and waited to be called into the call centre whose tinted-glass door was being guarded by a gun-toting bouncer.

I was called in first. I walked past rows and rows of cubicles in which young employees were staring at computer screens and speaking into microphones. I was asked to stop after reaching a gallery at the back of the office. A woman sitting behind a table was looking at my CV and circling entries with a pen. I told her that I had an appointment letter from a placement agency confirming this job. She said it meant nothing. 'Can you sell me this phone,' she said, tossing her own at the table. I repeated my past performance word for word. She asked me to follow my usher to a room across the floor for the next interview. This time, I sat across a table from two suited men and made a sales pitch for a mobile phone once again. After my colleague was put through the same drill, we were told to leave the building and wait to hear from the company.

By this time, I had interviewed four times for this job and couldn't wait to find out what I would be selling if I ever got in. One day I found someone who had mentioned the company's name as a previous employer in an online work profile. I sent her—a young woman with short hair and a cheerful smile—a message on Facebook, and she replied to say that she was glad someone saw the mention. 'I wanted people to know what the company is all about.'

Sona Kapoor, twenty-three, came to Delhi from western Uttar Pradesh in 2016 and joined the first company that offered her a job. A friend from home who was working there recommended her to an HR at the company. It seemed like a regular call centre job until, at the end of her training on the first day of work, she was handed a script. For two months thereafter, Kapoor called nearly fifty people—Indians and Indian migrants to the Gulf countries—every day off a list, opening with the same line again and again: 'Do you want a job or a job change?' If they said yes, she asked them if they had access to the internet. She then directed them to a jobs website run by her company and told them to register their profiles by making an online payment of ₹4000. Then, Kapoor transferred the call to a 'closer' who took the client back to the website to offer a suite of career-boosting services—Designer Résumé, Social Media Profile Builder, Live Interview Preparation, International Carrier Expert

Senior Level, and the like—crafted to close any remaining gap between them and their dream job. 'No one ever got any job. Nothing was what it seemed to be. Everything was a lie,' said Kapoor, who had learnt the truth about her job within a week. 'If clients called back threatening to file a police complaint, the company refunded the fee, but we got only four such calls every day.' Others chose to vent their pain on consumer complaint websites. I asked her why she participated in the con fully aware of what she was doing. 'You think the people who run these call centres are making so much money every day, you might as well make some of it while you are here,' said Kapoor.

It didn't surprise me to discover that entire neighbourhoods in Delhi specialized in this job scam. In every major Indian city, working-age people across sectors—banking, information technology, insurance—were getting calls from strangers who asked them if they wanted a job or a job change. Depending on their credulity and bank balance, the victims were cheated of anywhere between ₹1 lakh and ₹5 lakh. In case after case that the Delhi Police had investigated in the past three years, the 'modus operandi' consisted of fly-by-night companies, secret call centres and fake jobs websites. The profiles of the accused that the police filed in the case reports weren't very different from each other, either. Most of them were migrants from neighbouring states who had picked up the skills stumbling from one scam to another in the capital city, and had enough ambition to strike out on their own.

Her company made millions of rupees every month, according to Kapoor's estimate. The only way to scam Indians at such a scale, apparently, is by promising them jobs, a fulfilment of their most cherished dream. I now knew that at least some of those who respond to the suspicious job ads promising mass openings and unlimited incentives do land a job—even if that job is to scam other jobseekers. Most of Kapoor's colleagues—around 400 people work across the four-storey call centre—ended up at the company by following the same leads as me. Sona Kapoor left the job in a month, the moment she got her salary: ₹18,000. Her friend is still making cold calls to unsuspecting young Indians offering them their one chance at success.

Epilogue

ONCE I WOULD have judged someone like Sona Kapoor. However, by the time I discovered the world of call centre scammers, I had started to think a little like the people I spent three years talking to. If I had to boil their philosophy down to two words, it would be: whatever works. Like it or not, young India is what it is—unsatisfied, unscrupulous, unstoppable. Few young Indians I met had a clear sense of right and wrong; fewer gave a damn about it.

I could easily frame the lack of morality as a feature of their generation, but that would be a lie. They know what they are doing, but more tellingly, they know it's fine to do that. Pankaj Prasad isn't the first village fixer to charge people money for a free service, Vikas Thakur isn't the first aspiring politician to equate corruption with power, and Azhar Khan isn't the first wannabe superstar to pay an entry fee. How do three different people trying to make it in three different fields—governance, politics, show business—have similarly vague ideas of what's fair and unfair? Because their idea of success includes the ability to switch between right and wrong based on what they stand to win or lose.

The idea of personal benefit over public good isn't owned by them, however. It's at the core of India's value system. Sure, some young Indians will cheat their way to their dreams, but they don't see how they are different from anyone in the news—politicians, businessmen, celebrities. They have been abandoned by the country they claim to love with all their hearts, not once but twice. They haven't only been left to do as they wish with their lives, but left so without the barest education in moral responsibility. Not every twenty-year-old operates without principles, but some principles are more prized in contemporary India than others. Vinay Singhal is as much fashioned by his ideas as Richa Singh is by hers— they simply have different views of what India should be. Singhal wants India to be a global superpower—economic, technological, military—where systems work and people take responsibility. Singh wants India to first prove itself as a democracy where everyone—Hindu, Muslim, Dalit, woman—has an equal chance at freedom and opportunity. India isn't going to be either of these places in the foreseeable future, but the first is an engine for political populism, as Narendra Modi has been demonstrating since 2014, and the second a train wreck. I have known it a long time, but it still broke my heart to be reminded of it. After two months of campaigning for a seat in the Uttar Pradesh assembly, Richa Singh lost her bid in what was termed, once again, a Narendra Modi wave. The BJP won 312 of the 403 seats in the UP assembly; the SP was annihilated.

But that wasn't the real tragedy. Exulting in the unconditional support of aspirational Hindus, the BJP chose as the state's chief minister a man whose only qualification for the post was peddling hate for the *other*: Yogi Adityanath. As the first elected female president of the students' union of Allahabad University, Singh had stopped him from entering the campus on exactly the same grounds that now installed him in the chief minister's office in Lucknow, ruling what would be, if it were independent, the world's sixth largest country. After I heard the news, I wanted to phone her to find out how she felt about the development—it was the right thing to do as a reporter—but I couldn't bring myself to make the call.

Meanwhile, Singh had succeeded in leading more women into the university's politics. None took the risk in the year following her win, but in 2017's elections to the students' union, at least six girls contested various positions. A female member of the ABVP stood for the president's post, and turned down by the NSUI, a young woman left the Congress party's student wing to contest the vice president's post on her own. A young man from the Samajwadi Chhatra Sabha became the president.

The BJP's victory in the state elections wasn't Yogi Adityanath's alone, but belonged to every young Hindu man who had felt like a stranger in his own land. Many of them sent me messages celebrating the moment. 'We'll show them now,' said one. 'Mother India is in safe hands,' said another. I responded with vague emoji.

I could have felt better about it by thinking of the verdict as just another piece in the enabling of illiberal populism by abandoned youth—a global problem India didn't start and can't end. My job was to report what I saw. And I had seen enough to feel this was just the beginning. I was ready to argue that the BJP doesn't have to worry about elections as long as it can channel the anxieties of India's hopeless millions. But I saw, too, a glimpse of what lay at the end of that road. You can't give the young jobs or the infrastructure to make their dreams come true, but you can engage them in the most time-consuming enterprise ever known to youth: the politics of identity. It's a limited-period plan, though, and one known to backfire. I wondered what he would say to twenty-six-year-old Ratnikant Patel, red with rage as he demanded Modi rewrite India's Constitution or be ready for the consequences. I met him in Mehsana, a Patel-dominated district in Modi's home state, Gujarat, that gave the BJP its first seat in Parliament and has remained a party bastion. Now, thirty years after the favour, the community feels the BJP should return it by giving its youth quotas in educational institutions and jobs, for they no longer want to stay in villages and manage farms. But the party knows better than to mess with India's existing system of reservations that puts historical exclusion above all other criteria. So the young Patels declared war, flooding the streets of the state capital in numbers exceeding 5,00,000 and daring the police to shoot them in the face. Ratnikant Patel was one of them. He told me that his father had sold his village land to send him to an expensive school and then college. He expected to find a job as soon he was done studying, but found himself turned away from one government department after another. 'I applied for a teacher's job, then a peon's. Didn't get any,' he said, his face turning into a river of bulging veins. 'How can the prime minister of our country say that he will privilege one group of people over the others? *Yeh kaisa Hindustan hai* (What kind of India is this)?' He swore revenge.

Patel began by quitting his post as the manager of his neighbourhood's RSS unit. 'Religion is not more important than survival.' And nothing, he said, was more important than getting your due: 'If the Constitution can be written, it can also be changed.' I met young men who repeated the sentiment in places other than Gujarat. I stood frozen with dread as a group of teenage girls dressed in all-black outfits waved swords on a stage in western Maharashtra to let the BJP know it has two options: to punish Dalits for wounding the pride of the Maratha community, or to allow Marathas to shed blood. And while it mulled over those options, could the party perhaps also reserve for Marathas college seats and jobs? And so it went.

I couldn't possibly keep up with the quirks of India's 600 million young people, so I kept returning to those I understood a little better. Their lives were changing fast, even if not going according to plan. The scam soldiers were taking over the scams. They had picked up tricks of the trade and turned their backs on long shifts and late salaries. They were building networks of professional fraud by helping each other with the logistics of a call centre scam. What did you need to run a tech support scam? A team of five, a rented room, computers, mobile phones, a stash of software, a pop-up vendor, and a friend in the US or UK to lend you their bank account. And how were they operating these networks? On Facebook. It was social networking at its most efficient. An entire pocket of Facebook is commandeered to transact pieces of the framework. You could negotiate the rate for, say, pop-ups: 10 for ₹500 or 50 for ₹100. You could negotiate how scary you wanted the pop-up to be: take up a corner of the computer's screen, take up the whole screen, freeze it up or turn it black. You could negotiate where you wanted to plant the pop-ups, from porn websites to banking websites. Every petty scammer is now a mastermind and can have a go at the lifestyle—parties, fast cars, beautiful girls—as I could see in photos they share on Facebook. They had made it in life and they didn't care how many gullible elderly strangers in remote America lost their pensions in the process.

Some had decided to try their luck with honest work. The last time I spoke to Vikas Tanwar, he was developing the idea for a start-up with a bunch of friends he met in Gurugram—an Uber for spiritual services: 'Astrologers, priests, palm readers, tarot card readers.' A few years of call centre fraud, a veteran told me, is a common way to pull together a start-up fund. Amit Singhal is currently broke—he came to the point of asking me for a loan to pay a monthly instalment on his car loan—but full of faith in his ideas. 'There is too much stuff up here,' he once told us, jabbing his forehead to indicate the treasure it contained. Pawan Poojary briefly joined another, real, call centre days after leaving Phoenix 007. He regrets the decision. Half of his new colleagues called him a scammer and the other half a traitor for tipping off the Americans and bringing shame upon India. 'Indians are really strange people.' He has now decided that office work is not for him. 'They try to control you too much.' He is going to launch his own business.

The journey of WittyFeed took a sharp turn, too. A year after I first met the Singhals, at least 100 million people still visited the website every month, but almost half of them are now Indians. The local market for web content was exploding, said Parveen Singhal, the CCO, and the company would be foolish to ignore it. So they were now creating content in Hindi instead of Spanish. They were also slowly moving on from 'clickbait to clickable'. They have no option. 'Clickbait is over. Now you have to do other things to generate curiosity,' he said, sounding as excitable as ever. The website still publishes seventy stories every day, but it must force them through some filters. 'Now even Facebook only allows you to share high-quality content. You have to check facts, you have to be transparent, you have to give them high-definition photos, motion-graphic videos.'

The website now plays with subjects irresistible to the Indian audience: cricketers, Bollywood celebrities and Narendra Modi. No word of Modi's is left unreported and no action uncritiqued. The coverage switches between fanboyish ('Ten Times Narendra Modi Proved He Is a

Complete Rockstar' or 'Narendra Modi, the Selfie King') and prescriptive ('Seven Things Modi Government Should Ban Before 2019 General Elections'). What stands out is an open letter reminding Narendra Modi he is the only saviour of the Indian dream: 'We really need Individual like you who has helped us dream of a "Better India" to not step back in any manner and deliver what is expected from you. We have got this only ONE LAST chance to get our India to aspire for better future and you are with me in this!'

The American obsessions also stay firmly in place, but now the treatment is more news and less bait. ('President Trump Gets Trolled Hilariously on Twitter'. 'Marc Zuckerberg Reveals His Secret Marriage Story'. 'Dwayne Johnson Announces He Is Running for President in 2020'.) A part of the home page is dedicated to questions facing the future of American democracy, from Ivanka Trump's investments to the Russian interference in presidential elections. I could spot some old favourites of virality, from 'Fifteen Funniest Cat Videos' to 'Twenty-two Wedding Cake Fails', from the video of a puppy bathed in glue to the result of an upset mom texting a stranger instead of her daughter, so I assumed enough Americans must still be interested in viral content. The Haryana boys currently see less business sense in taking over America, though. The plan to set up an LA office is on hold, said Parveen Singhal. (What they have done is hire another twenty people for the office in Indore.) So is Vinay Singhal's dream to take off to Mars. In the meantime, I am sure, he continues to inspire his weekly audience of now more than 100 wide-eyed youngsters to dream their wildest dreams.

What will happen to the dreams of the rest?

Will Moin Khan become a world-famous motivational speaker? I don't know. Will he rule Ranchi's market for spoken English? Yes. Will Pankaj Prasad keep expanding his base of 'customers', adding floors to his house, buying symbols of his changing status, and throwing the most extravagant feasts? Most certainly. I have reason to doubt Azhar Khan will become a Bollywood superstar or Vikas Thakur an elected politician. But I do not, for a moment, think they will ever stop trying to become rich, powerful or famous. They can't go any further, they have nothing to go back to, so they will remain suspended between reality and their dreams. It's like flying into outer space without a return plan: No matter where you end up, the sun still shines brighter and the stars are at your fingertips.

Acknowledgements

My editors, Meru Gokhale, Manasi Subramaniam, Michael Dwyer and Sharmila Sen for guiding the book along. Everyone else at Penguin Random House India, Hurst and Harvard University Press for their hard work and patience.

Chiki Sarkar, for asking me to find out what young people in small towns were up to.

Friends who have either listened to or read these stories: Sonal Shah, Shivam Vij, Diksha Madhok, Taran Khan, Tripti Lahiri, Ajay Krishnan, Supriya Nair, Nikhil Kumar, Amulya Gopalakrishnan, Varun Rana and Alex Traub.

My family—Ved Prakash Narayan Singh, Punam Singh, Moneesha Sharma, Shweta Ved, Swati Ved, Sarah Ved, Abhimanyu Kumar, Gautam Kadian, Aletta Andre and Milan Andre Singh—for the unconditional love.

Arshia Sattar and Pushpesh Pant, for letting me into Sangam House and Jayanti Residency.

Bobby Ghosh, for giving me a job at the *Hindustan Times* and the space to follow some of the book's themes.

Samarth Bansal, for reporting one of the stories with me.

Everyone in the book, for letting me enter their lives.

Mihir Swarup Sharma, for everything else.

References

Chapter 1
Articles

4–5: Millions of people . . . likes on Facebook.
https://factordaily.com/wittyfeed-viral-content/
http://www.forbesindia.com/article/startups/wittyfeed-the-content-churner/48371/1
https://economictimes.indiatimes.com/small-biz/startups/wittyfeed-surpasses-twitter-and-instagram-becomes-20th-most-visited-website-in-india/articleshow/57292656.cms

9: Her first viral . . . it so far.
https://www.wittyfeed.com/story/7265/husband-divorced-his-wife-after-looking-closer-at-this-picture

13: Badlega India was . . . to this charter?).
http://www.badlegaindia.org/

13: The page was . . . people liked it.
https://www.facebook.com/AmazingThingsInTheWorld/

21: More than half . . . age of twenty-five.
http://www.livemint.com/Opinion/
2WSy5ZGR9ZO3KLDMGiJq2J/Indias-burgeoning-youth-
are-the-worlds-future.html

21: 'Never before have . . . our common future.'
https://www.unfpa.org/sites/default/files/pub-pdf/EN-
SWOP14-Report_FINAL-web.pdf

21: To call the . . . of 4200 colleges.)
https://www.csmonitor.com/World/Asia-South-Central/
2012/0116/In-India-the-challenge-of-building-50-000-colleges

21–22: Even if the . . . are immediately employable.
http://www.aspiringminds.com/sites/default/files/National%20
Employability%20Report%20-%20Engineers%20Annual%20
Report%202016.pdf

22: Only 2.3 per cent . . . in South Korea).
http://www.worldbank.org/en/news/press-release/2017/06/23/
new-world-bank-project-give-impetus-india-skills-agenda-to-
provide-over-8mn-youth-with-market-relevant-training

22: They want jobs . . . more productive jobs.
http://www.livemint.com/Opinion/
EZnQxosavPuFxrBznAonXM/The-challenge-of-
unemployment.html

22: The growing gap . . . and social instability.
http://www.ilo.org/global/about-the-ilo/newsroom/news/
WCMS_165465/lang--en/index.htm

22: Over the last . . . and rail networks.
http://www.financialexpress.com/india-news/andhra-pradesh-
kapu-protest-turns-violent-despite-cm-chandrababu-naidus-
reservation-assurance/205017/

22: In Haryana, they . . . the country's capital.
https://timesofindia.indiatimes.com/city/delhi/Jat-quota-
stir-Water-supply-cut-Delhi-may-go-dry-today/
articleshow/51073879.cms

22: In Gujarat, they . . . by the police.
http://indianexpress.com/article/india/india-others/patidar-
agitation-to-intensify-police-indulging-in-violence-hardik-patel/

22: In Maharashtra, they . . . under affirmative action.
http://www.hindustantimes.com/india-news/the-new-wave-
of-caste-wars-maratha-feel-their-social-order-is-under-
threat/story-fAhhIz8OEDcOYXZuoAHkLI.html

24: Between 2004–05 and . . . biases, and patriarchy'.
http://www.bbc.com/news/world-asia-india-39945473

24: They have the . . . ideas about success.
https://blogs.wsj.com/briefly/2015/07/22/indias-labor-force/

24–25: This is the . . . on world domination.
http://www.lokniti.org/pol-pdf/Keyfindingsfromthe
YouthStudy.pdf

26: Touring India during . . . to personal computers.
http://www.nytimes.com/1990/07/05/business/
entrepreneurs-flourish-as-india-makes-reforms.html
http://www.nytimes.com/1990/02/26/business/international-
report-pepsi-is-open-for-business-in-india.html

27: I wrote earnest . . . to *present* themselves.
https://india.blogs.nytimes.com/2013/07/05/developing-indias-
personality/

27–28: I spent nights . . . the Indian market.
http://www.caravanmagazine.in/reportage/casting-net

28: I spent days . . . to undertake it.
http://www.openthemagazine.com/article/books/the-new-heroes-of-mba-lit

28: Young Indians had . . . of the deal.
https://timesofindia.indiatimes.com/news/Election-results-2014-Lok-Sabha-Elections-2014/articleshow/35227336.cms

32: In May 2017 . . . for self-employment'.
http://www.hindustantimes.com/india-news/not-possible-to-provide-jobs-to-all-so-we-promote-self-employment-amit-shah/story-z1XMRYTdwOkBseTzjyrMIL.html

Books

V.S. Naipaul (1990), *India: A Million Mutinies Now*, Penguin Books.
Ed. Peter Ronald DeSouza, Sanjay Kumar and Sandeep Shastri (2013), *Indian Youth in a Transforming World: Attitudes and Perceptions*, Sage.
Parul Bansal (2012), *Youth in Contemporary India: Images of Identity and Social Change*, Springer.

Chapter 2
Articles

40: Most notably, spoken . . . 100 million Indians.
http://www.bbc.com/news/av/magazine-30729450/the-man-who-opened-india-s-first-call-centre

44–45: 'To be denied . . . creative or hardworking.'
https://blogs.timesofindia.indiatimes.com/The-underage-optimist/let-there-be-english-but-abolish-caste-system-around-the-language/

65: Perhaps that is . . . 2.5 million copies.
http://www.thehindu.com/society/motivational-speaker-shiv-khera-on-the-need-for-self-help/article19103320.ece

Books

Rashmi Sadana (2012), *English Heart, Hindi Heartland: The Political Life of Literature in India*, University of California Press.

Shiv Khera (2014), *You Can Win: A Step by Step Tool for Top Achievers*, Bloomsbury India.

M.K. Gandhi (1938), *Hind Swaraj or Indian Home Rule*, Navajivan Publishing House.

J.K. Tina Basi (2009), *Women, Identity and India's Call Centre Industry*, Routledge.

Chapter 3
Articles

82: Six weeks later . . . Congress got none.
http://www.elections.in/parliamentary-constituencies/2014-election-results.html

85: It was 2006 . . . needed passport-sized photos. Between 2004 and . . . roads, child nutrition.
http://www.unrisd.org/80256B42004CCC77/(httpInfoFiles)/134916AD19B8FC29C1257EEE0056063E/$file/India.pdf

86: Over the last . . . amounting to crores.
http://www.livemint.com/Politics/XeGU40jlsHGKrfwfJK1ccL/Govt-announces-Rs60000crore-loan-waiver-for-farmers.html

86: In 2009, the . . . or UID, project.
http://indianexpress.com/article/india/latest-news/aadhar-takes-off-pm-sonia-launch-uid-in-tribal-village/

86: In 2012, the . . . wages under MGNREGA.
http://www.thehindu.com/opinion/op-ed/aadhaar-and-mgnrega-are-made-for-each-other/article3599261.ece

88–89: Mineral-rich Jharkhand . . . over the state.
http://ngm.nationalgeographic.com/2015/04/india-coal/loyd-text

93: Within the first . . . longer front-page news.
http://www.business-standard.com/article/economy-
policy/jharkhand-turns-into-hotbed-of-corruption-
109102000100_1.html

93: And one of . . . worth $1.7 million.
http://www.thehindubusinessline.com/todays-paper/tp-
opinion/the-unfolding-koda-scam/article1068902.ece

93: A large proportion . . . fake job cards.
https://www.theguardian.com/world/2010/sep/07/india-
grain-farming-prices-poor
http://news.rediff.com/report/2010/may/23/study-finds-
massive-corruption-in-govts-flagship-nrega.htm
https://www.outlookindia.com/magazine/story/71-villagers-
say-theres-high-corruption-in-government-welfare-
schemes/237112

103: The country was . . . crippling agricultural life.
http://www.bbc.com/news/world-asia-india-36089377

103: Over 100 Indian . . . months of 2016.
https://timesofindia.indiatimes.com/india/116-farmer-
suicides-in-first-3-months-of-2016/articleshow/52002524.cms

105: On 8 November . . . them grew angrier.
https://qz.com/836378/one-week-of-narendra-modis-
demonetisation-in-india-the-good-the-bad-and-the-ugly/

106: India's cities might . . . in their accounts.
http://indianexpress.com/article/india/india-news-india/
demonetisation-hits-villages-tehsils-handful-of-banks-and-
limited-staff-rural-areas-feel-the-pinch/

106: 'Experience tells us . . . a televised appeal.
http://pib.nic.in/newsite/PrintRelease.aspx?relid=153404

Books
A. Raghuramaraju (2010), *Modernity in Indian Social Theory*, Oxford University Press.
Ed. Pamela Price and Arild Engelsen Ruud (2010), *Power and Influence in India: Bosses, Lords and Captains*, Routledge.

Chapter 4
Articles

119: I had grown . . . set things straight.
https://roundtableindia.co.in/index.php?option=com_content&view=article&id=5206:ranvir-sena-massacres-and-state-complicity

119–20: On 6 December . . . of Lord Ram.
http://news.bbc.co.uk/onthisday/hi/dates/stories/december/6/newsid_3712000/3712777.stm

120–21: Vivekananda wasn't simply . . . as Paulo Coelho's.
http://www.hindustantimes.com/india-news/swami-vivekananda-youngster-from-india-won-over-the-world/story-6xN7dIZYJiqTirMCwwloLI.html
http://indiatoday.intoday.in/education/story/swami-vivekananda-death-anniversary/1/706997.html

121: Vivekananda persuaded Hindus . . . do the same.
http://www.business-standard.com/article/current-affairs/full-text-of-swami-vivekananda-s-chicago-speech-of-1893-117091101404_1.html

122: The other major . . . in 20,000 colleges.
http://www.caravanmagazine.in/reportage/age-of-abvp

125: It's when the . . . as they please.
http://www.thehindu.com/news/national/andhra-pradesh/
valentines-day-vhp-bajrang-dal-warn-lovers/article8230633.ece

127: A city of . . . as 'riot-prone'.
http://ashutoshvarshney.net/wp-content/files_mf/
statesorcitiesstudyinghindumuslimriots.pdf

127: Its first sectarian . . . 'Institutionalized Riot System.'
http://www.paulbrass.com/files/Epwarticle.pdf

127–28: In 1987, in . . . Only three survived.
https://scroll.in/article/811062/hashimpura-may-22-1987-the-
forgotten-story-of-one-of-indias-biggest-custodial-killings
http://indiatoday.intoday.in/story/provincial-armed-
constabulary-faces-flak-for-controversial-role-in-meerut-
riots/1/337211.html

129–130: Sangeet Som first . . . the good fight.
http://indianexpress.com/article/who-is/who-is-sangeet-som-
taj-mahal-history-muslims-hindu-4893208/

132: A state-sanctioned identity . . . or its hide.
https://scroll.in/article/813871/will-haryanas-cow-protection-
ids-simply-be-a-licence-for-vigilantism

132: Not once in . . . western Uttar Pradesh.
http://www.bbc.com/news/world-asia-india-34409354

132: We have also . . . skinning cattle carcasses.
http://indianexpress.com/article/india/india-news-india/gujarat-
7-of-dalit-family-beaten-up-for-skinning-dead-cow-2910054/

133: The official logo . . . men across Haryana.
https://granta.com/cult-hindu-cowboy/
http://www.caravanmagazine.in/reportage/in-the-name-of-
the-mother

135: People are no . . . nation in 2016.
http://www.firstpost.com/india/beware-of-nakli-gau-rakshak-pm-modi-denounces-cow-vigilantes-for-the-second-time-2940986.html

136: Not twenty-four hours . . . the Pakistani-controlled side.
https://economictimes.indiatimes.com/news/defence/army-conducted-surgical-strikes-on-terror-launch-pads-on-loc-significant-casualties-caused-dgmo/articleshow/54579855.cms

136: The latter state . . . of Hindu vegetarians.
http://www.tribuneindia.com/news/comment/numbers-favour-dalit-muslim-unity-in-up/297311.html
http://www.huffingtonpost.in/2016/06/14/how-india-eats_n_10434374.html

136: Haryana was governed . . . support of Muslims.
http://in.reuters.com/article/india-politics-beef-modi-khattar-haryana/bjp-leader-urges-muslims-to-give-up-eating-beef-idINKCN0SA1HK20151016
https://timesofindia.indiatimes.com/elections/assembly-elections/uttar-pradesh/news/samajwadi-party-banks-on-muslim-yadav-formula/articleshow/56698505.cms

140: Between 2002, when . . . into the future.
http://www.businesstoday.in/magazine/case-study/case-study-strategy-tactics-behind-creation-of-brand-narendra-modi/story/206321.html
http://www.india-seminar.com/2013/641/641_shiv_visvanathan.htm

141: Many observers have . . . of jobs created.
http://www.livemint.com/Leisure/dLPCSc8BG725fx5dEB07uK/Whats-the-Gujarat-Model-and-whos-seen-it.html

http://www.epw.in/journal/2014/11/reports-states-web-exclusives/gujarat-model-development.html
https://scroll.in/article/855027/gujarat-model-the-gleam-of-states-high-growth-numbers-hides-dark-reality-of-poverty-inequality

141: Modi has tapped . . . in the world.
http://www.businessinsider.in/PM-Modi-is-the-most-followed-leader-on-social-media/articleshow/56687885.cms

145: In December 2014 . . . seats in Jharkhand.
http://www.financialexpress.com/india-news/jharkhand-assembly-polls-vote-counting-begins-in-24-centres/22239/

145: In a post-poll . . . for the BJP.
http://indianexpress.com/article/india/politics/its-opponents-divided-bjp-sneaks-through-the-gap/

145: The media duly . . . 'Narendra Modi wave'.
http://www.firstpost.com/politics/assembly-elections-jharkhand-swept-by-modi-wave-as-bjp-and-ally-set-to-from-govt-2003095.html

145: His man, Arjun . . . lost his seat.
http://indianexpress.com/article/india/politics/bjp-gets-clear-majority-in-jharkhand-arjun-munda-loses-election/

146: On 28 December . . . for chief minister.
http://indianexpress.com/article/india/politics/jharkhand-to-get-first-non-adivasi-cm-as-party-decides-to-elect-raghubar-das-for-the-top-job/

Books
Swami Vivekananda (2014), *The Complete Works of Swami Vivekananda*, Vols 1–8, Advaita Ashrama.

Christophe Jaffrelot (2011), *Religion, Caste and Politics in India*, Hurst.
Rohit Chopra (2012), *Technology and Nationalism in India: Cultural Negotiations From Colonialism to Cyberspace*, Cambria Press.

Chapter 5
Articles

149: This was one . . . carnival around it.
http://www.epw.in/hi/journal/1970/23/special-articles/
student-politics-allahabad-university.html

151–52: Most news reports . . . and handmade pistols.
https://www.ndtv.com/allahabad-news/student-riot-shuts-
down-allahabad-university-478910
http://www.thehindu.com/news/national/allahabad-varsity-
closed-as-vc-is-held-hostage-and-students-go-on-rampage/
article3359859.ece
http://www.theweek.in/content/archival/news/india/
allahabad-varsity-violence-22-held-case-against-2000.html

154: In 2006, the . . . to assert it.
https://scroll.in/article/805919/the-seeds-of-todays-ferment-
in-central-universities-were-sown-in-2006

154–55: Every major Indian . . . army: the ABVP.
https://www.thequint.com/news/politics/bjp-stumped-by-
young-idealists-gurmehar-kaur-rather-than-rahul-gandhi-
akhilesh-yadav

155: Four months before . . . a hostel room.
http://www.caravanmagazine.in/reportage/from-shadows-to-
the-stars-rohith-vemula

155–156: Barely a month . . . to the end.
https://timesofindia.indiatimes.com/india/JNU-student-
leader-arrested-on-sedition-charge-after-Afzal-Guru-protest-

event-sent-to-3-day-police-custody/articleshow/50963303.
cms

167: Singh's victory meant . . . dominated by muscle.
http://www.huffingtonpost.in/2015/10/01/allahabad-
university-elec_n_8225120.html

170: Singh called a . . . democratically elected body.
http://indianexpress.com/article/india/india-news-india/
ausu-president-says-wont-let-adityanath-enter-allahabad-
university-campus/

171: At 7 p.m. that . . . a hunger strike.
https://scroll.in/article/770358/in-pictures-allahabad-
university-students-protest-to-stop-yogi-adityanath-from-
entering-the-campus

173: At 11.30 a.m., news . . . by town officials.
http://indianexpress.com/article/india/india-news-india/
adityanath-barred-from-entering-allahabad/

176: Four months before . . . leaks, female suicides.
https://www.theguardian.com/lifeandstyle/2015/mar/30/
female-reporter-rural-india-khabar-lahariya-feminist-
newspaper

183: I had seen . . . turned to black.
http://www.hindustantimes.com/india-news/not-loving-thy-
neighbour-a-peek-into-the-mindset-of-nationalist-china-
bashers/story-jQDn7NXUePnmHDRXcgvTYK.html

Books
Neelam Saran Gour (2015), *Three Rivers and a Tree: The Story
of Allahabad University*, Rupa Publications.
Craig Jeffrey (2012), *Timepass: Youth, Class and the Politics of
Waiting in India*, Cambridge University Press India.

Dhirendra K. Jha (2017), *Yogi Adityanath and the Hindu Yuva Vahini*, Juggernaut.

Chapter 6

192: The newspapers had . . . seeking front-row seats.
http://inextlive.jagran.com/video/mr-and-miss-jharkhand-2014-show-in-ranchi-201408130007

195–96: And fashion shows: . . . and company galas.
https://timesofindia.indiatimes.com/home/sunday-times/deep-focus/The-small-town-sashay/articleshow/47314385.cms

221: Ghosh had first . . . in small towns.
https://www.nytimes.com/2014/09/19/arts/international/the-actor-salman-khan-is-focus-of-being-bhaijaan-documentary.html

Chapter 7

225: In 2016, 19,000 . . . the public sector.
https://timesofindia.indiatimes.com/city/bareilly/19000-graduates-postgraduates-MBAs-BTechs-apply-for-114-sweepers-jobs-in-UP-town/articleshow/50675268.cms
http://www.bankexamsindia.com/2013/03/sbi-po-recruitment-number-of.html
https://qz.com/823234/desperate-for-jobs-indias-graduates-are-working-as-drivers-maids-and-mechanics/

225–26: Regardless of their . . . the private sector.
http://www.thehindu.com/data/Entry-level-jobs-pay-more-in-Central-government/article14469396.ece

226: Unfortunately for the . . . jobs a month.
http://www.financialexpress.com/economy/3-years-of-modi-government-pm-has-failed-to-create-jobs-for-

the-desperate-young-people-who-gave-him-massive-mandate/686486/

227: A call centre . . . the United States.
https://economictimes.indiatimes.com/tech/ites/indias-technology-vendors-paddling-shaky-boats/articleshow/56543653.cms

231: Six months before . . . tip them off.
https://www.nytimes.com/2017/01/03/world/asia/india-call-centers-fraud-americans.html

236: The scam begins . . . as deadly threats.
http://www.hindustantimes.com/india-news/scare-and-sell-how-indian-call-centre-scammers-cheat-foreign-computer-owners/story-cTE5eHZIo3AkjvTJDhokAK.html

245: In every major . . . fake jobs websites.
http://www.hindustantimes.com/interactives/inside-fake-job-industry/

Epilogue

248: After two months . . . SP was annihilated.
http://www.thehindubusinessline.com/news/national/live-2017-assembly-election-results/article9579978.ece

249: Meanwhile, Singh had . . . on her own.
https://timesofindia.indiatimes.com/city/allahabad/more-women-candidates-contesting-ausu-elections/articleshow/61030541.cms

249: A young man . . . became the president.
https://timesofindia.indiatimes.com/city/allahabad/samajwadi-chatra-sabha-sweeps-ausu-polls/articleshow/61087664.cms

252: The website now . . . and Narendra Modi.
https://www.wittyfeed.com/

253: What stands out . . . me in this!'
https://www.wittyfeed.com/story/35683/2/an-open-letter-to-honourable-prime-minister-narendra-modi